D1130290

Please remember that this is a library book,
and that it belongs only temporarily to each
person who uses it. Be considerate. Do
not write in this, or any; library book.

WITHDRAWN

OLDER RURAL AMERICANS

WITHDRAWN

OLDER RURAL AMERICANS
A Sociological Perspective

EDITED BY

E. Grant Youmans

UNIVERSITY OF KENTUCKY PRESS · LEXINGTON · 1967

Copyright © 1967
by the University of Kentucky Press
Printed in the United States of America
Library of Congress Catalog Card
No. 67-23779

305.26
Y67r

Foreword

Private and public organizations in the United States have initiated a wide variety of programs for older people. The success of such programs depends, in large part, upon the accumulation of information about the behavior and living conditions of older persons in different social environments. Social gerontological studies have documented some of the conditions and circumstances of life among older persons living in metropolitan centers of the United States, but relatively little is published about older rural people. In this volume, sixteen social scientists from different regions of the nation have collaborated in presenting information about older people living in open country and in towns and in small cities removed from major metropolitan centers. Many of these rural older persons are outside the mainstream of American life and thus are deprived of the advantages and benefits available to others. The information presented in this volume points to some of the special problems of older rural people and should be useful to organizations and individuals who are planning and carrying out programs for these people.

John H. Southern, Director,
Economic Development Division,
Economic Research Service,
U. S. Department of Agriculture

William A. Seay, Director,
Kentucky Agricultural Experiment Station, and
Dean, College of Agriculture,
University of Kentucky

30152

JOYCE

Acknowledgments

The preparation of this monograph was sponsored jointly by the U. S. Department of Agriculture and the Kentucky Agricultural Experiment Station. Many persons contributed helpful suggestions and encouragement. Special acknowledgment is made to Louis J. Ducoff, former chief of the Human Resources Branch, Economic Development Division, Economic Research Service, U. S. Department of Agriculture, for advice and assistance. Special acknowledgment is made to A. Lee Coleman and to Thomas R. Ford of the Department of Sociology and Rural Sociology, University of Kentucky, for invaluable help during many critical phases of the project. Calvin L. Beale and Melvin R. Janssen aided in the project in many ways. Grateful acknowledgment for helpful suggestions on manuscripts is made to the following persons: Gladys Bowles, Milton Coughenour, James Cowhig, Charles Dean, George Hillery, Olen Leonard, Harry Schwarzweller, and Joseph Scott. Invaluable typing assistance was given by Irene Baker.

E. Grant Youmans

Contents

E. GRANT YOUMANS

Introduction

In recent decades public attention has been directed to the social, economic, and health conditions of older people in American society. Public awareness of these conditions has been augmented by the increasing number and proportion of the aged in the population and by the growing research literature on human aging. In 1850, about 3 percent of the United States population was aged 65 and over. One hundred years later it was 8 percent. In 1960 it was 9 percent, a proportion which included about 11 million aged men and women living in urban centers and almost 5 million living in rural areas of the nation. During the first half of the century (1900-1948), about 18,000 publications on aging were reported.[1] Between 1949 and 1961 about 34,000 publications appeared.[2] It is a reasonable expectation that research activity on human aging will continue to expand.

In a research field that is growing so rapidly, there is a notable omission. This is the extremely small number of reported publications that focus on older persons who live in rural environments—in small towns, in open country, and on farms. Despite the sizable number of older persons living in these places, very few researchers have studied older rural populations in a systematic manner.

The materials presented in this volume give a sociological perspective on older persons living in rural environments of the

1

United States. The first five chapters are concerned with perspectives and social roles. Four succeeding chapters deal with the social, economic, and health conditions of older rural persons. Older persons in three subcultures are the subjects of three chapters. The final chapter deals with programs for the rural aged.

In the first chapter, Arnold Rose points out that an understanding of the rural aged requires examining three sets of factors: the aging process in American society, characteristics of rural life today, and characteristics of life in small towns and in open country some sixty years ago when the present generation of older rural people were in their formative years. In limiting his analysis to these three sets of factors, Rose states that he does not deny the importance of others upon older people but that "these three sets of influences have worked on *all* older rural people, whereas any others must have had a more limited influence."

Ward Bauder and Jon Doerflinger describe the rapid changes occurring in occupational roles in rural and urban areas of the United States and raise a basic question: can a transition "be made without taking too heavy a psychological toll of the rural aged whose occupations and retirement are tied to the rural systems of the past?" In their chapter on "Work Roles Among the Rural Aged" these authors examine rural-urban differences in work, participation of older rural people in work, and retirement practices and adjustments in rural areas of the United States.

Joseph and Jean Britton examine the research literature on family behavior in the middle and later years and raise the question of the extent to which rural or urban residence is an important differentiating variable. This chapter includes a section on historical changes affecting the rural family and a rationale for the use of a developmental approach to the study of the family. Literature on the "middle years" is discussed under such topics as "role behavior," "the middle-aged and their grown children," "the middle-aged and their parents," and "marriage in the middle years." Literature on the "the later years" is placed under such headings as "living arrangements," "relationships of older persons with their families," "isolation of older persons from their families," and "family norms for aging in rural communities."

In his chapter on "Community Roles and Activities," Walter McKain states that two major values—the importance of work and the emphasis on youth—have important implications for the use of free time by older persons in American society. McKain points out that the community roles and activities "of older rural people bear the imprint of rural values and rural customs." He provides documentation about the formal and informal social participation of older rural people and examines some of the factors associated with their participation.

One of the current explanations of human aging as social-psychological phenomena is found in disengagement theory. In his chapter on "Disengagement Among Older Rural and Urban Men," Grant Youmans examines disengagement among elderly men living in their respective communities. The chapter focuses on disengagement in economic life, in family life, and in hobbies and community activities. Three central questions are asked of empirical data: (a) What evidence exists of disengagement in these three areas of life? (b) What relationships exist between social disengagement and the men's subjective life? (c) What influence does rural and urban residence have on the disengagement process?

Henry Sheldon, in his chapter on the "Distribution of the Rural Aged Population," raises a basic question: Does the age structure of the rural population merely reflect that of the general population or does it arise from its rural condition? By use of reported census statistics, Sheldon examines the proportions of aged persons living in urban and rural areas of the United States, documents changes in the rural age structure from 1950 to 1960, and offers some speculations about future trends in the age structure of the rural population.

Juanita Kreps gives special attention to the economic status of the rural aged. The data she has assembled on urban and rural older persons offer striking evidence that "the combination of old age and rural residence makes the rural aged one of the lowest income groups in the United States." Mrs. Kreps analyzes some implications of technological change and recent occupational shifts upon the economic position of the rural aged.

In his chapter on "Housing of the Rural Aged," James Montgomery gives evidence of the many changes that have confronted rural older people in their living arrangements and housing conditions. He points to some of the deprivations associated with housing among the rural aged, examines the factors affecting housing needs in rural areas, and discusses attempts to improve housing for older rural people in the United States.

Basic objectives of medical research on the health of older persons in the United States have been to understand the degenerative processes that occur with age, to combat these, and to prevent their occurrence as much as possible. In his chapter on "Health Status of the Rural Aged," Bert Ellenbogen examines the physical health conditions of older rural people, aspects of their mental health and psychological outlook, the health services and programs available to the rural aged, and potentials for improving the health care of the older rural population. Wherever possible he makes comparisons between the rural and the urban aged.

There is need for cross-cultural comparisons of aging in various minority and ethnic groups. Three chapters, those by Levy, Leonard, and Smith, deal with older persons in three subcultures of the United States. Jerrold Levy, in his chapter on "The Older American Indian," points to the difficulty of generalizing about North American Indians, who encompass a wide diversity of cultures and languages. Levy describes the aboriginal period of Indian life and gives special attention to the status of the aged in aboriginal America. In the third portion of his chapter, Levy examines the conditions of life of the contemporary aged Navajo, who share the culture of the largest single Indian tribe in the United States.

"The Spanish-speaking people in the United States are second only to the American Indians in the length of time they have occupied American soil." So states Olen Leonard in his examination of the social, economic, and health status and the family and community roles of the older Spanish-speaking people of the Southwest. One of the acute problems confronting the aged, according to Leonard, is the rapid assimilation of the young Spanish-speaking population into the dominant culture of the nation. It is mainly the older people, particularly those in the more isolated rural areas, who retain the traditions of Spanish culture.

Stanley Smith "brings together some of the limited materials about older Negroes who live in rural areas—a population possessing three poverty-linked characteristics: old age, rural residence, and minority-group status." By means of census and regional data, Smith documents the educational, employment, and income levels of older rural Negroes in the United States and gives evidence of their deprivations and exclusion from the mainstream of American life.

The final chapter in this volume, by Marvin Taves and Gary Hansen, examines "Programs for the Rural Elderly." The authors trace the development of local, state, and federal programs for the aged, describe some of the salient federal legislation which affects older rural people, and give examples of cooperative efforts of federal and state agencies, private institutions, business and voluntary organizations, and various civic groups in meeting the needs of older rural persons.

The monograph is written primarily for social gerontologists, for social scientists and other persons interested in rural gerontology, and for organizations and individuals who are developing programs for older rural persons.

NOTES

[1] Nathan W. Shock, *A Classified Bibliography of Gerontology and Geriatrics* (Stanford, Calif.: Stanford University Press, 1951).

[2] Nathan W. Shock, *A Classified Bibliography of Gerontology and Geriatrics, Supplement One*, 1949-1955 (Stanford, Calif.: Stanford University Press, 1957), and *A Classified Bibliography of Gerontology and Geriatrics, Supplement Two*, 1956-1961 (Stanford, Calif.: Stanford University Press, 1963).

ARNOLD M. ROSE

Perspectives on
the Rural Aged

In analyzing the rural elderly, three sets of factors must be kept
in mind: (*a*) factors associated with aging in American society,
(*b*) characteristics of life today in small towns and the open
country, and (*c*) characteristics of life in small towns and the
open country some sixty years ago when the present generation of older people were in their formative years. The reason
for distinguishing the third set of factors from the other two
is that rural life, which was much different sixty years ago in
the United States than it is today, has had a profound effect
on the present generation of older people. This generational
influence is to be sharply distinguished from the influence of
aging as such since it is much more temporary. Rural life today
is much less distinguishable from urban life. When the present
generation of rural adults becomes old, their generational characteristics and problems will be little different from those of the
urban elderly but much different from the generational characteristics and problems of present rural older people.

In separating out the influence of these three sets of factors—
which we shall call, respectively, the factors of aging, of rural
life, and of generation—it is to be understood that this is an
analytic distinction. Their influence on the elderly is in fact
inextricably intertwined. In limiting our analysis to these three
factors, we do not deny the importance of others upon older
people. These three sets of influences have worked on *all* older

rural people, whereas any others must have had a more limited influence. Obviously the well-to-do are going to be different from the impoverished, the southern-born from the northern-born, the "Old Americans" from those with minority ethnic ties, and so on, but it is not within the scope of this paper to distinguish among such subcategories of the rural aged, except insofar as they are pertinent to the discussion of the generational factor.

AGING IN AMERICA

In distinguishing the factor of aging[1] from the generational influence, we did not intend to imply that the former was unchanging while the latter was changing. The condition of being an older person is not merely a function of relatively immutable biological characteristics but also of cultural characteristics, which happen to be changing at a rapid pace in contemporary American society. The limitations on the elderly, the opportunities before them, the attitudes of younger generations toward them, and their attitudes toward themselves or older people are— since the 1950's—undergoing changes of almost revolutionary proportions.

Before considering these changes, let us first examine the social psychology of the typical older person in present American society. There are two outstanding social psychological problems of older people in American society today, and they are related in part: one is the loss of social roles and the other is the development of negative attitudes toward the self.

LOSS OF OCCUPATION

Most employed persons are obliged to retire from their jobs sometime during their sixties, and occupation is a chief life role for most men and for a significant proportion of women. The chief life role for most women is childbearing and child-rearing, and this has been accomplished for most American women in their fifties or, increasingly because of the younger age at which women now voluntarily stop having babies, in their forties. After they are no longer engaged in childrearing, many American women find new roles in employment or voluntary associations, but these also are greatly reduced by the mid-sixties.

The loss of the chief life function—occupation for a man and childrearing for a woman—may be damaging to the conception of the self, especially if all the individual's values have been concentrated on this function and if he has no other valued activities that can provide him with substitute goals and satisfying roles. On the other hand, if he has the latter and feels a growing strain between carrying on the chief life function and the physical ability or interest in doing so, retirement can be a relief and an avenue to a happier life. There is evidence that, for many males in our society, particularly in the lower- and middle-income classes, retiring from the job is looked forward to with pleasure and anticipation. Still, there is a great deal of individual variation, and, from the standpoint of life satisfaction and mental health, forced retirement is undesirable. The difficulty arises less from the reduction of income, since various pension plans now in existence prevent income from falling too low and there are fewer expenses, than from forced and rapid role change. Simple substitution of leisure for work is seldom satisfactory unless the individual is so physically deteriorated that he can work only with extreme difficulty, because work is highly valued in our culture, even if the work happens to be unpleasant. Americans do not learn how to spend leisure time in ways that they themselves and their fellows consider desirable.

Complete and sudden retirement is almost unique to industrial society. In most other societies, there is a gradual sloughing off of the primary occupation, and although the roll and the group participations associated with it change, the individual's conception of himself does not change rapidly. In agrarian areas many farmers are able to cut down on their work role gradually, thereby reducing the sense of loss which often accompanies abrupt retirement.

Sudden retirement, common in urban America, is often the source of mental problems. If retirement is complete, there is a sharp reduction in income for most persons. Social security and private pensions seldom compensate completely for loss of wages or salary. Although expenses tend also to be lower for older persons, this is not true of medical expenses. Many older persons live in fear that their savings will not cover their rising medical expenses, especially if they have chronic diseases. Loss of income generally restricts activity and travel and even more greatly restricts the sense of psychological freedom.

ATTITUDES TOWARD AGING

Both men and women in their sixties tend to be excluded from voluntary associations, although some new organizations are being established by and for older people, particularly in urban centers. Some voluntary associations are connected with occupation, and when occupation disappears, so does participation in the related voluntary associations. Other voluntary associations—especially those centered on sports, childrearing, and self-education—no longer hold much interest for older persons because of the change in their physical and social conditions as they enter old age. In many cases, older members are forced to reduce their participation in still other voluntary associations— those concerned with civic life, social welfare, or even just sociable activities—partly because they lack the strength to keep up with the pace and partly because energetic younger adults replace the elderly in positions of leadership. Of the non-age-graded associations, only those connected with the church do not tend to push out older persons. The often noted increased participation of older persons in religious activities is not solely a result of the increasing interest of people in religion as they approach death but also a result of the fact that this is one area of life that does not tend to exclude older people. Exclusion from participation and loss of roles in voluntary associations as well as in occupation tend to create negative self attitudes.

The problems of retirement are intimately connected with the problem of the reduced prestige of aging. In past centuries, wisdom was associated with age, but today the pace and complexity of events have prompted us to attribute wisdom only to the expert. Also, the elderly person was relatively rare in the past; today, the percentage of those over 65 years of age in the population has climbed to 1 in 11. This inflation may have helped to reduce the popularly evaluated worth of the elderly person. Respect and praise in our society are generally accorded for achievement, and valued achievement is mainly a product of occupation, including childrearing for women. Loss of occupation in retirement removes the occasion for manifestations of praise and respect.

CHANGES IN FAMILY ROLES

Old age often brings changes in family roles. Even before one reaches the age of 65 today, one has lost the childrearing role and assumed the grandparental role. The latter generally does not occupy as much time as the former and is frequently more pleasant, if the older couple and the younger families are in separate households. With retirement there is often a change in husband-wife roles; when he was employed full-time there was a natural division of labor and power between them; upon retirement, he tends to intrude into her sphere. Either he wants some chores to keep himself busy or he feels he ought to help out when she is busy and he has nothing to do. He expects to take on these tasks as an equal (or sometimes, if he had a directive role in his occupation, unconsciously he expects to be a superior). Previously his wife has had little interference in running the house. Under the circumstances, either he meets rebuff, with some damage to his self-conception, or he starts a permanent conflict, or he threatens his wife's conception of herself, or they work out a new division of labor. This problem is less likely to occur if the man is a farmer and gradually retires from that occupation.

If either or both of the old couple move in with one of their married children's families, the required role adjustment is even more drastic. In other societies, and in our own society until about fifty years ago, the family included the older generation, but today in our society the older person is regarded as an extra member. The older couple living with their adult children in past centuries very often were regarded as the heads of the household, whereas today they are generally the subordinates. Either of the older folks intrudes on the functions of the younger wife, except when she needs a baby sitter. The young couple's interests are generally different from those of the older persons, and there is always a question whether the latter should be included in the young couple's or family's activities. Entertainment of friends is often difficult in someone else's home, and if the move into the younger couple's home has entailed a movement into another community, there are often no friends nearby for the elderly person to invite.

In most cases, movement into the home of a married child involves some depreciation in self-conception arising from the down-grading of a role from an independent to a dependent person. Even the role of grandparent is not a satisfying one in our society if the grandparent lives in the same home: the younger family tends to be child centered today, but older persons often regard children as subordinates or pets. To have to accommodate to a dominating child is an annoyance to a grandparent who lives in his own home; it can be traumatic to the grandparent who lives in the child's home. The difficulties of elderly parents living with their adult offspring in our society generally have kept them from living together; today this living arrangement is the atypical rather than the typical one, although research literature shows that other kinds of intergenerational relationships are maintained today.

When one of an older couple dies, the remaining person is cut off from his major social relationship. Both a role change and a narrowing of the self-conception is involved. Whereas there always may have been psychologic dependency on the spouse, awareness of this does not always exist until the spouse is dead. If there are strong group memberships, the psychologic dependency of the surviving person can be transferred partly to them. But the groups to which the older person belongs—especially the informal ones—are likely to consist also of older persons who die at an increasingly rapid rate. With each friend's death, the older person loses another role, another source of prestige, another social support, and part of himself. No loss of prestige is involved in the status of widowhood itself. However, the widowed woman may experience a strong sense of loss if she depended heavily for her social relationships on friends of her deceased husband rather than on her own personal friends.

DECLINE IN PHYSICAL POWERS

With the inevitable decline in physical powers, most older persons recognize that the future will bring even more incapacities and eventually death. For some, physical decline is so gradual and the unwillingness to face old age so strong that the realization that one is old may come as a traumatic shock that may result in depression of some duration. This depression may take the form of a disorganization of one's roles and of a strongly negative self-conception. For the majority, evidences of physical decline intrude themselves in one's self-conception as early as the thirties, so that the traumas occur in numerous small bits over a quarter of a century and leave no sudden, shocking realization for the individual to cope with. Still, it is probable that no individual is pleased with or is fully adjusted to the thought that he may become permanently infirm. Whatever the general level of aspirations of the individual, he probably hopes to continue his freedom of movement, but when that seems to be disappearing, he probably feels there is little left to which he can aspire.

For many aging persons there is some awareness of declining mental powers, and this may be as painful an experience as that of declining physical powers. However, declining mental powers usually involve less awareness, with the result that their total impact on emotional health may be less.

Deteriorating health of the older person tends to create one or the other of two mental health problems. The first is hypochondriasis. The aging individual becomes aware of an increasing number of specific disabilities and of a general weakening of his body. Sometimes he reacts by complaining to others of these things and by going to the doctor frequently or by taking copious quantities of patent medicines in an effort to stave off his physical decline. The opposite reaction, equally a problem, is likely when the individual has never been much bothered by poor physical health during his life. When age brings physical disabilities, he refuses to recognize them and resists medical care. This attitude is especially likely if a person spent his youth in a rural area of the country or has had a low income throughout his life, so that seeking medical advice and care is foreign to his experience.

FEAR OF DEATH

Whereas death may not be so terrifying as in the days when there was an active belief in hell and many individuals had private reasons for predicting that this was to be their residence in the afterlife, the fear of the permanent unknown probably is still strong in most persons. Generally, death is welcomed only by those who are suffering great physical or mental pain or who have reached such a condition of lassitude that one nothingness seems to be an inconsequential substitute for another. The fear of death is so powerful that individuals who have little to live for and whose life offers them nothing but misery still refuse the release of death. The perception of the world is a personal one, and few individuals can conceive of the world without themselves, except perhaps in an academic sense. Most older people probably reconcile themselves to the thought of death, but once the conception has been formulated, it casts a shadow over a person's thoughts and over his expectations for the future by which he lives.

SUMMARY

Although old age may bring a release from a boring job and from striving for scarcely attainable goals, resulting in a mellowness that comes to some old people, for most persons it brings disturbances to one's roles and self-conceptions that tend to result in minor forms of ill health. There tends to be a movement from head of household to dependent, from lack of awareness of psychologic dependency to poignant awareness, from rise in prestige to decline, from having a meaningful life role to having to search for a new role, and from being an active person to being a partial invalid. Opportunities for developing negative self-conceptions multiply, and mild depressions or neuroses thereby are more likely to result. It is even conceivable that the high rate of psychosis among older people is at least partly stimulated by these conditions. All of these mental states create problems for all the younger people who have to cope with older persons or who have responsibility for them in any way.

THE RURAL SETTING

Rural areas include both the open country, where farming is the usual occupation, and small settlements, where chief occupations range from mining and forestry to trade, transport, and service. A much larger proportion of rural than of urban residents are self-employed, and self-employed people are less likely than employees to retire completely and suddenly at a fixed age. The more gradual retirement of the farmer or small-town merchant eases many of the problems mentioned below as characteristic of retirement from occupation. With gradual retirement there is also less strain on income, and there may be less anxiety over declining income in the later years in the rural areas of the United States than in the urban areas. There is one significant additional burden on the income of the aging rural person, however, and that is the necessity of journeying and living away from home to get medical care for the more serious chronic diseases. This can add a serious additional strain on economic resources and also tends to stimulate anxieties about living among strangers at a time of personal crisis. It is likely that the rural aged make less use of medical facilities for these reasons.

THE COMMUNITY DOMINATED BY OLDER PEOPLE

With a decrease in the number of persons engaged in certain rural occupations, especially in agriculture and mining, there has developed a population imbalance. Most of those leaving rural areas are young adults, and they leave behind a disproportionate number of older persons. The nation has become familiar with localities to which older people migrate—such as St. Petersburg, Asheville, Tucson, and San Diego—but much less attention has been paid to the rural counties in many other states which also may have large numbers of older people.[2] Even when the older couple abandon the family farm (usually by selling it to a large-scale operator), they characteristically move into a nearby village or town. In some midwestern rural counties, half of the adult population is over sixty years of age.

Although such communities may not be actually controlled by the aged, these communities often reveal the pervasive influence of older people. Political actions are geared to their interests. It is difficult to get school bond issues passed, there is strong opposition to the real property tax, a considerable share of local tax receipts are devoted to the county's share of Old Age

Assistance payments, and the town is more likely to have a park than a playground. The general outlook of the community is marked by the large number of older inhabitants: the drug stores display items appealing to older people, merchants make benches available in front of their establishments, homes tend to be shabbier because their elderly inhabitants are neither physically nor financially able to paint them, and the aged are everywhere in evidence. Political representatives from declining rural areas in state legislatures are as likely to reflect the generally conservative attitudes of the disproportionate number of older constituents as they are the economic interests of the farmer and small-town merchant.

HOUSING

In many American cities new housing programs have been initiated to fill the special needs of older people. The building of these apartments, both publicly and privately owned, dates mainly from the mid-1950's. An apartment house designed for older inhabitants usually has several of the following features: entranceways without steps, all units on the ground floor or accessible by elevators, handrails in the corridors, handrails in the bathrooms, electric outlets that can be reached without bending, shelves that can be reached without standing on ladders or chairs, and small units supplemented by common rooms. Little of this kind of housing is yet available in rural areas, although government financing is equally available and presumably private contractors are available to build it.

Many small-town elderly hold on to the large old houses in which they reared their families, even though such houses are no longer suited to their needs. The lag is partly social psychological and partly economic. It is difficult to find a buyer for a large old house in an area of declining population. But there is also an attachment to the old home, despite its inadequacies. It is a place where the adult offspring, with their growing families, may visit. To move from it would require disposal of much furniture and other personal property to which there are personal attachments. If the old home happens to be located along a highway or in a tourist area, it is frequently turned into a tourist home as a means of supplementing income. This provides the older or widowed homeowner with a range of outside social contacts, although superficial ones.

OPPORTUNITIES FOR SOCIAL LIFE

Because of the high proportion of older people in many rural areas of the United States, most of them have ready physical access to other persons of their own age. Of course, if they remain on the farm, they are often dependent on the automobile as a means of visiting their friends. If they are too physically handicapped to drive an automobile, the rural setting may isolate them. Unless they have the means and the inclination to travel, or unless they happen to live in a tourist area, both of which circumstances are rare, rural old people are largely cut off from broader social relationships. On the other hand, it is probable that rural old people are not so age graded and isolated by voluntary associations as are older people in the cities.

Just as rural areas have been laggard about accepting the modern forms of housing for older people, they have been slow about developing the modern forms of recreation for older people. Especially since 1950, the cities of the United States—through the initiative of social workers, churches, civic groups, or of older people themselves—have created a wide variety of recreational and social organizations. Many of these have names that reflect an optimistic view of old age: Golden Age Club, Live-Long and Like-it Club, Life Begins at Eighty Club. Any large northern city may boast of more than one hundred such clubs, although those familiar with them estimate informally that they attract no more than 5 to 10 percent of the population over 65 years. These clubs seem to do a great deal for the morale of those who participate in them.

But these clubs and organizations have been practically absent from rural areas, largely because local governments or private organizations have done little to create them. In Minnesota, a committee set up to prepare for the White House Conference on Aging in 1961 devoted many of its resources to an experiment of stimulating the establishment of recreational, social groups as well as other programs for older people in rural areas.[3] Where the local community could be persuaded to sponsor such clubs, the response from the older people was tremendous. In one area where the town and surrounding area numbered less than 1,000 inhabitants, about 70 percent of those past 65 years of age attended the first meeting, and attendance decreased very slightly after that. The typical experience of the Minnesota program was that 40 to 50 percent of the older residents attended the clubs—a turnout many times greater than that obtained in Minneapolis, or any other large northern city.

The need for such activities seems to be very great among older people. Frequently it was noted that persons who had not seen each other in decades would finally meet at clubs, even though they lived only 10 or 20 miles apart. It is apparent that many rural older people are lonely and do not take advantage of the fact that a large proportion of the population consists of persons of their own age. Their loneliness is probably accentuated by the fact that—especially among the farming population— the adult children have mostly migrated to the cities.

THE GENERATIONAL FACTOR

Many of the attitudes of today's rural elderly population can be explained by the fact that they grew up in the years around 1900. Whether they grew up in rural areas of the United States or, less frequently, of Europe, their way of life was very different from that of the youngsters in rural areas today. Rural life is not greatly distinguishable from urban life today in most northern states: the farm is run like an industry, the stores offer the same range of merchandise, travel to cities is frequent, and radio and TV keep people in constant touch with the world. The farm and the small town of sixty years ago was much more closed, limited, and isolated. One could escape it only by migrating to the big city, as many did. But those who stayed retained much of the old-fashioned, almost frontierlike, mentality, even as changing technology and economic organization changed the way of rural life for their offspring. In the South, chronic economic depression and technological backwardness, coupled with the pervasiveness of the caste system and the extreme social isolation, made the rural white or Negro of the lower income group into a peasant.

CONSERVATISM

The evident conservatism of today's elderly citizens has led many observers to conclude that aging brings conservatism. That may be, but it has not yet been demonstrated. A simpler explanation of the conservatism of most elderly people today, especially the rural ones, is that they always were conservative.

But the conservatism of the rural areas of the United States in 1900 went far deeper than politics. Modern technology had made little impact on the farms by then, and although some farmers were prosperous, they were not affluent, as many farmers are today. If they had migrated from Europe, many had been peasants, and theirs was essentially a medieval mentality. There was tight control of the children by the parents and even a good deal of patriarchal domination of the whole family. Fundamentalism in religion was probably stronger in rural areas then than it is today. Education seldom went beyond the primary grades and even then was usually provided in one-room school houses by poorly educated teachers. Rural life in the United States in 1900 did not often produce bold, open, inquiring minds in its young people, and when it did, the young people migrated to the big cities.

INFLUENCE OF POVERTY

The tight control of the American economy after the Civil War by the big city bankers, industrialists, and railroad owners helped to prevent prosperity on the farm—except for the brief period of World War I. The fact that agriculture was so competitive and so risky, especially as an efficient technology was being adopted in the first four decades of the twentieth century, kept most farmers poor until 1940. Many of the rural aged today have experienced bankruptcy and mortgage foreclosure. Poverty and consequent lack of access to the advantage of modern household technology have helped to mold the attitudes of the contemporary rural aged.

As they perceive the affluence of the younger generation—on the farms as well as in the cities—many older persons who have been economically deprived through most of their lives must feel some resentment. Of course, they feel some compensation in their attachment to the old-fashioned virtues, but the envy is still there. Prosperity came to the farms too late (during the 1940's) to benefit most of the elderly of today, and they are still poor and deprived. The amenities of modern life, and even such necessities as good medical care, are still not theirs. A significant number among them are resentful and crabbed.

THE CHANGING OUTLOOK FOR THE RURAL AGED

When we speak of the future of the elderly rural population of the United States, two things must be understood. One is that we are making a prediction on the basis of existing major trends; we neglect minor trends and we necessarily neglect major forces not yet operating on the social scene. Thus, our prediction must be highly tentative and incomplete. Second, because the present population of the aged will soon die, we are speaking about the next generation of the elderly—those who are middle-aged today.

The generational influence will obviously change rapidly. As the rural elderly become those who were formed during the prosperous period of World War I or the radical period of the 1930's, the generational influence will become different in character.

The changing character of rural society, both in the small towns and in the open country, has been studied by rural sociologists and agricultural economists and summarized in the many textbooks on rural sociology. Farming in the future will be almost entirely a commercial enterprise requiring considerable capital and expert knowledge. Farmers will be only slightly different from self-employed businessmen, and farm laborers will be like semi-skilled laborers. Income will be much more secure, especially as the movement away from the farms slows to a virtual halt. As the remaining inefficient farmers disappear and the economically minimum proportion of farmers in the population is reached (within a decade or so), the rural population will gradually return to a more normal balance of the age groups. The communities dominated by old people because the younger ones have migrated will be a phenomenon only of the next thirty years or so.

The lags in rural society will be eliminated gradually. Housing and recreational programs for older people are now beginning in the small towns, and they can be expected to become at least as available as in the large cities. If there are improvements in public transportation, rural older people will gain much advantage from them, but if the private automobile continues to be the main source of transportation and the roads continue to be crowded, the elderly will be even more confined to their homes than they are now. But as they become better off financially, elderly farmers can be expected to retire more frequently to the towns and cities. As programs are developed to provide medical care for older people, much of their concern about health will be greatly diminished.

Perhaps the most significant changes of long-run significance will be in the factor of aging. The elderly are likely to develop new social roles for themselves, since they have been excluded from the former ones. Already one sees a minority engaged in more constructive roles in voluntary associations, especially those primarily composed of older people. These range in function from purely social and recreational, through those with social welfare and social improvement functions, to those with civic and political functions. Older people are becoming more aware of themselves as a social group with common problems and with potential power if they take collective action. Younger people are becoming more aware of the problems of older people, and the society is beginning to take action to help solve some of the problems of older people. The first effort along these lines was the passage of the Social Security Act in 1935 to ameliorate the income problem; in the 1950's governmental efforts were directed to improve employment, housing, and recreational problems of older people. In 1965, a long struggle to provide free or insured medical care for older people was finally resolved by the passage of Medicare. The status level of older people is beginning to rise; with increasing frequency they are included in public activities of one sort or another, rather than ignored. Rural areas lag somewhat behind urban areas in this respect, but they are also making progress.

Improvements in medical knowledge, availability of medical care, and willingness to use medical knowledge are creating an older population in better health and with greater physical vigor than was formerly the case. Greater social participation and higher social status further aid their morale. They are gradually learning how to make pleasant and profitable use of their leisure time. Although fear of ill-health and death remain, these are being postponed for most elderly persons. Long-range social trends and organized political action are combining to solve many of the current problems of the aging in both rural and urban areas of the United States.

NOTES

[1] The discussion of the aging factor is largely a revision of two earlier analyses by the author, adapted to the aging in rural society: "Mental Health of Normal Older Persons," *Geriatrics*, 16 (Sept. 1961), 459-64; and "The Subculture of the Elderly: A Framework for Research" in *Older People and Their Social World*, ed. A. M. Rose and W. A. Peterson (Philadelphia: F. A. Davis Company, 1965), Ch. 1.

[2] Jon A. Doerflinger and Douglas G. Marshall, *The Story of Price County, Wisconsin* (Madison: University of Wisconsin Agricultural Extension Service, 1962).

[3] Bernard Nash and Gerald Bloedow, "The Five-County Demonstration Project" in Arnold M. Rose (ed.), *Aging in Minnesota* (Minneapolis: University of Minnesota Press, 1963).

WARD W. BAUDER

JON A. DOERFLINGER

Work Roles among
the Rural Aged

No treat' e on the rural aged would be complete without a discussion of their work roles and their retirement from these roles. Work, which is expected of the adult male in our society, serves to fix his position in the social order, to maintain him in a meaningful reference group, to regulate much of his life activity, and it is a source of many satisfactions and emotional experiences. The central position of work in American society is emphasized by Miller and Form:

> The impact of work routines is found in almost every aspect of living and even in the world of dreams and unconscious fantasies. During "vacations," for example many people find the departure from work routines a disturbing thing. Others find rejuvenation in being released from occupational duties. Both instances demonstrate the importance and pervasiveness of work. It is not an overstatement to suggest that work is not a part of life, it is literally life itself.[1]

This chapter examines the work roles of the rural aged in the United State⁻ Emphasis is given to rural-urban differences in work, labor-force participation of older people, patterns of and factors in retirement, adjustment to retirement, and some speculations regarding the direction of trends and future prospects.

WORK IN RURAL AND URBAN SOCIETY

Preliterate societies, as a rule, do not sharply distinguish work from other activities in the daily round of life. This is not the case in contemporary American society, for work in and of itself is a major focus of attention. As Durkheim observed many years ago, preliterate societies were bound together by custom and tradition and by the authority of elders. In contrast, complex modern society is held together by a network of mutually dependent and highly specialized occupational groups.[2] Although Durkheim was not comparing rural and urban society of the United States in the twentieth century, many of his observations are applicable. Rural society today retains many of the characteristics of preliterate societies.

At one time our nation was composed of those who lived in the cities, the urban segment, and of those who lived on farms, the rural segment. The growth of towns in rural areas, in order to collect farm produce and distribute nonfarm goods and services to farmers, changed this picture. By 1920 the townspeople had become inextricably bound to the neighboring farmers in a network of social relations. The term "rural" took on new meaning. It had come to mean a more complex population, including open-country farmers, plus open-country nonfarm people, and a network of nucleated population in the villages and small towns, all bound together by mutual service. Today, farmers are not bound to their immediate community but experience more far-reaching relationships. Likewise, people of smaller towns have relations with larger centers. Each person lives in an expanding world.[3]

With industrialization and the growth of large corporations, specialization occurred and many new occupational roles appeared. In urban centers, proprietorship declined as a prerequisite to high status, and management and scientific skills increased in importance.[4] The proliferation of new occupational roles in urban society created a sharply defined status hierarchy. In rural areas, where nearly everyone was farming, the status differences were less pronounced. Of course, there were big farmers and little farmers, good farmers and poor farmers. There were proprietors and professional farm managers. However, the tie between work and proprietorship was more dominant in rural than in urban society.

Many authors have commented on the nonrational factors which characterize farming as an occupation.[5] For many farmers it is a way of life and not merely a means of production. This nonrational element is evident in studies of farm boys and farm operators who claimed they were willing to accept low incomes in order to enjoy the "independence" of being a farmer. In many ways, farming sets a style of life for rural communities, and, wittingly or unwittingly, the inhabitants in small towns and in open country tend to conform to this life style.

LABOR-FORCE PARTICIPATION AMONG THE RURAL AGED

One feature of the occupational structure of rural areas is that it tends to be manned by an older labor force than is found in urban areas. Although the residential classification of the population into urban, rural nonfarm, and rural farm may not be the most meaningful classification of populations on a rural-urban continuum, it is the only one for which data are readily available. Census data on labor-force participation rates by 5-year age groups for the male population aged 50 and older show residential differences (Figure 1). Rural nonfarm participation rates are the lowest and rural farm rates are the highest in each age group, with urban rates intermediate. Beyond the generally accepted retirement age of 65, labor participation rates among rural farm males are more than double the rates for either the rural nonfarm or the urban population.

It is clear from the data in Figure 1 that rural-urban differences in labor-force participation of the aged are primarily differences between the farm and the nonfarm population and are, therefore, more properly termed occupational than residential differences. From a community point of view, however, it is reasonable to speak of rural-urban differences. The rural nonfarm and the rural farm data combined are generally descriptive of rural communities, and a combination of the farm and nonfarm components of the rural population still exhibits a contrast with the urban. The low participation rates among older nonfarm men are partly a function of the migration of retired farmers to small towns. Furthermore, part of the difference between farm and nonfarm labor-force participation rates can, no doubt, be traced to the difficulties of placing a threshold on the criteria for participation. Perhaps larger proportions of aged farmers might be in the labor force if social security regulations did not prohibit their participating in significant work while drawing benefits.

Figure 1. Labor-Force Participation by 5-Year Age Groups of Men Aged 50 and Older for Three Residence Classes in the United States, 1960

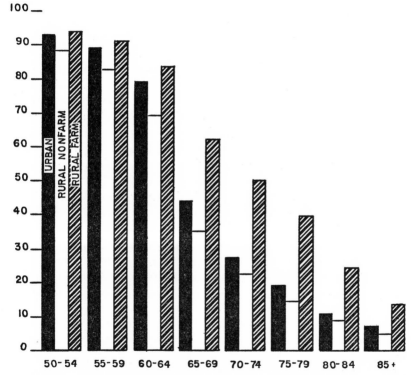

Source: U. S. Bureau of the Census, *United States Census of Population: 1960,* U. S. *Summary, Detailed Characteristics,* PC (1)-1D (Washington, D. C., 1961), Table 194, pp. 490-96.

Next we can consider how labor-force participation differs with age in the major occupational categories. Unfortunately, the census does not publish occupation by age and residence, so we must make inferences regarding residential differences from occupational category differences. Labor-force participation of older persons varies with occupational category. However, some occupations are more typical of one residence class than another, and only limited inferences can be made regarding differential participation of older workers by residence. To illustrate: among farmers who are almost universally rural, the proportion 65 and older in the labor force in 1960 was 14 percent and the proportion 45 and older was 60.7 percent. Among operatives who are mostly urban the proportions were 2.4 and 34.9 percent, respectively, in the same age categories.

THE RETIREMENT PROCESS

Students of society in America have concentrated on the first half of the life cycle with theories of development. This is part of the emphasis on youth in American society, and it reflects the preponderance of youth in the population. As advances in medical science and nutrition have brought larger proportions of the population well into the second half of the cycle, efforts were made to extend developmental theories to explain the changes that occur in later life.

Recently a formal theory called "disengagement" has been developed to explain the changes that occur in older age.[6] Since this topic is discussed in another chapter of this volume, only brief reference is made here. Perhaps some anthropological perspectives may suggest other alternatives. One has but to reflect upon the contrasting status afforded the aged in classical Chinese culture and among the polar Eskimos to appreciate the range of cultural variety. It is our impression that many primitive societies do not disengage their older members but continue to integrate them into one whole round of existence. In some instances integration continues even after death, through the use of a religious system.

Townsend has noted a sex difference in the life cycle.[7] He observes that men become more and more passive with the advanced years, whereas women become more actively dominant. For men, the principal mode of engagement in modern Western society is through the occupational role. In general, men work for a living and women attend to the family and household. As more and more women spend major parts of their lives in the labor force, this division of labor is changing, but even for most working women, family and household roles remain the dominant modes for relating to other people. For men, disengagement means retiring from their main life activity, a process which involves learning new skills more suitable to less instrumental roles.

It may not be retirement from work per se that creates a crisis for many men but rather the loss of social relationships that accompany work. Modern work roles provide an important basis of association. Withdrawal from work roles is an important change in daily life patterns and can be a critical point in the life cycle. The seriousness of the adjustment problems experienced will obviously vary with the manner in which work roles are integrated into other role complexes.

Retirement from an occupation may not necessarily constitute significant disengagement, for one can withdraw from a particular job and substitute another, or one can substitute family, community, and other roles. Some men modify their activities so as to engage more intensely within their own age group to form what Arnold Rose has called the subculture of the aged.

Whatever theory one accepts regarding the social aspects of aging, it is clear that the retirement process presents a problem to workers and to society. The magnitude of this problem for society can be seen in the sheer numbers of individuals who are now living to an advanced age. The problem has been created in part by improvements in health practices that have been responsible for extending average life expectancy. The problem of the aged in our affluent society appears to be an ethical problem. As Rosow states: "Although many specific needs are involved, the old in America suffer primarily from a lack of status and function."[8]

RETIREMENT PRACTICES IN RURAL AREAS

Systematic documentation of retirement practices in rural areas has not yet been done, but scattered studies of retirement plans and attitudes toward retirement suggest some modal patterns. Most of these studies have been concerned with farmers; the small-town business and professional persons largely have been ignored.

Although we do not know the exact rural patterns, a discussion of the possibilities will suggest some of the practices that may exist or are emerging. Four dimensions of retirement are considered: (*a*) the degree to which work is diminished, (*b*) the changes of residence which accompany retirement, (*c*) the financing of retirement, and (*d*) the timing of retirement. If we apply the evidence available to these dimensions, we can infer some patterns of rural retirement.

DIMINUTION OF WORK

The complete cessation of work, as found in many urban areas, is not common in rural areas. There is some evidence to support this as concerns farmers. In the 1950's, for example, only 15 percent of Connecticut farmers intended to retire,[9] only 12 percent of Texas farmers had definite plans for retirement,[10] and two-thirds of Wisconsin farmers had given little or no consideration to the problems of retirement.[11] One can interpret these results as meaning that retirement defined as cessation of work is a relatively hazy concept to most farmers.

There is substantial evidence that the typical rural pattern of retirement is associated with reduction of work rather than cessation of work. Our previous discussion has indicated that the rural labor-force structure and ethos would allow for and induce this practice. Taylor found that Illinois farmers distinguished between partial and complete retirement and that partial retirement covered a wide spectrum of adjustment in labor and management roles.[12] A recent study of farmers in South Dakota reinforces this thought, for only 21 percent of these farmers thought retirement would mean that physical labor would be eliminated entirely and 44 percent felt that management would be reduced completely.[13]

It is necessary to distinguish between working at a life occupation and other work as this pertains to retirement. For example, a large portion of the custodial staff of Iowa State University is composed of retired farmers. In the South Dakota study, one-fifth of the farmers who expected to continue work after retirement expressed a preference for nonfarm work. Generally, the nonfarm work done during retirement is wage work, but there are many cases of farmers who have retired to town and purchased a small business as a retirement business.

CHANGE OF RESIDENCE

One common pattern of farmer retirement involves moving to town and preferably to the same town that had serviced the farm family during its active farm career. The advantage of such a move is to be closer to those services that are thought to be more essential in old age. The South Dakota study indicated that this pattern is still practiced, for the majority of those farmers who thought of retirement as meaning a change of residence favored a short move to the open country or to a nearby community.[14]

Demographic evidence indicates the results of this practice, for the rural village of today exhibits the highest proportion of aged of any residence class. However, this phenomenon is due to out-migration of youth as well as in-migration of aged farmers. Also, aging rural proprietors caught in expanding trade areas may be forced to live out their lives with their business in the village setting. Whatever the cause, the consequence has been that many rural villages have become retirement communities, by historical accident if not by design.

Most rural people express a desire for independence of residence in their retirement. In studies that have asked such questions, responses have indicated an almost unanimous preference for living in their own homes rather than living with a child or in a home for the aged. Considering the traditional rural pattern of three-generational households, this may represent an example of rural-urban convergence in retirement practices.

FINANCING RETIREMENT

Because of the preponderance of self-employment in rural areas, investments and earnings from part-time labor constituted the principal means of financing retirement before the extension of Old Age, Survivors, and Disability Insurance (OASDI) coverage to the self-employed.

Pre-OASDI studies effectively shattered the widely held myth that mother earth offered the greatest security in old age to the farmer.[15] Over 70 percent of Wisconsin's farmers said that they felt that farming provided no more security for old age than other occupations, and in other states only about half felt financially secure about their old age.

Farming, like other entrepreneurial occupations, demands a capital accumulation; but the patterns of capital manipulation to finance retirement are extremely varied, and it is doubtful that any standard patterns have yet emerged. The picture is complicated by the alternatives of intergenerational property transfers. Generally, two main types of transfer may be distinguished: (a) those that occur within the lifetime of the owner and (b) those that take place after the owner's death. The aging farmer is faced with a dilemma: how to provide for his own retirement while insuring a start in business for those descendants who are interested in carrying on in business. The owner must also consider the problem of treating fairly those descendants who choose to follow another occupation.

North Central Regional Publication 127 lists the following six goals of family farm transfer:

(a) Reasonable degree of income security for parents.

(b) Reasonable degree of opportunities for farm operating son.

(c) Equitable treatment of other children.

(d) Minimization of impacts of taxes and probate costs.

(e) Maintenance of the farm on an efficient basis.

(f) Agreement to the plan by the entire family, if possible.[16]

Needless to say, a rational transfer of property which allows for a reasonable degree of income security for the parents is seldom achieved. It is our impression that frequently a joint arrangement is achieved after the fact, and the arrangements are seldom agreeable to all.

Pre-OASDI studies indicated varying degrees of confidence that income from investments would cover retirement costs (40 percent in Kentucky, 50 percent in Connecticut, 40 percent in Wisconsin).[17] At any rate, half of the farmers were not sure that they could finance their own retirement.

Extension of OASDI to farmers and other self-employed persons provides an important means of financing retirement. In some ways, OASDI presents an income advantage to farm owners or owners of small businesses in that benefit payments are not necessarily reduced by rental income. Thus, it is possible to combine business ownership and the status advantages that go with it and social security benefits.

Studies made since the extension of OASDI coverage to farmers indicate that OASDI payments are an important source of retirement income for a majority of those already retired, and among those not retired almost all are counting on OASDI payments to finance retirement.

Another pattern of financing retirement for rural entrepreneurs may be termed "living up your capital pattern." For those not fortunate enough to have sufficient capital to finance retirement without selling their businesses and who cannot or will not sell their businesses at the heavy discount required to move property in towns with declining populations, an alternative is gradually to liquidate the business capital. This may be done by letting stocks decline and by not replacing worn-out or out-moded equipment. In many cases there is the anticipation that death will precede the exhaustion of the capital.

TIMING OF RETIREMENT

We have noted that the farm population tends to remain in the labor force longer than the urban and that the rural nonfarm population participation rates at advanced ages are less than for urban workers. These figures, however, may not reflect preferences but rather opportunity and necessity. Several recent studies show that farmers prefer retirement to begin at a younger age than the generally accepted age of 65.[18] The most recent of these, the South Dakota study, indicated that the median preferred age of retirement for farmers of all ages was 62, but that the older the farmer the older the preferred age of retirement. However, the average preferred age of retirement did not exceed 65 for any age group.

FACTORS INFLUENCING RETIREMENT
IN RURAL AREAS

Factors influencing retirement in rural areas and urban areas differ in at least six ways: (a) age grading, (b) self-employment versus wage and salary work, (c) work and nonwork roles, (d) transfer of property, (e) relationships between the sexes, and (f) filial responsibility.

AGE GRADING

Age grading is one way of defining who may play certain roles in society. It keeps the young out of key work positions until they know enough to fill them and removes the old before their skills become obsolete. Age grading is structurally compatible with an occupational organization that stresses experience and training as qualifications for jobs, and it is also compatible with an organization that must concern itself with the rapid obsolescence of skills by technological advance. Thus, we find that promotion and retirement policies in many industries are based on the principle of advancing and retiring age groups. Such a policy is often rationalized in terms of making way for younger men.

In agriculture and many other rural occupations, age grading is less pertinent to occupational roles. Since farming has traditionally placed more value on experience than on book learning, one might expect that age grading would be more rigid in rural areas, but the greater opportunity for intergenerational cooperation in many farm tasks and the greater importance of family interaction have had the opposite effect. Peer relationships, although existing among farmers and small-town business and professional persons, are not nearly as important as in urban areas. The farmer either works alone or in groups composed of parents and children more often than he works in groups of peers. Similarly, the small-town businessman interacts less with his peers in his work than the businessman in the metropolitan center. Dependence on peers and the use of instrumental skills in relating to peers is, therefore, much less extensive among farmers and small-town business and professional persons than among urban workers generally. Consequently, withdrawal from work roles in rural areas involves less change in interaction patterns.

SELF-EMPLOYMENT AND WAGE WORK

A fundamental dichotomy pertinent to the process of retirement is the division between those who work for themselves and those who work for others. The data in Tables 1 and 2 indicate the high frequency of self-employment in rural agricultural occupations. The proportion of self-employed workers in agriculture is six times the proportion in nonagricultural employment. This difference has major significance for the older person, since the self-employed man can exercise more control over the manner of his retirement.

Table 1. Number of Employed Persons in Agricultural and Nonagricultural Labor Force by Class of Worker in the United States, 1960

Labor force	Class of worker			
	Wage and salary	Self-employed	Unpaid family	Total
Agricultural	1,209,000	2,755,000	603,000	4,567,000
Nonagricultural	52,944,000	6,194,000	562,000	59,700,000
Total	54,153,000	8,949,000	1,165,000	64,267,000

Source: U. S. Bureau of the Census, *Statistical Abstract of the United States: 1960,* Eighty-first Edition (Washington, D. C., 1960), p. 216.

Table 2. Percentages of Persons Employed in Agricultural, Nonagricultural, and Total Labor Force by Class of Worker in the United States, 1960

Class of worker	Labor force		
	Agricultural	Nonagricultural	Total
Wage and salary	26.5	88.7	84.3
Self-employed	60.3	10.4	13.9
Unpaid family	13.2	0.9	1.8
Total	100.0	100.0	100.0

Source: U. S. Bureau of the Census, *Statistical Abstract of the United States: 1960,* Eighty-first Edition (Washington, D. C., 1960), p. 216.

Retirement for the self-employed is different from retirement of workers from industry and large corporations. When an employee in an industrial organization has reached a given age, he is required to terminate his employed status. This decision is based on the policy of the organization and usually includes a provision of reduced payments or pension. Without these payments retirement would be little different from being discharged or laid off. Generally, the status of a retired person is higher than that of an unemployed person of the same age who still is part of the labor force.

Retirement for the self-employed is usually a voluntary decision, for by definition the self-employed person determines his own work status. Although health, financial resources, the opportunity to dispose of or transfer the business, family roles, and attitudes may condition the decision, the individual is relatively free to make it himself.

WORK AND NONWORK ROLES

The work ethic may be stronger in rural than in urban areas, but more pertinent to retirement are the differences in definitions of what constitutes "real" work and how work roles are related to nonwork roles. The combination of self-employment and family business, such as is found on a farm or in a small-town retail store, preserve the rural work ethos and make for less tolerance of nonwork roles by rural people. At the beginning of the life cycle, the son or daughter on a family farm or business can count on an early introduction to the world of work. There is a higher incidence of unpaid family work among rural people than among urban. Even if rural youth are engaged in "nonwork" roles, such as student, many are likely to have the experience of working in the "real" world of work. Schooling is often not viewed as work in rural areas; "real" work tends to be synonymous with physical work. In rural areas, only office work that involves ownership and management of property is classed as "real" work. Even the work of the professions is sometimes not thought of as "real" work. "Keeping bankers' hours" is the way many rural workers describe what they do when they take it easy or slacken their work schedules.

At the other end of the life cycle, the multiple-role character of most rural occupations provides an opportunity for gradual and controlled retirement. A farmer, and to a lesser degree many other rural workers, plays many different roles in his occupational activity. He is manager, employer, laborer, entrepreneur, mechanic, teacher, and engineer. When he approaches retirement age, he can reduce or drop roles which unduly tax his physical capacity. He can adjust his activity schedule by concentrating on fewer roles. The entrepreneurship role affords an opportunity to continue a management status through the maintenance of ownership status. This is in sharp contrast to the typical large urban business where ownership is usually divorced from management through a corporate structure in which capital is furnished by a distant public so as to produce a diffused and generally uninvolved ownership.

Because of the close association of management and ownership, the older owner-operator of a farm or small business can preserve his work status simply by maintaining ownership. The farmer may substitute a son, or the store owner a clerk, to perform most of the functions connected with his business, but his ownership status still places him in the active work category in the local public eye, even if the amount of work done is only a convenient fiction perpetuated for status reasons.

TRANSFER OF PROPERTY

In rural areas, retirement is frequently associated with the transfer of the business. Property ownership holds a high position in the rural ethos of America. It has long been a symbol of status. Although not as pervasive in the determination of life patterns as in earlier postfeudal days when it attained its maximum importance, property ownership retains a strong hold on the pattern of life and world view of rural people. Transfer of the enterprise to another person often results in the older person's retaining a substantial portion of the property rights, an arrangement that can create problems in the operation of the business.

For many small businessmen in rural towns, particularly for those in retail trade, personal retirement is synonymous with the retirement of the business. A declining population has reduced the market value of many businesses. Business assets in such a situation may be valuable to the present elderly owner as a source of retirement income but worthless to someone wanting to start a career. In other words, the best alternative available may be gradually to retire the business with the man.

RELATIONSHIP BETWEEN THE SEXES

Among rural families there is a sharp division of labor between the sexes. However, family ownership of the enterprise tends to increase the opportunity for cooperative effort between the sexes. The spirit of family life tends to foster the attitude that everyone should pitch in to help. In such a situation, freer substitution of tasks is possible. It is not uncommon to observe women doing field work on farms or wives clerking in rural hardware stores. In farming, the seasonal peaks in labor demands tend to encourage total family participation regardless of sex. In small-town stores, the long hours usually maintained encourage the use of female family members.

The world of work is experienced by women in rural communities through active participation. It is expected, therefore, that the adjustment problems of retirement for rural women would differ from those of urban women. One could expect a more sympathetic understanding of the meaning of loss of work to the rural male, since both sexes have been closely involved in work activities.

FILIAL RESPONSIBILITY

Sociologists have maintained that the forces of industrialization and urbanization have tended to isolate the nuclear family. Spatial mobility, separation of home from work, specialization of skills, and abrupt retirement would mitigate against intergenerational solidarity in urban centers. Physical separation reduces the help that children can give to their aged parents. In rural areas, filial responsibility for aged parents is commonly expressed by sharing living quarters, an arrangement often brought about by economic necessity. It may be concluded that the more common filial support for aged parents in rural than in urban areas is prompted by the imperatives of the situation as well as by the adherence to traditional values.

RETIREMENT TO RURAL AREAS

We have discussed retirement practices of persons who live in rural areas, but we have failed to mention that rural areas frequently are attractive places for urban old people to reside in retirement. Cheap land and cheap living have an appeal to those who must retire on limited incomes. Developers have capitalized on these assets, for retirement communities frequently have rural sites. Operating a retirement farm is a way of supplementing retirement income. In a recent study of Florida retirement farms, Alleger pointed out that 64 percent of the operators listed a non-farm preretirement occupation, which suggests that farming is emerging as a retirement alternative for nonfarm workers.[19]

ADJUSTMENT TO RETIREMENT IN RURAL AREAS

In a society that places high value on work as an end in itself, conflict can arise between the need to feel useful and the practice of retiring from occupational roles. In rural areas evidence of this conflict is found in compulsive efforts to rationalize leisure or nonwork activities and the embarrassment that is often shown on being caught loafing or at leisure.

Adjustment becomes necessary when a change upsets previously existing patterns of relationships and activities. Retirement from work can be such an upsetting change. Loss of status and reduction of income are two principal upsetting elements in withdrawal from work.

We have already noted that self-employment provides opportunity for a less disruptive transition from full employment to retirement than does wage or salaried employment. The transition from full operation as owner-manager of a farm or business frequently is a very gradual process, the result being a status very close to the beginning status.

Rural workers who can retire and still be owners of businesses or managers of real property (in contrast to stocks or bonds, which have never been popular investments in rural areas) escape in part the need to acquire status-giving substitutes for occupational roles. For many rural workers who have not achieved ownership status, full retirement has been out of the question. OASDI has been a boon to this group and to those among the property ownership class whose property was limited to a home, a business, or a farm too small to provide sufficient rental income for a minimum living standard.

Although in many respects adjustment to retirement is easier for rural than for the urban aged, there are two areas of adjustment that are more difficult in rural areas. These are income and health. The rural aged may enjoy some nonincome advantages, such as more space, fresh air, and the peace and quiet of rural surroundings. However, the fact that median incomes for rural persons at retirement age (65 or older) were 25-30 percent less than those of urban persons in the same age bracket in 1959 is substantial evidence of a low-income problem in rural areas.

Money may not solve all the problems of retirement, but lack of it can aggravate the situation. In a commercial society such as ours, income not only provides for the amenities of life but serves as a vehicle for maintaining social relationships that tend to preserve status and function to maintain engagement with the society.

Health is almost universally recognized as a major factor in adjustment for the aging person. The significance of health in retirement is obvious. For many, the decision to retire or not to retire is determined by the person's state of health, regardless of other circumstances. The rural aged share with the urban aged the adjustment problems occasioned by failing health, with the important exception that health facilities are less readily available in most rural areas.

The retirement experiences of three generations of one family cannot duplicate all the adjustment problems of farmers, but they can serve to illustrate some common experiences and the changes that have occurred over the past 50 years in the Midwest. The grandfather of the present farmer moved from Iowa to establish a homestead in unsettled land in Nebraska in the 1880's. By 1909, his family of three boys and three girls were grown to maturity, and two of the boys were ready to start farming for themselves. Having accumulated enough land for two farms, the grandfather retired at the age of 49 and rented the land to the two sons who aspired to be farmers. After two years of renting, the sons "purchased" the farms. Although the grandfather was a landlord only two years, the sales involved no down payment and the purchasers were his sons; thus, he continued in an advisory capacity of a landlord for many years, spending much of his time, particularly during the summer months, helping out on the farms.

The sons who started farming in 1909 followed their father's example, even to expanding their holdings in anticipation of having more than one farm to pass on in turn to their sons. The Depression altered these plans, and one son lost both the original farm and the one he had purchased in 1930. The other managed to retain his farm and, by postponing retirement, used the period of favorable farm prices during World War II to pay off his debts. The son who lost his farms "retired" in the mid-thirties to odd jobs as a day laborer. The other retired in 1946 at the age of 60 and moved to a small city, selling part of his farm to a son, who took over operation of the entire farm, but remaining actively involved with the farm as his father before him had. Although the second-generation farmer had accumulated a larger farm than his father had, it was only large enough for one farm when he retired.

Like many of his generation, the current farmer had to delay starting his farming career until his father was financially able to retire. His waiting time was occupied with college training, nonfarm employment, and service in World War II. Although already older than his grandfather was at retirement, he has only been farming about 20 years, and retirement still seems far away. He owns part of the land he farms, but the rest of the farm is tied up for an indefinite period in a life estate for his widowed mother. His efforts to achieve full owner-operator status and to insure transmission of the farm intact to the next generation have not been fulfilled. One of his sons left the farm for a high school teaching job and the other is still in school. The possibility of using a family corporation as a mechanism for keeping the farm intact and facilitating its transfer from one generation to another is under consideration.

PUBLIC PROGRAMS AND RETIREMENT
AMONG THE RURAL AGED

The classification of farmers with factory owners and businessmen was largely responsible for the decision of Congress to omit farmers from OASDI coverage when the original social security legislation was passed. The assumption was that farmers would not be interested in participating, which probably was true in 1935. By 1950, however, the full effects of the Depression and the effects of technological changes in agriculture during World War II had altered opinion. The Depression and the rapid capitalization of agriculture during the war and immediate postwar period offered convincing evidence that farm owneroperatorship was no longer feasible for many nor was it essential for success in farming.

The complexity of the socioeconomic organization of society had by 1950 produced a conviction that the differences between self-employed and wage workers in their control over their welfare was not as great as had been assumed. Security mechanisms had been initiated for wage and salary workers in the form of negotiated wage contracts, workmen's compensation, pension systems, group insurance, and social security. Self-employment as an owner of a small business (on the farm or in the small town) had lost some of its luster. As a consequence, opinion surveys of farmers in the early 1950's revealed that a majority were willing to participate in a public program to insure income for old age or dependence caused by the death of the worker.[20]

IMPLICATIONS AND PROSPECTS

Rural society is changing; indeed, the rate of change in rural areas may exceed that in urban centers. Farming in the United States is becoming more technical and commercialized. The significant question is whether a transition can be made without taking too heavy a psychological toll of the rural aged whose occupations and retirement are tied to the rural social systems of the past.

We have seen that many smaller rural places have become retirement communities. Can these villages provide the atmosphere and services that are conducive to a healthy (both mental and physical) old age for their citizens or will they, as well as the individuals, become "disengaged" from the mainstream of American society?

In some ways, retirement in rural areas is less difficult than in urban centers. A principal advantage in rural areas is the preponderance of self-employment, which means that relatively few rural people are faced with the abrupt transition from full employment to no employment at all. There is a better chance for continuity of life styles as the worker moves into later life. When there is cultural preparation for a new way of life, the results are less likely to be disastrous. Other factors that facilitate retirement in rural areas are:

(a) An integration of work with nonwork roles so that the diminution of work roles does not involve a violent break with previously established patterns of age grading.

(b) The preservation of work status by the older man who keeps the farm or business in the family and exercises management functions.

(c) More sympathetic understanding between the sexes about problems of retirement.

(d) Greater filial support of aged parents by their adult children.

The discussion above pictures the ideal for retirement in rural areas, but there are also some negative aspects. For example, small-town businessmen are often pressed toward larger operations and may be forced to live with their business until their death. In addition, smaller operations may not be able both to finance retirement and to insure a good start for children.

The prospects of rural work roles and retirement are bound up with the trends in national culture, for there is evidence that rural-urban cultural convergence is occurring. If this process culminates in a more-or-less uniform national culture, it will not mean that problems of work and retirement will have been solved for older persons. The concept of retirement is a relatively new one and does not as yet have universal acceptance in either urban or the rural society, nor is there extensive agreement on its meaning. It may be concluded that more experimentation with various alternatives will be necessary before acceptable and beneficial norms regarding work and retirement will emerge.

NOTES

[1] Delbert C. Miller and William H. Form, *Industrial Sociology* (New York: Harper, 1951), p. 115.

[2] Emile Durkheim, *The Division of Labor in Society*, trans. George Simpson (New York: Macmillan, 1933).

[3] Brian J. L. Berry and Allen Pred, *Central Place Studies, Bibliography Series Number One* (Philadelphia: Regional Science Research Institute, 1961).

[4] Robert W. Hodge, Paul M. Siegel, and Peter H. Rossi, "Occupational Prestige in the United States, 1925-1963," *American Journal of Sociology*, 70 (Nov. 1964), 286-302.

[5] Daryl J. Hobbs, George M. Beal, and Joe M. Bohlen, *The Relations of Farm Operator Values and Attitudes to Their Economic Performance* (Iowa Agricultural and Home Economics Experiment Station Project 1492, Department of Economics and Sociology, Iowa State University, Rural Sociology Report No. 33; Ames, Iowa: June 1964).

[6] Elaine Cumming and William E. Henry, *Growing Old* (New York: Basic Books, 1961).

[7] Peter Townsend, *The Family Life of Old People* (Glencoe, Ill.: Free Press, 1957).

[8] Irving Rosow, "And Then We Were Old," *Transaction*, 2 (Jan./Feb. 1965), 20-28.

[9] Walter C. McKain, Jr., Elmer D. Baldwin, and Louis J. Ducoff, *Old Age and Retirement in Rural Connecticut: 2. Economics Security of Farm Operators and Farm Laborers* (Storrs Agricultural Experiment Station Bulletin 299; Storrs, Conn., June 1953).

[10] William G. Adkins and Joe R. Motheral, *The Farmer Looks at His Economic Security* (Texas Agricultural Experiment Station Bulletin 774; College Station, Texas, 1954).

[11] William H. Sewell, Charles E. Ramsey, and Louis J. Ducoff, *Farmers' Conceptions and Plans for Economic Security in Old Age* (Wisconsin Agricultural Experiment Station Bulletin 182; Madison, Wis., Sept. 1953).

[12] John S. Taylor, *Farmer's View of Retirement in Relation to Post-Retirement Work Activity* (Northwest Missouri State College Bulletin 52; Maryville, Mo., May 1959).

[13] Howard M. Sauer, Ward W. Bauder, and Jeanne C. Biggar, *Retirement Plans, Concepts and Attitudes of Farm Operators in Three Eastern South Dakota Counties* (Rural Sociology Department, Agricultural Experiment Station, South Dakota State University, Brookings, in cooperation with Farm Population Branch, Economic Research Service, U. S. Department of Agriculture, Bulletin 515; June 1964).

[14] *Ibid.*

[15] McKain, *et al.*, *Old Age and Retirement in Rural Connecticut*; Sewell, *et al.*, *Farmers' Conceptions and Plans*; Adkins and Motheral, *The Farmer Looks at His Economic Security*; I. M. Baill, *The Farmer and Old-Age Security: A Summary of Four Studies, 1951-1954* (Agriculture Information Bulletin 151; Washington, D. C., 1955); and Robert E. Galloway, *Farmers' Plans for Economic Security in Old Age* (Kentucky Experiment Station Bulletin 626; Lexington, Ky., 1955).

[16] Elton B. Hill and Marshall Harris, *Family Farm Transfers and Some Tax Consideration* (North Central Regional Publication 127 and Michigan State University Agricultural Experiment Station Special Bulletin 436; Sept. 1961).

[17] Galloway, *Farmers' Plans for Economic Security*; Sewell, *et al.*, *Farmers' Conceptions and Plans*; McKain, *et al.*, *Old Age and Retirement in Rural Connecticut.*

[18] Ward W. Bauder, *Iowa Farm Operator's and Farm Landlord's Knowledge of, Participation in and Acceptance of Old Age and Survivor's Insurance Program* (Iowa Agricultural and Home Economics Experiment Station Research Bulletin 479; June 1960); Ward W. Bauder, Otis Durant Duncan, and James D. Tarver, *The Social Security and Retirement Program of*

Oklahoma Farm Operators and Farm Landlords (Oklahoma Experiment Station Bulletin B-592; Stillwater, Okla., March 1962); Sauer, *et al., Retirement Plans, Concepts and Attitudes.*

[19] Daniel E. Alleger, *Rural Farm Retirement* (University of Florida Agricultural Experiment Station Bulletin 583; Feb. 1957).

[20] McKain, *et al., Old Age and Retirement in Rural Connecticut;* Sewell, *et al., Farmers' Conceptions and Plans;* Adkins and Motheral, *The Farmer Looks at His Economic Security;* Baill, *The Farmer and Old-Age Security;* Galloway, *Farmers' Plans for Economic Security.*

JOSEPH H. BRITTON

JEAN O. BRITTON

The Middle-Aged and Older Rural Person and His Family*

Probably no institution has greater potential for lifelong influence upon human behavior than the family. The family is defined as "a socially sanctioned grouping of persons united by kinship, marriage, or adoption ties, who generally share a common habitat and interact according to well-defined social roles created by a common culture."[1] The family is of central importance to all other social institutions. It is the first institution by which the child is socialized and it provides a setting to satisfy the physical, social, and psychological needs of its members. The three-generation extended family plays a vital role in meeting the needs of the elderly, especially for those whose capacity for independence may be limited.

HISTORICAL CHANGES AND THE RURAL FAMILY

The rural family in early days was largely a self-sufficient and isolated unit, which tended to foster a strong sense of inter-

* Submitted as Research Publication 237, College of Home Economics, Pennsylvania State University, University Park, Pa. The preparation of this chapter was aided by Public Health Service Grant 1 R01 HD 01757-01, from the National Institute of Child Health and Human Development.

dependence among members. As families migrated to this country and to the West this familial interdependence was important, although the larger kin group was not maintained intact. The traditional rural family tended to be patriarchal, and care of the sick and the aged was the expected pattern.

In the traditional rural family children were economically advantageous and there were more children per family and fewer childless families than in urban areas.[2] They worked closely with their parents, learning skills of farming and homemaking. Not only was little time or energy available for leisure activities, but work was a virtue in itself. Every family member's help was needed, and there were many jobs the old could do around the house and the farm. Daily farm chores tied farmers and their families to the farm, and they traveled little and seldom moved.

Many rural families are losing their rural characteristics, and the differences between the rural and urban are disappearing.[3] Technological advances have enabled fewer persons to produce more with less physical effort. With industrialization, young farm people are seeking jobs away from the home. Mechanization has made farming specialized and the farm family tends to be a commercial unit dependent upon outside cash markets. Improvements in transportation and communication have lessened the physical and social isolation of the rural family. The decrease in rural-urban differences is illustrated by a national study of how Americans view their mental health. Gurin, Veroff, and Feld found that "a young, educated, male farmer is more like a young, educated, male New Yorker than either of these people is like his own father. Although cultural subgroupings based on geographical distinctions may have had meanings in the past, before the mass media and the transportation revolutions, they are probably becoming less critical today."[4]

Smaller families, smaller living quarters, changes in educational patterns, and increased social mobility also had their effects. It became more feasible for women to work outside the home. Families came to depend upon other social institutions for educating the young, for entertaining the family, and for caring for the sick and the aged. New patterns of buying, new desires for material comforts and conveniences and even luxuries, for travel and vacations, in effect brought a new way of life to rural families.

What special meanings did these changes have for the rural

aged? Older adults were left with land and an occupational commitment to farming. Compared with young people, they were less well educated and less inclined or able to move from their farm homes. They knew farming not simply as a way of earning a living but as a way of life. The belief that one's own land would provide sustenance in times of need may have made them resistant to change. The older person's children in many cases had become urbanized and often lived some distance away in housing which typically had no space for guests—including the old.

New patterns of support of the aged and care of the ill and the dependent had emerged. Professionalization of services tended to reduce the status of the old person in his family and in the community. The reliance upon governmental and industrial pension systems and insurance programs and the use of public rather than familial assistance suggest an orientation that differed greatly from the traditional pattern. The old farmer himself could now draw his social security benefits or, if necessary, accept public assistance for his support in the absence of family or farm.

All these far-reaching changes may have left the older rural person feeling that the old values are no longer tenable, and yet he is uncomfortable with the new ways of believing and behaving. Perhaps it can be said that if there is a rural way of life today it persists only in the old.

A DEVELOPMENTAL APPROACH TO THE FAMILY

A "developmental approach"[5] to the study of the family views change over time as a major variable. As described recently by Hill and Rodgers, this approach to the study of the family uses the family life cycle as a "demographic independent variable" and as a "process."[6] The family is viewed as a "unity of interacting personalities" and the behavior of its members is dependent upon the structure of this unity and upon the functions, or "tasks," these persons have at one point in time and extended over time. Important in such an analysis of the family are the peculiar positions the members occupy and the roles (and role "clusters" and "complexes") they perform in the system. Also important are the "sequential regularities" of the family over its life history, including the "role sequences, careers of family positions, intercontingencies of careers, and stages of development." In addition, the features of the family as purposeful and goal-seeking give direction to its behavior as a social system within a larger social system. Rodgers[7] discusses the bases of this developmental approach:

> As the individual grows older, the societal and family age and sex norms relevant to his roles change. At the same time, the abilities of the individual—motor, intellectual and social—also change. . . .
> Secondly, as times moves on, situations within the family and in society at large change. . . . These changes bring about redefinitions of situations within and outside the family, and, concomitantly, changing role patterns.
> Finally, from within the individual (and aside from his physical growth) there develops a kind of personal "life view" which will bring pressure for change in systemic organization.[8]

The life cycle of the family begins when the man and woman marry and establish their family, moves on to an "establishment" stage, then to an "expectant" stage. At a "childbearing" stage and as a family with preschool children, its major goal is to reorganize itself around the needs of infants and small children and later to fit into the expanding world of school-age children. Still later it becomes a family with "adult trainees," and its task then is to loosen the family ties to permit greater freedom and heavier responsibilities to its younger members.

When the family releases its young adults, it is in the "launching stage." Typically this span of time encompasses about eight years, from the first child's leaving to the time the last child leaves, when the husband and wife are usually in their early fifties.[9]

In the "middle years" or the "postparental" or "empty nest" stage, the family's goal is to reorganize itself around the marriage pair and, perhaps, prepare a "strategy of 'disengagement.' "[10] During this period, the couple typically become grandparents, an event that entails new roles and activities. At retirement from job, the couple's goal may be to initiate disengagement, or withdrawal, then more or less gradually to retire selectively from outside activities or become active in new pursuits. Following this period comes widowhood, from the time of the death of one spouse to the death of the survivor.

During these stages the various members of the family have their own individual developmental tasks to accomplish, resulting in complex interpersonal relationships and patterns of motivation and behavior. In addition, individuals have tasks to master at various stages of their occupational careers. The intricacies of how the tasks of work life and family life occur simultaneously are illustrated by Rapoport and Rapoport.[11]

THE MIDDLE YEARS

A developmental approach views individual and family behavior in the context of time. It recognizes behavior in young adulthood, for example, as related to behavior in childhood and adolescence, and old age as related to the periods of life which preceded it. In this review, concern is primarily in the middle and later years of the life span. Here middle age means the time when the individual parent is in the "postparental" or "empty nest" stage of the family cycle. This is a period which for *couples* is historically new; at the turn of the century the typical (median) husband died before his last child left home, whereas in 1950 he lived 14 years beyond his last child's departure.[12] This suggested to Martel that the present generation of middle-aged people might be called "cultural pioneers."[13]

The middle years have been described as a time when the individual is confronted with uncomfortable physical changes, when he recognizes that he has reached the top of his career, and when he realizes his future is limited.[14] Some writers have spoken of the new freedoms of the middle years[15] and the perspective and opportunities this time provides. As Donahue has said, "The human mental machine is now, at last, ready for its prime performance."[16]

Although middle-aged people apparently have personal and family problems, these problems have not been studied widely.[17] The studies that have been conducted on middle age and family behavior have been concerned with role behavior, intergenerational relationships, responsibility for aging parents, and marriage in the middle years. Generally, the studies have used urban subjects. The findings, therefore, do not necessarily apply to middle-aged persons in rural families. It is hoped that questions of rural-urban differences in these uncharted areas will be raised for investigation.

ROLE BEHAVIOR

Several studies have focused on the functioning of middle-aged persons in their familial environments. These studies of role behavior indicate that middle-aged persons often reorganize their roles. Adults of varying ages perceive younger and older aged persons differently, which in turn influences their own role behavior. Rating the role performance of a sample of Kansas City residents aged 40 to 70, Havighurst delineated five major patterns of role performance, two of which were "family-centered."[18] People with these patterns tended to employ a large part of their energy in the roles of parent, spouse, and homemaker and to neglect the extrafamilial roles of citizen, friend, and association member. There were social class differences, but the differences between sex and age groups were very small.

Rose provided questionnaire data on role behavior which he obtained from the parents of university students.[19] His findings verified the hypothesis that "the life satisfaction of middle-class women as they enter middle age is a function of the degree to which they are able to assume another central role to substitute for their necessarily declining role as homemakers."[20]

In their study of 60 Chicago women in the climacteric years (aged 44-57), Wood and Neugarten examined patterns of role change from age 40 onward.[21] About 20 percent of the women enlarged their role behavior and 25 percent were "shifters" who expanded their roles in some areas, constricted them in others. Another 28 percent had changed their roles very little since age 40. And 27 percent tended to have had low activity levels in both family and extrafamilial roles and tended to have constricted these further since age 40. And although women with "empty nests" expanded their roles, the investigators were surprised to find that women who showed most role expansion were those with the youngest child 14 years of age or younger still at home. The group of women whose youngest child at home was 18 or older had least role expansion. They suggested that "general life satisfaction" may be a mediating variable.[22]

To study role-images of husbands, wives, sons, and daughters, Neugarten and Gutmann used a specially-designed picture showing a young man, a young woman, an older man, and an older woman.[23] It was presented to 131 urban men and women aged 40 to 70 of two social class levels. Their findings showed some perceptions of age and sex roles in the family:

> The Young Man was generally seen as a somewhat detached figure in the family setting. . . . The Young Woman was a bland figure . . . around whom family issues were initiated and resolved. She provided the tie between younger and older generations. . . . The Older Woman, was seen as the key figure in the family, and the one who usually had the greatest impact upon the resolution of family issues. . . . The Older Man, by comparison with the Older Woman, was a neutral figure . . . seen as conforming to the wishes of others or as withdrawn altogether from family interaction. . . .
>
> The role-images of all four figures varied consistently with age and sex of respondent, but not with social class. Most striking was the fact that with increasing age of respondents, the Older Man and Older Woman reversed roles in regard to authority in the family. For younger men and women (aged 40-54) the Older Man was seen as the authority figure. For older men and women (aged 55-70) the Older Woman was in the dominant role and the Older Man, no matter what other qualities were ascribed to him, was seen as submissive.[24]

THE MIDDLE-AGED AND THEIR GROWN CHILDREN

What are the relationships of middle-aged persons with their grown children and with other family members? Several studies by Sussman have been concerned with "intergenerational family continuity," i.e., the character of and the extent to which relationships are maintained between succeeding generations of the family and thus are contributing to the "on-goingness" of the family's original values, attitudes, and other behavior.

In one such investigation, a sample of Cleveland-area couples between the ages of 45-60 whose children had married and permanently left the parental home was used.[25] Interview material was evaluated in terms of family continuity and change in role behavior since the leave-taking of the last child. Some of the findings were the following:

> Family continuity was found to be inversely related to social class. Half or more of the couples reported changes in the four roles of parent, spouse, user of leisure time, and church member; but changes in the roles of worker, sibling, child of aging parents, aunt or uncle, club or association member, citizen, or friend, were relatively infrequent. It appears that intergenerational family continuity is a more important factor than social class in affecting changes in social roles among post-parental couples.[26]

In a broader context, Sussman and Burchinal summarized evidence concerning the function of aid within the kin group, concluding that there exists an American kin family system with complicated matrices of aid and service activities which link together the component units into a functioning network.[27] "The network . . . is composed of nuclear units related by blood and affinal ties. Relations extend along generational lines and bilaterally where structures take the form of sibling bonds and ambilineages, i.e., the family circle or cousin club."[28]

It has been assumed that historical changes, especially those related to shifts in rural to urban living, have resulted in a common pattern of the isolated nuclear family—one in which there is little or no interaction among kinsfolk or between adult generations. In this family, middle-aged couples have little contact with their adult children or with their aged parents. Sussman and Burchinal attacked this notion, concluding that understanding the family "as a functioning social system interrelated with other social systems in society is possible *only by rejection of the isolated nuclear family concept.* Accepting the isolated nuclear family as the most functional type today has led to erroneous conclusions," they said, in social service practice and other social systems.[29]

In a paper on geographic mobility and family cohesion, Litwak emphasized that persons separated from their families maintain ties with extended family members and that a "modified" extended family provides assistance—financial, psychological, and social—associated with moves of the young nuclear family. He pointed out that for bureaucratic occupations, at least, those nuclear families on "career plateaus" were not likely to move, or, if they did move, they moved toward their extended families. They also may encourage retired parents to settle near them.[30]

In another study of the extended kinship system, Reiss interviewed variously aged adult members of 161 middle-class Boston families concerning frequency of interaction among kinsfolk.[31] His data showed that the degree of kin relationship and the geographical distance (not age or family cycle phase) were the most important variables in accounting for frequency of interaction. Half of his respondents felt that interaction had not been frequent enough; there was "a desire for kin to live closer than they now do—but not too close. Common residence with kin is strongly disapproved." Reiss concluded: "In general, it appears that in the middle class the pattern of independent nuclear families is well institutionalized and that there is concern that the nuclear family be not also isolated from extended kin. Geographic mobility is the factor upon which the question of isolation hinges."[32]

In a study of parental aid to married children in a North Carolina city, Adams showed that the length of the marriage, residential propinquity, occupational strata, and sex of the child were important factors in parental aid.[33] However, 20 percent of the sample said there was no pattern of helping the young couple at all.

Adams concluded that research is needed on the attitudes of young adults toward their own and their spouse's parents as they do or do not receive help from them. It might be added that similar research is needed to learn how the parents, in their middle years, feel toward giving aid, perhaps as a part of the "launching" process, and to determine the circumstances under which they feel they in turn can or should receive assistance from their grown children. Since these interrelationships are laid in a historical context of some decades, the special meaning they take at one point must be seen with the additional perspective of the long-range sequence. Knowledge of these attitudes could add to an understanding of the dynamics of the actual operation of the family network, between and within generations, over time.

THE MIDDLE-AGED AND THEIR PARENTS

What is the "duty" of grown children toward their aging parents? Schorr dealt with this question in *Filial Responsibility in the Modern American Family*.[34] His analysis showed this to be an issue of the interpersonal rights and obligations of adult generations, complicated by changing moral and legal sanctions and by a cash economy. He noted that 35 states expect adult children to contribute money to their parents, but that this was "an expectation that differs from customary American family practice and from the assumptions underlying other (financial) programs."[35] Filial relations in the United States, Schorr said, are characterized by a "spontaneous exchange of help and services," little influenced by support laws.[36] When support requirements are enforced, the result is that the parents and children live together not by choice but by necessity, and, Schorr added, "Often the results are damaging and contrary to what the people involved would choose."[37]

Related to Schorr's last point is a finding from research on three-generation families.[38] Data from several community studies showed that the proportion of families in which three generations were living together varied from an estimated 1.9 percent in an Illinois community to 8.4 percent in one rural community in Pennsylvania. Smith, Britton, and Britton studied such families in two small Pennsylvania communities. Nearly two-thirds of the families consisted of the first generation and daughter and her family. For about half, economic reasons were given as most important in the decision to live together, and usually it was for benefit of the older rather than the middle generation. As to preference of living arrangement, about 6 out of 10 of both first and second generations said they preferred to live in their own homes alone.

Smith interviewed 490 persons in two Pennsylvania urban areas.[39] Of the persons interviewed 71 percent said it was the responsibility of families either wholly or in part to help older family members.

Dinkel reported the attitudes of a group of high school and college students toward supporting aged parents.[40] His findings indicated that the obligation of children to support their aged parents is no longer well established. Still, more students accepted than rejected the obligation when the situation did not present unusual hardships.

Consistent with the finding reported earlier that the nuclear family is not isolated from kinsfolk is the finding of Shanas, from a study of health care of older people.[41] A nationwide probability sample of persons 65 or over, living outside institutions, was interviewed along with the relatives and friends to whom they would turn in time of need; 9 of every 10 would turn to children, most often to daughters. What is important here is that these middle-aged children themselves expressed willingness to "assume obligations which are traditionally associated with the relationships of aged parents and adult children."[42]

These studies suggest the significance of the discrepancy between social norms and personal aspirations, on the one hand, and actual behavior within families in caring for their aged members.

MARRIAGE IN THE MIDDLE YEARS

Little research has concerned marriage in the middle years of life, a point emphasized by Gravatt, who commented on the conflicting notions about how placid or turbulent these years of marriage might be.[43] He interviewed and tested couples whose children had grown up and left home, and he learned that the middle years were seen neither as "fraught with fears and difficulties" nor a time when the couple is drawn closer together.[44] Those subjects of his study who had had a satisfactory marital adjustment prior to the children's departure maintained a satisfactory marital adjustment; those whose adjustment was unsatisfactory remained unsatisfactory. Gravatt concluded that "there is continuity to personality adjustment within the family, even when the major changes of middle and later life . . . demand changes in behavior patterns."[45]

Deutscher investigated the attitudes of 49 Kansas City husbands and wives concerning the postparental phase of the family cycle.[46] His data indicated that this phase is "not generally defined unfavorably by those involved in it," a finding consistent with that of Axelson,[47] in spite of the newness of this phase of the family cycle and the little opportunity for "anticipatory socialization."

Some longitudinal data on marriage in the middle years were provided by Pineo's research.[48] He was able to retest 400 of the 1,000 couples Burgess and his associates had studied during engagement and early marriage. After 20 years of marriage, marital satisfaction and other characteristics were again assessed, so that the early and middle years of marriage could be compared. Losses were found on almost all of 18 indexes, with significant losses on several—for both husbands and wives.

The question of how these 400 couples might have differed from the nonparticipants is not answered in Pineo's report. For the couples participating in the study, at least, there was a drop in marital satisfaction and adjustment and a loss of intimacy, a process Pineo called "disenchantment." He suggested that the effects of "exaggerated idealization of the mate or of intense romanticising" are probably felt in the early years of marriage. In the middle years, Pineo said, "it is the unforeseen changes in situation, personality, or behavior, which contribute most to the disenchantment," and since these changes could not have been foreseen, he added, some process of disenchantment is to be expected.[49]

These few exploratory studies of role behavior, intergenerational relationships, and of marriage during middle age raise many questions that merit the attention of family specialists—including both research workers and practitioners in clinical and instructional settings. Until such research is conducted, using rural-urban living, for example, as one differentiating variable, it will not be clear when and how pertinent these findings are to families in the middle years.

THE LATER YEARS

As the middle-aged couple completes its adjustment to the climactic and climacteric years, they experience new relationships. They may have new feelings of freedom—freedom from occupational, financial, and familial pressures, new feelings of comfort and companionship, and sometimes, new feelings of boredom, disenchantment, and despair.

These relationships may persist until some change forces the couple to recognize a new situation that demands a new adjustment. Although old age does not occur abruptly, in current American society onset of old age is arbitrarily marked by compulsory retirement at age 65 or at age of eligibility for social security or retirement benefits. For many self-employed business men and farmers, retirement may not be so abrupt. Other changes, normal for this stage, present themselves,—declining physical strength and chronic illness, widowhood, or financial crises. Each of these by itself would be burdensome, but the older person may face all of them within a short time. And in a culture where there is an apparent reluctance to face such changes, the older person is often unprepared.

The family constitutes persons of potential significance for providing strength for each other in times of need and for creating and sharing pleasures with each other. What is known about the family and its behavior in the later years, especially the rural family? In the sections that follow, research findings concerning living arrangements, intergenerational relationships, isolation, and norms for aging in rural communities will be presented.

LIVING ARRANGEMENTS OF OLDER PERSONS IN RURAL AREAS

The social relationships of older persons with members of their families depend in part upon where older members live and where they prefer to live. When adults are asked where they plan to live in old age, most say they will continue to live in their own homes.[50] Rural persons overwhelmingly prefer to live in separate homes with their spouses. This is borne out by studies of Bauder in South Dakota,[51] Sewell, Ramsey, and Ducoff in Wisconsin,[52] and Bauder, Duncan, and Tarver in Oklahoma.[53] Only 14 percent of the Connecticut farm operators in McKain, Baldwin, and Ducoff's study thought they would like to spend their retirement years with their children. Only 6 percent of regular hired farm laborers said they wanted to live with their children.[54]

Although rural older people may want to live alone or with their spouses, what are their actual living arrangements? In a small Connecticut community, McKain and Baldwin found that over half the older persons lived either alone or with their spouses; one-fourth lived with their children.[55] More of the widowers were living with their children than widows. In this town 90 percent of the older adults had relatives living in the same town.

Barron surveyed men over 60 in six predominantly rural counties in New York.[56] He found that more retired men lived alone, without spouse and children, than did employed respondents. In Thurston County, Washington, Stone and Slocum reported that 23 percent of older persons who had children lived with them.[57] Homes were shared with children by a larger proportion of the people living in the open country than by those living in small towns or cities. Often it was the children who shared the parents' household.

In a study of older people in Pepin County, Wisconsin, Loeb and his associates found that about two-thirds of the older people lived alone or with spouse and about 15 percent lived with their children and grandchildren.[58]

A report on an Iowa survey of life after 60 showed that most of the persons interviewed were homeowners living in their own homes.[59] More than 25 percent of the people in their sixties and 35 percent of those past 70 reported that they lived alone. Women more than men lived alone, and among women in rural counties who were past 75, nearly half were living alone. In urban areas, such women tended to move in with their children. Three-quarters of the respondents had one or more living children, but only 20 percent were actually living with a son or daughter. About half of the parents had no children living in the immediate vicinity, and one-fourth said they did not see any of their children as often as once a month. In spite of distance, however, most parents in the sample did maintain regular visiting with at least some of their children and they derived important satisfactions from these relationships. Over half said they had visited with a son or daughter during the week preceding the survey, and more than 40 percent had spent time with grandchildren.

Muse compared the plans of middle-aged couples with the actual living arrangements made by older couples, widows, and widowers aged 65 and over in rural Vermont areas.[60] She reported that almost all the middle-aged couples believed that as long as husband and wife are both living they would continue to maintain their own households and have no one else with them. These couples had given little thought to living arrangements in case of death of one spouse. More than half of them thought they would then probably live alone in the same houses. Almost all of the elderly couples in the study were living in their own households and most had no one else living with them.

Montgomery studied 510 persons 65 years of age and older living in a small town in central Pennsylvania.[61] Of the respondents, 57 percent were married and living in their own households, and in 12 percent of the households relatives were present, usually a son or daughter. Nearly one-half (48 percent) of the widows received regular assistance from their relatives, as compared with 22 percent of the single and 14 percent of the married respondents.

In a study of Lutheran church members aged 65 and older of a central Pennsylvania synod, it was found that although 30 percent of the group had no living children, 82 percent lived within nine miles of their nearest kin. Two-thirds of the older people studied had kin living in the same community. When they were asked about the most satisfactory living arrangements, nearly two-thirds felt it was most satisfactory to live independently, either with spouse or alone, if single or widowed. About 66 percent of the group lived either with spouse or alone, and only 16 percent lived with their children.[62]

The foregoing studies have shown that older rural persons most often are living alone or with their spouses. These are the arrangements generally preferred. Less often older persons live with their children. This is an arrangement less frequently preferred.

RELATIONSHIP OF OLDER PERSONS WITH THEIR FAMILIES

How often do older rural persons visit with their children or other relatives or call upon them for help? How satisfied are they with these relationships? Youmans interviewed over one thousand men and women aged 60 and over in a rural county and a city in Kentucky.[63] He found that more rural than urban older people had both living children and living brothers and sisters. Somewhat more rural than urban respondents lived in the same household as their children. Both rural and urban tended to visit their children more often than their siblings, but rural more than urban persons depended upon children to initiate the visits. Youmans suggested that such a difference reflected the poor transportation and limited finances of the older persons in the rural area.

Fuller, et al., studied 695 persons 60 and older in an Iowa

county, finding that older people living in the open country had the largest number of living relatives.[64] Aged persons in small towns planned visits with relatives and friends more often than others. One-fifth of the aged in open country and in the urban areas had had no relationship with relatives or friends during the month preceding the interview, as compared with one-tenth of those living in small towns. The fact that the month in this case was February is probably pertinent to this finding.

For the aged in Wellington County, Ontario, Stevens reported that 77 percent of the rural (open-country *and* small-town) aged lived with spouse and/or children, compared with 63 percent of the urban aged.[65] Thus 90 percent of the rural aged said they saw their immediate families daily or one or more times a week; only 65 percent of the urban aged reported this frequency of visiting with members of their families.

Warren interviewed all adults 65 and over, 143 men and women, in Almond, New York, with a population, 1,234. He found that about half of the group said they got together with family or close relatives on important holidays or birthdays.[66]

Ström investigated the living conditions and health of 1,389 persons aged 70 or older in Norway; they were largely rural dwellers. He found that 74 percent were in daily contact with their families. Among 123 elderly people with "poor" family contacts, 22 percent were "physically unfit."[67] Studying the family life of old people in East London, Townsend also noted a relationship between incidence of health and financial problems and the lack of contact with family members.[68] He said that "elderly isolates seemed likely to make disproportionately heavy claims on health and welfare services. A supplementary investigation of a geriatric hospital, of welfare homes and of a local domiciliary service, . . . showed this to be so. People with daughters at hand made least claim of all. Various estimates suggested that but for the care given by female relatives the number of old people seeking admission to hospitals and welfare homes would have been three to five times greater."[69]

In his study of older persons living in an Illinois city, Phillips reported that almost half the respondents saw their children less often than at age 50, but that most of the sample saw their children rather frequently.[70]

Several investigators have assessed how much satisfaction older people derive from visiting with their families. It might be hypothesized that since older people tend to participate less frequently in formal and informal groups outside the family, the relationships they have with their children and with other relatives assume greater importance in maintaining their morale in old age.[71]

In the New York study by Warren, over half the group felt that relatives were more important to them as time went by, and about the same proportion felt quite satisfied with the help and consideration they received from relatives.[72] In comparing what older adults expect of their children with the actual behavior of their children, both as viewed by the older respondents, Phillips learned that children tended to do far more than their aged parents expected them to do.[73] In 95 percent of the cases the parents reported that they were quite satisfied with their children and 83 percent said they enjoyed seeing their children almost more than anything else.

Brown's study of a sample of 161 older residents of the city of Durham who had living children showed that in spite of geographic mobility of the children, changed structure of the family, and social isolation of the older parents, the elderly did not feel neglected. In only one segment of his sample—the upper status group—did Brown find that social isolation was related to feelings of neglect. He suggested that social isolation produces feelings of neglect only when older people expect a very close parent-child relationship. He cautioned that the older population is not a homogeneous one and that changes attributed to the American family do not affect older family members uniformly.[74]

The studies concerning visiting between older persons and members of their families must be viewed in terms of living arrangements and expectations. Most older adults seem to be satisfied with the relationships they do have. Rural persons tend to have more relatives to visit, but residence in the open country, small towns, and urban centers apparently makes a difference.

ISOLATION OF OLDER PERSONS FROM THEIR FAMILIES

Social isolation is often interpreted to mean separation from one's family, particularly from one's children. A distinction must be made between physical isolation and feelings of isolation of older people. Several writers have commented upon this.[75] Living with others, even with children, does not guarantee freedom from feelings of isolation. Conversely, living alone is not necessarily social isolation. Living alone means different things to persons of different backgrounds, experiences, personalities.

In a paper concerning family tensions between the old and the middle-aged, Cavan reported that attitudes rejecting old people by middle-aged persons are supported by such "rationalizations" that in-laws cannot live peaceably together, that the middle generation owes sole attention to the oncoming generation, and that old people are better off in institutions than in close association with their children.[76]

Research on the social isolation of older persons is meager. In their study of a London suburb, Willmott and Young confirmed the notion that "most people are not solitary," and that "old people without children are on the whole no more isolated or neglected than those with them." These investigators pointed out some common ways that older people find substitute arrangements when they are childless or without relatives: "Childless people treat nephews and nieces as their own children; their grandnephews and grandnieces as their grandchildren. Single people turn to their siblings and form a sort of nuclear family. Single people without relatives make quasi-siblings out of single friends and thus form a kind of family."[77]

In a report from a nationwide sample survey of all noninstitutionalized persons aged 65 and over in the United States, Shanas wrote: "More detailed analysis of family visiting patterns of the aged will probably reduce the estimates of old people in the United States who are socially isolated to something less than 6 percent. . . . However, an even smaller proportion of the elderly perceive of themselves as isolated."[78]

Kurtz and Smith reported that almost one-third of the sample members in a rural-urban fringe area rarely visited with any families in the area; 40 percent said they never visited local members of the family.[79]

In research concerning 6,300 persons aged 65 and over living in both rural and urban communities in five midwestern states, it was found that 80 percent of the respondents had at least one living child, and 60 percent of them reported that their children lived in the same town or within 25 miles. About 80 percent had living siblings and 40 percent had brothers and sisters living in the same town or within 25 miles' distance.[80]

Taietz studied the family life of old people in the Netherlands and found that "of the sons who live in the parents' community, those who are mobile with respect to their parents tend to visit their older parents less often than sons who are in the same stratum as their parents." When he interviewed 355 old people in two Dutch townships, there was some indication of avoidance of joint living arrangements and an absence of common meanings and values between the aged and their children. He found a high proportion of old people who felt negatively toward the extended family. Taietz claimed, however, that these trends do not necessaily mean isolation of old people from their adult children.[81]

In a study of intergenerational closeness or separation, Albrecht found no difference in degree of independence from children of people aged 65 to 69 and those over 80 years.[82] Married parents and men were more likely to allow their children to become independent and to maintain their own independence when they are old. Some lower socioeconomic groups tended to keep children dependent longer or to become dependent on them in later years. Care of aged parents was a responsibility of only 11 percent of the children—usually by those children who were single or widowed.

Evidence of differences in dependency between rural and urban older people is included in Steven's study of older adults in Ontario.[83] He asked them, "If you had to move, who would assist you in finding a place suited to your needs?" Of the urban aging 57 percent said they would depend upon themselves, and 52 percent of the rural aging said they would depend upon their children.

In his study of 490 urban Pennsylvania families regarding plans for their later years, Smith found that about three-fourths of the respondents had had some experience in "doubling up" and most wanted neither county homes nor children's homes for their retirement years. It appeared that couples maintain closer relationships with the parents of wives than with the parents of husbands.[84]

In her study of 70 four-generational families in which representatives of the three adult generations were interviewed, Boyd found that propinquity, personal attention and services, shared group activities, and desirable personal qualities were mentioned as factors which strengthened intergenerational ties.

Spatial and social distance, differing beliefs and ideologies, pre-occupation with affairs separate from the wider family, infrequent get-togethers and visits to one another, illness, age, and debility were factors seen as weakening intergenerational relationships.[85]

Glasser and Glasser concerned themselves with role reversal and conflict between aged parents and their children.[86] Their data, gathered in Detroit among 120 persons aged 60 or over receiving aid from the Jewish Family and Children's Service, suggested that parents and children expected to maintain close psychological ties but that children were not expected to provide material support for their aged parents. The Glassers noted a lag between expectation and actual provisions for the aged, creating role conflict between older parents and their children. This conflict is intensified by changing social norms which force many older people into dependent roles within their families, a reversal of the roles they played with their own children.

The research evidence indicates that, contrary to popular belief, the majority of old people in the United States do not live alone. Most older people live with their spouses, their children, and with other relatives. Only about a fifth live alone and, of these, most are women. Only about 5 of every 100 old people who have children and who are widowed and live alone live as far from their nearest child as a day's journey or more.[87]

FAMILY NORMS FOR AGING IN RURAL COMMUNITIES

The standards by which family behavior of adults is approved or disapproved are implied by some of the findings already reviewed. How do norms differ for the aged? Britton and his associates studied this problem in one rural Pennsylvania community.[88] They interviewed an adult in each household in a rural village and the surrounding township to determine what these adults expected of older persons. Open-ended and anecdotal questions were used. Following each anecdote, the interviewer asked the respondent to tell what he thought about the behavior just described. For example:

> Because she is pretty lonesome after the death of her husband, Mrs. Sayles rented out her own home and moved

in with her married daughter. (Q. What do you think of this?)

Emily lives alone. Although her hands are swollen she manages most things pretty well. The heavier housekeeping jobs, however, are practically impossible for her. (Q. What do you think of this?)

Interviewees commented freely and their responses were recorded verbatim on the schedule. Free responses given by major proportions of the interviewees concerning living arrangements and family relationships are shown in Tables 1 and 2.

The data in Table 1 show that in some ways young, middle-aged, and older adults differed according to what they consider appropriate behavior for older persons. For example, older adults were more convinced than younger ones that older persons ought to live alone and that older parents could advise their children,

Table 1. Selected Responses of Interviewees of Different Ages Concerning Living Arrangements and Family Relationships by Percentage

| | Age of interviewee | | | |
Response	39 or less; N=168 (X)	40-59; N=198 (Y)	60 or over; N=120 (Z)	Significant comparison*
An older person should live alone if at all possible.	23.2	24.2	39.2	X-Z Y-Z
It's all right for two generations to live together if they can get along.	18.5	20.7	30.8	X-Z
It's all right for parents to advise; they can help the children.	17.3	28.8	30.0	X-Y X-Z
Children can't always come home on holidays because they have plans of their own.	64.9	52.2	51.7	X-Z X-Y
It is all right for an older person to remarry if he wants to and can find a suitable mate.	91.9	81.8	68.3	X-Y Y-Z X-Z
So long as a grandmother does not care to be with her grandchildren it is all right.	20.3	31.8	27.5	X-Y
Most grandmothers love their grandchildren.	51.8	34.8	39.2	X-Y

* Significance of difference between percentages.

but less often than younger adults, did they think it appropriate for an older person to remarry.

As to norms concerning the family's role in solving older persons' problems (Table 2), younger adults saw family members assisting their elders significantly more often than the older persons saw them doing so—be it to take a senile member to the doctor or to help with money or with housework. In the example of the senile old women, middle-aged adults more often than oldsters suggested that the family had to care for her the best they could.

Table 2. Selected Responses of Interviewees of Different Ages Concerning Ways of Solving Older Persons' Problems by Percentage

Response	Age of interviewee			Significant comparison*
	39 or less; N=168 (X)	40-59; N=198 (Y)	60 or over; N=120 (Z)	
When an older woman acts "queer" her family should take her to the doctor.	39.3	33.8	21.7	X-Z Y-Z
When an older woman acts "queer" the family should care for her the best they can.	19.0	30.8	31.7	X-Y X-Z
The family should help an older couple almost out of money.	28.6	27.8	15.0	X-Z Y-Z
The family should help a woman who is physically unable to do her housework.	37.0	22.2	17.5	X-Y X-Z

* Significance of difference between percentages.

In this study social norms for older persons differed somewhat according to age, but social and educational differences were also correlated.[89] In a later phase of this investigation (1956), data were obtained on older (65+) persons themselves as to their activities and their attitudes and feelings concerning self.[90] Almost three-fourths of these 59 men and 86 women were living with family members; almost one-half were married and living with spouse; over one-third were widowed. Few felt neglected or believed their families interfered in their affairs. All but a few agreed that it was the family's responsibility to help an older couple who lacked money, but one-third of them said that this was often difficult since "they have their own families to look after."

When the survivors of these older adults were re-interviewed six years later (1962), at a time when all were 72 or over, 87 percent had had no change in marital status and 97 percent had not lost any children by death. Over one-half said they had more visits with their children than earlier, and another third said there had been no change in the number of visits with children. Most continued to feel neither neglected nor interfered with. Thus, in this investigation, little change in family norms had occurred and during the 6-year period there was little or no change in personalities and adjustments.[91]

CONCLUSION

Methods of research with the rural aging have not been given deserved attention. Problems of sampling are crucial among studies of adults, since no representative "captive" groups are available. Those adults who are available and willing to be interviewed are not necessarily representative of the total group. Frequently the research reports have not made clear the means by which subjects were selected nor the particular methods of obtaining data. Often the context of the study is not clear, and variation of responses according to social class, ethnic and religious background, or even sex are not always pointed out. Probably more restrictions on the findings reported would have been necessary if such conditions had been met. Many studies of family behavior have been cross-sectional descriptive investigations of the middle-aged or the aged. They have *not* been of aging as a process of change over time. More theorizing about the dynamics of change during the middle and later years is needed to lay the base for longitudinal research.

As shown by the research that has been done, these major findings emerge: there is a mutual desire of adult generations generally to live separately. Older people continue to relate satisfactorily to the younger generations in the family. The great majority of older people in the United States are not socially isolated from their middle-aged children and grandchildren.

They live near them, see them frequently, observe holidays together, and perform services that are mutually beneficial.

Many questions have not been answered by the available data. Fundamental is the question of the extent to which rural-urban residence is an important differentiating variable. Most investigators have assumed that behavior of the middle-aged and the aged with members of their families occurs without relation to location of residence. This variable, moreover, should be clearly distinguished from social, educational, occupational, or other cultural differences.[92]

Granting the expressed desire of adult generations to live independently, what changes occur when the generations must live together? What patterns of familial adjustment occur when an older person moves from a rural setting to an urban or suburban setting in order to live with his children? How are differences in value systems accommodated? What are the criteria of success in marriage of rural couples in the middle and later years?

Although it has been established that older people in the United States usually maintain relationships with their families, more knowledge is needed concerning the nature and meaning of these and the extent to which they satisfy the needs of older people over a period of time. And what meanings do these relationships have for adult children and grandchildren as they grow older? What factors further intergenerational solidarity among rural families? How is solidarity affected by social mobility? What factors promote mutually satisfying relationships between adult generations? What are satisfactory substitutes for the loss of family members? How do older persons cope with social change?

More understanding is needed concerning the reversal of parent-child roles in the event of physical and mental deterioration. What happens to ego functioning under these circumstances? How do such events affect expenditures of money and energy for the education and nurturing of grandchildren? How will new government-sponsored financial and medical benefits affect the family behavior of middle-aged and older adults? What kinds of living arrangements meet the diverse needs of the older rural persons who are widowed, sick, or disabled?

Problems of defining new roles for rural older people need study. What are substitute roles for persons to whom work has been a consuming interest and a primary source of satisfaction and livelihood? What about persons to whom strictly leisure-time activities seem immoral or excessively egocentric? How important are extrafamilial roles in maintaining and enhancing morale in middle and old age?

Randall has summarized the meanings of family life of middle-aged and older adults:

> The vital element of "inclusion" in the family circle—a strangely shaped circle these days—is not that all members of that family live under one roof. Rather it is the maintenance of the feeling of being one of the family in its culture—in its contribution to the community and to society generally—of being strengthened by the fact that one's own people care what happens to one, of their sharing in the good and bad things of life, even though they may be able to do little to prevent or to alleviate in a practical way the misfortunes or the losses which come to most of us as we grow older.[93]

NOTES

[1] Alvin L. Bertrand (ed.), *Sociology: An Analysis of Contemporary Rural Life* (New York: McGraw-Hill, 1958), p. 210.

[2] U. S. Bureau of the Census, *Statistical Abstract of the United States: 1962* (83rd ed.; Washington, D. C., 1962), p. 29.

[3] Glenn V. Fuguitt, "The Growth and Decline of Small Towns as a Probability Process," *American Sociogical Review,* 30 (June 1965), 403-11.

[4] Gerald Gurin, Joseph Veroff, and Sheila Feld, *Americans View Their Mental Health: A Nationwide Interview Survey* (New York: Basic Books, 1960), p. 230.

[5] Reuben Hill and Donald A. Hansen, "The Identification of Conceptual Frameworks Utilized in Family Study," *Marriage and Family Living,* 22 (Nov. 1960), 299-311.

[6] Reuben Hill and Roy H. Rodgers, "The Developmental Approach," in Harold T. Christensen (ed.), *Handbook of Marriage and the Family* (Chicago: Rand McNally, 1964), pp. 171-211.

[7] Roy H. Rodgers, "Toward a Theory of Family Development," *Journal of Marriage and the Family,* 26 (Aug. 1964), 262-70.

[8] *Ibid.,* p. 268.

[9] Paul C. Glick, "The Life Cycle of the Family," *Marriage and Family Living,* 17 (Feb. 1955), 3-9.

[10] Hill and Rodgers, "The Developmental Approach," p. 188.

[11] Robert Rapoport and Rhona Rapoport, "Work and Family in Contemporary Society," *American Sociological Review,* 30 (June 1965), 381-94.

[12] Glick, "The Life Cycle of the Family."

[13] Martin U. Martel, "Changing Marriage Relationships and Adult Sex Roles," in W. W. Morris (ed.), *The Middle Years: A Time of Change and Preparation* (Proceedings of the Sixth Annual Conference on Gerontology, Iowa City, Iowa, Oct. 7-8, 1957), pp. 21-29.

[14] Robert J. Havighurst, Middle Age—the New Prime of Life?" in Clark Tibbitts and Wilma Donahue (ed.), *Aging in Today's Society* (Englewood Cliffs, N. J.: Prentice-Hall, 1960), p. 142.

[15] Vivian Wood and Bernice L. Neugarten, "Social Role Change and Mental Health in the Climacteric Years," unpublished paper presented at the American Sociological Association, Washington, D. C., Sept. 1, 1962.

[16] Wilma T. Donahue, "The Human Machine at Middle Life," in Tibbitts and Donahue, *Aging in Today's Society*, p. 116.

[17] That there may be problems in middle age is indicated by a symposium entitled *Potentialities of Women in the Middle Years*, ed. Irma H. Gross (East Lansing: Michigan State University Press, 1956); by a volume by Edmund Bergler with the ominous title of *The Revolt of the Middle-Aged Man* (New York: Grosset and Dunlap, 1957); and by a book, *You and Your Aging Parents*, by Edith M. Stern and Mabel Ross (New York: A. A. Wyn, 1952), which carried the caption on its jacket, "How to Keep Your Parents Happy *While Living Your Own Life*" (italics in original).

[18] Robert J. Havighurst, "The Social Competence of Middle-Aged People," *Genetic Psychology Monographs*, 56 (1957), 297-375. See also Robert J. Havighurst, "The Nature and Values of Meaningful Free-Time Activity," in Robert W. Kleemeier (ed.), *Aging and Leisure: A Research Perspective into the Meaningful Use of Time* (New York: Oxford University Press, 1961), pp. 309-44.

[19] Arnold M. Rose, "Factors Associated with the Life Satisfaction of Middle-Class, Middle-Aged Persons," *Marriage and Family Living*, 17 (Feb. 1955), 15-19.

[20] *Ibid.*, p. 19.

[21] Wood and Neugarten, "Social Role Change and Mental Health in the Climacteric Years."

[22] *Ibid.*, p. 7.

[23] Bernice L. Neugarten and David L. Gutman, "Age-Sex Roles and Personality in Middle Age: A Thermatic Apperception Study," *Psychological Monographs*, 72 (1958), Whole No. 470, pp. 1-33.

[24] *Ibid.*, pp. 32-33. This study, along with seven others was presented in a volume by Bernice Neugarten and her associates, *Personality in Middle and Late Life* (New York: Atherton Press, 1964). The studies were directed toward discovering some characteristics of normal development of personality during adulthood. They were based on "relatively large study populations" drawn from a pool of over 700 cases in use with the Kansas City Studies of Adult Life.

[25] Marvin B. Sussman, "Intergenerational Family Relationships and Social Role Changes in Middle Age," *Journal of Gerontology*, 15 (Jan. 1960), 71-75.

[26] *Ibid.*, p. 74.

[27] Marvin B. Sussman and Lee Burchinal, "Kin Family Network: Un-

heralded Structure in Current Conceptualizations of Family Functioning," *Marriage and Family Living*, 24 (Aug. 1962), 231-40.

[28] *Ibid.*, pp. 238-39. In another paper these writers discuss possible consequences of parental aid to married children: See Marvin B. Sussman and Lee Burchinal, "Parental Aid to Married Children: Implications for Family Functioning," *Marriage and Family Living*, 24 (Nov. 1962), 320-32.

[29] Sussman and Burchinal, "Kin Family Network," p. 240.

[30] Eugene Litwak, "Geographic Mobility and Extended Family Cohesion," *American Sociological Review*, 25 (June 1960), 385-94. See, however, M. F. Nimkoff, "Changing Family Relationships of Older People in the United States During the Last Fifty Years," *The Gerontologist*, 1 (June 1961), 92-97.

[31] Paul J. Reiss, "The Extended Kinship System: Correlates of and Attitudes on Frequency of Interaction," *Marriage and Family Living*, 24 (Nov. 1962), 333-39.

[32] *Ibid.*, p. 339.

[33] Bert N. Adams, "Structural Factors Affecting Parental Aid to Married Children," *Journal of Marriage and the Family*, 26 (Aug. 1964), 327-31.

[34] Alvin L. Schorr, *Filial Responsibility in the Modern American Family: An Evaluation of Current Practice of Filial Responsibility in the United States and the Relationship to It of Social Security Programs* (Washington, D. C.: U. S. Department of Health, Education, and Welfare, 1960).

[35] *Ibid.*, p. 37.

[36] *Ibid.*, p. 33.

[37] *Ibid.*, p. 37.

[38] William M. Smith, Jr., Joseph H. Britton, and Jean O. Britton, *Relationships Within Three-Generation Families* (College of Home Economics Research Publication 155; University Park, Pa.: The Pennsylvania State University, 1958).

[39] William M. Smith, Jr., "Family Plans for Later Years," *Marriage and Family Living*, 16 (Feb. 1954), 36-40.

[40] Robert M. Dinkel, "Attitudes of Children Toward Supporting Aged Parents," *American Sociological Review*, 9 (Aug. 1944), 370-79.

[41] Ethel Shanas, *The Health of Older People: A Social Survey* (Cambridge, Mass.: Harvard University Press, 1962).

[42] Ethel Shanas, "Family Responsibility and the Health of Older People," *Journal of Gerontology*, 15 (Oct. 1960), 411.

[43] Arthur E. Gravatt, "Family Relations in Middle and Old Age: A Review," *Journal of Gerontology*, 8 (April 1953), 197-201.

[44] Arthur E. Gravatt, "An Exploratory Study of Marital Adjustment in Middle Age" (unpublished Master's thesis, Department of Sociology, University of Oregon, 1951).

[45] *Ibid.*, p. 200.

[46] Irwin Deutscher, "The Quality of Postparental Life: Definitions of the Situation," *Journal of Marriage and the Family*, 26 (Feb. 1964), 52-59. See also Deutscher's "Socialization for Postparental Life," in Arnold M. Rose (ed.), *Human Behavior and Human Process* (Boston: Houghton Mifflin, 1962), pp. 506-25.

[47] Leland J. Axelson, "Personal Adjustment in the Postparental Period," *Marriage and Family Living*, 22 (Feb. 1960), 66-70.

[48] Peter C. Pineo, "Disenchantment in the Later Years of Marriage," *Marriage and Family Living*, 23 (Feb. 1961), 3-11.

[49] *Ibid.*, p. 7.

[50] G. H. Beyer and M. E. Woods, *Living and Activity Patterns of the Aged* ("Cornell University Research Program on Housing for the Aged," Research Report No. 6; Ithaca, N. Y., 1963). See also, William S. Folkman and C. Horace Hamilton, *Impact of the Social Security Old Age Retirement System on Agriculture and Rural Life in Eastern North Carolina* (Agricultural Experiment Station Bulletin RS-40; Raleigh, N.C., 1961); and R. L. Skrabanek and Louis J. Ducoff, *Social Security and the Texas Farmer* (Agricultural Experiment Station Bulletin 928; College Station, Texas, 1959).

[51] Ward W. Bauder, "The Concept of Retirement Among Farm Operators in South Dakota," unpublished paper presented at Rural Sociological Society, Los Angeles, 1963.

[52] William H. Sewell, Charles E. Ramsey, and Louis J. Ducoff, *Farmers' Conceptions and Plans for Economic Security in Old Age* (Wisconsin Agricultural Experiment Station Bulletin 182; Madison, Wis., Sept. 1953).

[53] Ward W. Bauder, Otis Durant Duncan, and James D. Tarver, *The Social Security and Retirement Program of Oklahoma Farm Operators and Farm Landlords* (Agricultural Experiment Station Bulletin No. 13-592; Stillwater, Okla., March 1962).

[54] Walter C. McKain, Jr., Elmer D. Baldwin, and Louis J. Ducoff, *Old Age and Retirement in Rural Connecticut: 2. Economic Security of Farm Operators and Farm Laborers* (Storrs Agricultural Experiment Station Bulletin 299; Storrs, Conn., June 1953).

[55] Walter C. McKain, Jr., and Elmer D. Baldwin, *Old Age and Retirement in Rural Connecticut: 1. East Haddam: A Summer Resort Community* (Storrs Agricultural Experiment Station Bulletin 278; Storrs, Conn., June 1951).

[56] Milton L. Barron, "Survey of the Rural Aged," in Milton L. Barron, *The Aging American: An Introduction to Social Gerontology and Geriatrics* (New York: Thomas Y. Crowell, 1961).

[57] Carol Larson Stone and Walter L. Slocum, *A Look at Thurston County's Older People* (Washington Agricultural Experiment Station Bulletin 573; Pullman, Wash., May 1957).

[58] Martin B. Loeb, Allen Pincus, and Jeanne Mueller, *Growing Old in Rural Wisconsin* (School of Social Work, University of Wisconsin, Oct. 1963).

[59] Martin U. Martel, "Housing and Living Arrangements," Part VIII of "A Report of the Iowa Survey of Life after Sixty," in *Adding Life to Years* (Supplement No. 8, Institute of Gerontology, State University of Iowa; Iowa City, Aug. 1961). See also H. Lee Jacobs, "Attitudes Toward Nursing Homes and Homes for the Elderly," in Supplement No. 5 (May 1961), and Martel, "Family and Friendship Patterns of Older Iowans," in Supplement No. 7 (July 1961).

[60] Marianne Muse, "Homes for Old Age," *Journal of Home Economics,* 57 (March 1965), 183-87.

[61] James E. Montgomery, *Social Characteristics of the Aged in a Small Pennsylvania Community* (College of Home Economics Research Publication 233; University Park, Pa.: The Pennsylvania State University, 1965).

[62] West Pennsylvania Conference, Lutheran Inner Mission, *A Study of Older Persons: Supplementary Report* (Harrisburg: Central Pennsylvania Synod, United Lutheran Church, May 16, 1960).

[63] E. Grant Youmans, *Aging Patterns in a Rural and an Urban Area of Kentucky* (Agricultural Experiment Station Bulletin 681; Lexington, Ky., March 1963). See also E. Grant Youmans, *Leisure-Time Activities of Older Persons in Selected Rural and Urban Areas of Kentucky* (Agricultural Experiment Station Progress Report 115; Lexington, Ky., March 1962).

[64] Wayne A. Fuller, Ray E. Wakeley, Walter A. Lunden, Pearl Swanson, and Elisabeth Willis, *Characteristics of Persons 60 Years of Age and Older in Linn County, Iowa* (Iowa Agriculture and Home Economics Experiment Station, Special Report No. 33; Ames, Iowa, June 1963).

[65] Vernon S. Stevens, *The Aging Population of Wellington County* (Guelph, Ont.: Department of Agricultural Economics, Ontario Agricultural College, 1959).

[66] Roland L. Warren, "Old Age in a Rural Township," in *Age Is No Barrier,* New York State Joint Legislative Committee on Problems of the Aging, Legislative Document No. 35 (Albany, N. Y., 1952), pp. 155-66.

[67] Axel Ström, "An Investigation of the Living Conditions and Health of 1389 Persons Aged 70 or More in Norway," *Journal of Gerontology,* 11 (April 1956), 178-86.

[68] Peter Townsend, *The Family Life of Old People: An Inquiry in East London* (Glencoe, Ill.: The Free Press, 1957).

[69] *Ibid.,* p. 206.

[70] Bernard S. Phillips, *The Aging in a Central Illinois Community* (Small Homes Council-Building Research Council Research Report 62-4; Urbana, University of Illinois, Oct. 1962).

[71] Irving Rosow, "Relationships of Older Persons to Family and Friends," *Welfare in Review,* 3 (July 1965), 15.

[72] Warren, "Old Age in a Rural Township."

[73] Phillips, *The Aging in a Central Illinois Community.*

[74] Robert G. Brown, "Family Structure and Social Isolation of Older Persons," *Journal of Gerontology,* 15 (April 1960), 170-74.

[75] For example, see Bernard Kutner, David Fanshel, Alice M. Togo, and Thomas S. Langner, *Five Hundred Over Sixty: A Community Survey on Aging* (New York: Russell Sage Foundation, 1956), and Robert F. Winch, "The Adult and His Parents," in Robert F. Winch, *The Modern Family* (New York: Holt, Rinehart, and Winston, 1963), pp. 533-62.

[76] Ruth Shonle Cavan, "Family Tensions Between the Old and the Middle-Aged," *Marriage and Family Living,* 18 (Nov. 1956), 323-27.

[77] Peter Willmott and Michael Young, *Family and Class in a London Suburb* (London: Routledge, 1960), p. 58.

[78] Ethel Shanas, "The Older Person at Home—A Potential Isolate or Participant," *Research Utilization in Aging: An Exploration,* U. S. Depart-

ment of Health, Education and Welfare, Public Health Service Publication No. 1211 (Washington, D. C., 1964), p. 84.

[79] R. A. Kurtz and Joel Smith, "Social Life on the Rural-Urban Fringe," *Rural Sociology* 26 (March 1961), 24-38.

[80] Gary D. Hansen and Samual S. Yoshioka, *Aging in the Upper Midwest: A Profile of 6300 Senior Citizens* (Kansas City, Mo.: Community Studies, Nov., 1962).

[81] Philip Taietz, "The Extended Family in Transition: A Study of the Family Life of Old People in the Netherlands," *Sociologia Ruralis*, 4 (No. 1, 1964), 63-76.

[82] Ruth Albrecht, "Relationships of Older Parents with Their Children," *Marriage and Family Living*, 16 (Feb. 1954), 32-35. See also Albrecht, "Relationships of Older People with Their Own Parents," *Marriage and Family Living*, 15 (Nov. 1953), 296-98.

[83] Stevens, *The Aging Population of Wellington County.*

[84] Smith, "Family Plans for Later Years."

[85] Rosamonde Ramsay Boyd, "The Valued Grandparent" and "The Emerging Social Roles of the Four-Generational Family," unpublished papers, Converse College, Spartanburg, S. C., 1965.

[86] Paul H. Glasser and Lois N. Glasser, "The Role Reversal and Conflict Between Aged Parents and Their Children," *Marriage and Family Living,* 24 (Feb. 1962), 46-51.

[87] Shanas, "The Older Person at Home," pp. 81-86.

[88] Joseph H. Britton, William G. Mather, and Alice K. Lansing, "Expectations for Older Persons in a Rural Community: Living Arrangements and Family Relationships," *Journal of Gerontology*, 16 (April 1961), 156-62, and Joseph H. Britton and Jean O. Britton, "Expectations for Older Persons in a Rural Community: Solving Personal Problems," *Geriatrics*, 17 (Sept. 1962), 602-608.

[89] Alice Kendrick Lansing, "Behavior of Older Persons as Viewed by People in a Rural Pennsylvania Community" (unpublished Master's thesis, The Pennsylvania State University, 1956).

[90] Joseph H. Britton, "Dimensions of Adjustment of Older Adults," *Journal of Gerontology*, 18 (Jan. 1963), 60-65.

[91] J. H. Britton, "Change in Adjustment of Older Community Residents after Six Years," *Abstracts of Papers Presented, Sixth International Congress on Gerontology, Copenhagen, Denmark, 1963* (Amsterdam: Excerpta Modica Foundation, 1963), p. 137, and Joseph H. Britton and Jean O. Britton, "Consistency of Personality Evaluations in Old Age," *American Psychologist*, 20 (July 1965), 567. See also Jean Dail Davidson, "Change in Adjustment of Older Adults as Related to Situational and Personal Factors" (unpublished Master's thesis, The Pennsylvania State University, 1963).

[92] The methods of the Barkers might be useful. See Roger G. Barker and Louise Shedd Barker, "The Psychological Ecology of Old People in Midwest, Kansas, and Yoredale, Yorkshire," *Journal of Gerontology*, 16 (April 1961), 144-49. See also Roger Barker's discussion of "behavior setting size and individual behavior" in "On the Nature of the Environment," *Journal of Social Issues*, 19 (Oct. 1963), 17-38. In addition, see William H. Harlan,

"Social Status of the Aged in Three Indian Villages," *Vita Humana*, 7 (Nos. 3-4, 1964), 239-52.

[93] Ollie A. Randall, "The Older Person in the Modern Family Structure," in *Growing with the Years*, New York State Joint Legislative Committee on Problems of the Aging, Legislative Document No. 32 (Albany, N. Y., 1934), pp. 81-84.

WALTER C. McKAIN, JR.

Community Roles and Activities
of Older Rural Persons

The older person whose children have left home and who has retired from work often finds himself confronted with free time
and no socially acceptable way to use it. He may have learned to
consider his retirement income as a kind of deferred fringe benefit, but he has never quite accepted the notion that free time is
also a benefit earned during the working years. Instead, he often
regards his free time as a burden, one of the penalties imposed
upon older people.

Two values widely held in American society reinforce the rejection of most leisure-time pursuits for the elderly. One is the
importance attached to work as an end in itself and the other is
the emphasis on youth. Each has been established firmly in the
ideological system of the United States and the task of modifying
them will require the efforts of more than one generation.

A young man entering the labor force 50 years ago expected to
work until he died or until he became incapacitated. As a child
he was told work was good and idleness evil. As a young man he
was trained to work, and during the middle years work and
work-related activities dominated his life. Only the ne'er-do-well
or the dilettante permitted hobbies or social activities to interfere with his job. Most social clubs and community organizations
concealed their recreational function with names, stated objec-

tives, and public utterances that emphasized work rather than play.

As a result, the older person today probably subscribes to the middle-class belief in the nobility of work yet lives in an affluent society that can afford the luxury of leisure. His use of free time that has been thrust upon him is guided by attitudes that had their origin at a different time and under far different circumstances. An abundance of leisure time poses a serious problem to the present generation of older people, since earning a living and rearing a family are considered the basic roles in an action-paced society.

The emphasis on youth in our society is another hurdle in the path of the older person who wishes to remain active in community affairs. In a work-dominated society, free-time activities tend to be youth-centered. There is an emphasis on competitive sports and strenuous games. A premium is placed on the physical attractiveness associated with youth. Communities look to younger and employed persons when making important assignments. Aging is considered undesirable, hence effort is made to delay the process.

The impact of these values both on the content and on the scale of free-time activities has been great. A basic distinction is drawn between the activities of older persons that are personal and those that are service-related. Those activities which purport to go beyond the satisfaction of personal needs have achieved a measure of respect. They are consistent with the work ethic. Activities that provide immediate, fleeting, and personal pleasures are held in low esteem. Recreation is often equated with indolence. Social participation must be justified on the grounds that it results in community service, that it maintains the health of the individual, or that it is educational. It is a means to an end, never an end in itself.

The glorification of work has influenced the content of free-time activities in the later years; the glorification of youth has affected the scale of these activities. Since many leisure-time activities are based on the attributes and the convictions of young people, the apathy that characterizes so many older people in their use of free time is more readily understood. The disengagement of older persons from the life around them can be expected when one of their major resources is free time and free-time pursuits are predominantly reserved for the young.

RURAL-URBAN DIFFERENCES

The broad chasm that once separated the urban from the rural world in American society no longer exists. Certain differences still remain and, what is more important, the present generation of older people in the rural population spent most of their lives in a rural environment at a time when sharp contrasts existed between urban and rural patterns of behavior. The community roles of older rural people bear the imprint of rural values and rural customs. In some ways a rural background facilitates the use of free time in the later years; in other ways it places obstacles in the way of its use.

Rural persons probably are less likely than urban people to have basic fears of nonstructured activity. The urban worker, more than the rural worker, is subject to external controls in his job. He reports regularly to work; his duties are usually specific and more or less repetitious. Frequently his work is machine-paced and when machines don't structure his operations other human beings do. At retirement he may become lost with so many hours of uncommitted time. Rural workers, particularly those in agriculture, may have a long hard regimen of work but the pattern can be varied by individual choice and is always subject to the caprice of nature. Rural workers, in most cases, are not accustomed to a structured work day to the same degree as urban workers, and thus in later years they may be better prepared for the art of keeping busy.

Older rural people usually enter full retirement later in life and continue to do some work long after they have retired from a regular job. They have acquired a variety of skills, one or more of which may be put to use on a limited basis as long as they live. Gradual retirement is more consistent with the work ethic than complete withdrawal from the labor force. Status in the community under these conditions can be maintained and even transferred to roles that are associated with free-time activities.

The structure of rural social organizations in some ways makes it easier for the elderly person to remain active in the community. Organizations in the city tend to have limited objectives and their participants tend to be homogeneous. In rural areas most organizations are rather diffuse in both goals and membership. These multipurpose organizations make use of both young and old. When human resources are scarce, the emphasis on youth is diminished, and the older person can more easily retain active membership in community organizations.

In some rural communities the older persons are well known. Their interests, abilities, needs, and problems may be common knowledge. An older person's withdrawal from society is less likely to occur under these conditions.

In many other ways the older person in rural areas lives in a hostile environment with respect to the use of free time. The concept of the virtue of work is strongly entrenched in rural society and the idle person tends to lose respect perhaps more in the country than in the city. He equates idleness with the lack of gainful employment. For this reason he often comes unprepared to the years when he can no longer work; he does not wish to call attention to his retirement from work by engaging in nonwork activities.

The settlement patterns in rural areas also tend to limit participation in community affairs. Transportation poses a problem that becomes more difficult in the later years. Meetings usually are held at night in deference to the importance of daytime work and the elderly person may not wish to hazard the risks of walking or driving at night. The low density of the population often precludes the possibility of organized services for the elderly. Recreation centers, clubs for older persons, friendly visiting, meals on wheels, congregate living, and many other services of this kind are largely confined to the more densely populated urban areas.

Strong family ties that exist in rural areas are helpful to the older person, but when they are broken they may leave the older person desperately alone. The death of a marriage partner and the departure of children to homes of their own can be expected, yet the one who is left behind is often unprepared. The present generation of rural oldsters grew up in the day when grandparents, aunts, uncles, and other unattached adults found refuge in the family. Today many are left alone and in their resentment often withdraw further.

THE USE OF FREE TIME

Older persons in the United States seek self-expression in a variety of forms after retirement but in almost every category their participation in community life declines.[1] This is particularly true for the physically active forms of recreation that involve skill and daring and for the sex-social activities that are so important in the younger years.

Most research, but not all, suggests that older persons reduce their recreational activities, withdraw from community participation, and devote increasing amounts of time to rest and sleep. The older person makes only limited use of his free time with the exception of such sedentary activities as reading or watching television. Tasks that formerly were performed rather quickly are now stretched out over a relatively long period of time. The added hours of free time have resulted in less rather than more social participation and they have yielded less rather than more social recognition. Research that has been conducted in rural areas tends to support the foregoing analysis.

AMOUNT OF FREE TIME AVAILABLE

Older rural men either retire from work or reduce their working hours, giving them an abundance of free time. Older rural women work fewer hours after their children leave home. Both have more time to use as they please. In Thurston County, Washington, 68 percent of the older persons living in open country had more than four hours each day for leisure-time activities.[2] Older residents in the rural urban fringe, in the small towns, and in the cities had even more free time. In East Haddam, Connecticut, 60 percent of the older persons had free time in excess of four hours a day.[3] A larger proportion (73 percent) of the persons over 74 years of age had at least four hours a day available for leisure-time activities. Nearly one-third of the persons in their sixties who lived in a rural Mississippi town had "all day free."[4] Over one-half of those in the seventies and 83 percent of those in the eighties made the same report.

Wayne A. Fuller and his associates made a detailed analysis of activities in the daily life of persons over 60 who lived in Linn County, Iowa.[5] The number of hours spent in each activity was recorded. The leisure-time activities included personal recreation, social recreation, and hobbies. The hours spent in each category were shown for men and women by various age groups and by place of residence (urban, rural place, open country). Weekday and Sunday activities were recorded separately.

Older persons who lived in rural places or in the open country spent an average of 6.4 hours a day on leisure-time activities; those who lived in the city averaged just under six hours a day. The amount of time devoted to recreational activities as a whole tended to increase with age. Personal recreation accounted for more hours a day than social recreation and the number of hours increased with the age of the older person. Hobbies accounted for less than an hour a day. The Sunday schedule in both rural and urban areas included more hours for recreation than did the weekday schedule. In the rural areas social recreation, in particular, was higher on Sunday.

FORMAL SOCIAL PARTICIPATION

As early as 1940 Landis had observed that older rural men seldom participated in group organizations and that older rural women were also quite inactive.[6] A few years later McKain noted that older persons living in a California retirement community had very low social participation scores.[7] In 1950 Samson and Mather summarized their findings in Wayne County, Pennsylvania, as follows: "The obvious lack of interest and enthusiasm for organizations, including the church, was clear."[8] Since then research in other rural areas has told just about the same story. Many rural people in the later years are not members of any social organization. Some have never been "joiners"; others are in poor health; the cost is prohibitive for some; and transportation, always a problem in rural places, becomes an insurmountable problem in old age.

In Thurston County, Washington, 60 percent of the older persons living in open country did not belong to any organization and only 54 percent of the older members attended regularly.[9] Less than 20 percent of the older persons in Casey County, Kentucky, participated regularly in any group activity, excluding church attendance.[10] In East Haddam, Connecticut, 74 percent of the older respondents did not have an affiliation with any social organization and among the foreign-born the percentage of nonmembers was even higher.[11] In Mississippi less than one-half of the elderly attended meetings.[12] Only a few rural old persons in Minnesota were members of any organizations other than religious or professional.[13]

Nearly one-half of the older persons living in the open country and one-third of those living in other rural places in Linn County, Iowa, did not name a single organization that they had attended during the previous month.[14] Many were nominal members of a group but did not participate actively. Albrecht discovered that 74 percent of the older men and 45 percent of the older women in a midwestern town had no interest and no participation in formal social groups.[15]

Mayo in his study in Wake County, North Carolina, reported that the social participation scores declined with age for both males and females and for both whites and Negroes.[16] Taietz and Larson reported similar findings in four rural New York communities but observed that a sharp decline did not occur until age 80.[17] They found that 28 percent of the older persons between 65 or 74 were nonparticipants and 43 percent of those over 75 did not participate in any organization, excluding church.

Obviously many older persons living in rural areas do not take part in formal social organizations. The findings suggest, however, that some older persons are members of formal groups and attend the meetings and other events sponsored by these groups. Within the wide range of organizations open to older persons there is considerable variation in membership and participation.

Clubs for older persons do not attract many rural residents. The "Golden Age" type of club did not become popular until after 1950. Before then, organizations such as the Townsend Club performed somewhat the same function but neither kind of organization has drawn much rural support. In Linn County, Iowa,[18] and Thurston County, Washington,[19] less than 4 percent of the older persons were members of clubs for older persons and in Casey County, Kentucky,[20] none of the rural people belonged to such an organization.

In both Washington and Kentucky, rural older persons were more likely to be members of lodges and farmers' organizations than members of social, service, or veterans' organizations. In Paradise, California, persons 65 and over represented 23 percent of the population but they accounted for 33 percent of the members of social clubs, 22 percent of the special purpose clubs, 12 percent of the service clubs, and 9 percent of the veterans' organizations.[21]

There is conflicting evidence regarding church membership and church attendance. Although most research suggests that religion becomes more important in the later years, many investigators have discovered that a substantial proportion of older persons do not participate in this activity. In Thurston County, Washington,[22] and in Almond Township, New York,[23] one-third of the older persons never attended church services. In a rural area of Connecticut, 44 percent of the older persons never attended church[24] and Landis reported in his Iowa study that almost one-half of the aged seldom went to church.[25] In a small midwestern town 53 percent of the men and 30 percent of the women seldom attended church.[26]

Other researchers have reported substantially higher participation in religious activities. Von Mering and Weniger suggest that church and political behavior are the two areas that offer older persons the best opportunity to remain active in the community.[27] Youmans found that for the great majority of older persons in Casey County, Kentucky, church was the only community activity that claimed their attention.[28] He found that 83 percent of the aged in Casey County participated in a religious organization and that the percentage was even higher in urban Lexington. In rural Minnesota, 76 percent of the rural respondents were members of a church.[29] In Linn County, Iowa, 54 percent of the older persons in the open country areas were members of church and the mean attendance was 2.3 times a month.[30] In the rural places of Linn County 76 percent were members and attendance averaged 3.2 times a month. Taietz and Larson used Chapin's index for church participation and learned that in the rural communities of New York the scores remained high until very late in life.[31]

Variations among the aged in participating in community activities are undoubtedly related to many variables. To some extent they can be explained by the habits of the general population in each area. The composition of the population with respect to socioeconomic status, nativity, and age itself is also involved. Transportation and health are important considerations for many older persons in determining their participation in community functions.

INFORMAL ACTIVITIES

Social activities available to older persons in communities are not entirely performed within the framework of formal associations. Unstructured free-time activities such as visiting and hobbies exist apart from or in conjunction with special-purpose organizations. Thus, informal conversation may take place in the home and on the street or it may accompany an auction, a church service, or the meeting of a farm organization.

Informal free-time activities have been classified in a number of ways. One of the basic distinctions is between those activities that are solitary and those that involve other persons. Another difference is based on the role of the individual. Is he a participant or an observer? In some instances the purpose of the activity or its locale serve as classificatory devices. Is the activity largely recreational or creative? Does it take place in the home?

Youmans in his Kentucky research presented a fourfold classification of leisure-time activities: (a) immobile pastimes including reading or watching television, (b) explorative activities such as travel or sightseeing, (c) creative activities such as gardening, hunting, and most hobbies, and (d) social pastimes such as informal visits.[32] Gerontological research in rural areas has not consistently defined these categories but most researchers have included one or more of these types in their analyses.

Older persons spend a large part of their free time in activities that are passive and do not require much effort or mobility. Reading, listening to the radio and, more recently, watching television, just sitting and thinking, or watching the activities of others are pursuits mentioned by a high proportion of older persons in the New York,[33] Washington,[34] Connecticut,[35] Kentucky,[36] and Vermont[37] bulletins.

There is some evidence that reading may not occupy as much time as the respondents suggest. In her study of Vermonters who were approaching the later years Muse found that none of the farm families had more than 12 books and that only 11 percent of the husbands 60-64 years of age and 25 percent of the wives 60-64 had read one or more books during the past year.[38] In a rural area of Connecticut over one-fourth of the older persons do not have a newspaper available to them and over one-half do not have access to a magazine.[39] In Thurston County, Washington, where reading was the most popular pastime mentioned by older persons, not quite one-half of them read any books with the exception of the Bible.[40] And, although over 90 percent of the older persons had a daily newspaper and almost as many read magazines, the median number of hours spent each week in reading was less than nine.

Radio and television were ranked high among the interests of older persons in all sections of the country. This particular form of involvement does not require much effort and its intensity can be regulated according to the desire of the listener. Furthermore, most rural people grew up in an oral society where communication was by the spoken word and not so much by newspapers, motion pictures, or television.[41] In New York state listening to the radio was rated high among all leisure-time activities topped only by chatting with friends.[42] In Connecticut also listening to the radio was the second most popular pastime.[43] This activity among the oldest group in Vermont ranked third, just behind reading and visiting.[44] Hoar noted that older persons in Mississippi had garden projects in their sixties and then shifted to radio listening in the seventies.[45]

In some respects these relatively immobile pursuits represent a withdrawal from the community. One elderly man in Connecticut put it this way, "Sure, I read and listen to the radio. But half the time I just sit here and think while the radio plays. And then my wife comes in and finds me sound asleep."

Man's quest for new experience may be dulled in the later years but it certainly is not obliterated. Many older persons have embarked on new careers or expanded their horizons in other ways. The particular ways in which free time is used is some indication of this drive. One explorative use of leisure time is travel. These would include trips to new places, ranging from a Sunday afternoon walk or drive to world travel. It would cover visits to children and friends and forays into the village or city for shopping, entertainment, or just sightseeing. Certain hobbies are also explorative in nature.

Many persons plan to use part of the free time made available to them later in life in travel. Thus, Muse discovered that travel ranked first among the activities for which more leisure time was desired by Vermont women approaching 65 and ranked second for the men.[46] However, among the husbands and wives who were 60-64 only 25 percent and 66 percent respectively had been away from home as long as a week during the previous year.

Older persons who have access to an automobile may go for rides, although these are usually related to some other activity such as shopping or visiting. In Thurston County, Washington, approximately one-half of the older persons listed "going for rides" as one of their leisure-time activities.[47] The New York study indicated that as people grow older their interest in this activity tends to decline.[48] In Kentucky and Connecticut less than 10 percent of the older persons reported travel or automobile rides.[49]

Very few older people attend the movies and the proportion that do declines with age. Shopping as a leisure-time activity also drops off in the later years. Older persons who live in small towns and villages maintain this activity longer than the open-country residents, probably because the opportunity is greater.

Research procedures may operate to exclude those older persons who have exploratory tendencies. The older person who wants to travel after his retirement may, in fact, do so and then be overlooked since he is not at his usual place of residence when the interviews are made.

Creative activities are closely related to the work ethic and are frequently mentioned by elderly persons when leisure-time activities are discussed. Working around the house both inside and outside, hunting and fishing, hobbies of many kinds, sewing, writing letters, and music are among the many creative pastimes listed by older persons. There is a reluctance on the part of older persons to identify any of their pursuits as "hobbies," although specific hobbies are sometimes mentioned by name. The word "hobby," as opposed to sewing, gardening, or handicrafts, does not carry the connotation of being work related.

In Almond, New York, 41 percent of the older persons had

no hobbies[50] and 39 percent of those in Linn County, Iowa, reported no hobbies.[51] Only 15 percent of the older persons in Thurston County, Washington, worked on a hobby during the week prior to the interview.[52] According to the Linn County summary older persons living in the rural areas spent 15 minutes or less a day working on hobbies.[53]

When a listing is made of the leisure-time activities a different picture emerges. Gardening was reported by 27 percent of the older persons in the Kentucky study,[54] by 64 percent of open-country residents in Thurston County,[55] by 69 percent of the older persons in New York,[56] and by over three-fourths of the older persons in Vermont.[57]

Sewing among older women was popular. Approximately one-half of the older women reported in the Kentucky[58] and Washington[59] bulletins listed this activity. In some instances the respondents included sewing among their regular household duties. One elderly woman remarked, "I have no time for hobbies. I'm too busy making clothes for my grandchildren."

Hunting and fishing are popular activities among older men. In Kentucky,[60] Washington,[61] and New York[62] from one-fifth to one-half of the older male respondents listed this pastime. It ranked highest among the activities anticipated by older men in Vermont.[63] These sports were also mentioned by several older women, one of whom had not "missed a deer season in fifty years."

Only a few older persons mentioned such hobbies as handicrafts, stamp collecting, painting, or music. Usually these activities are begun early in life and if a person does not become interested then, he does not undertake them in his later years.[64] There is some evidence that persons approaching retirement expect to engage in creative activities when they have more free time. Only a few of them succeed in this ambition. Lack of continuing interest, poor health, and reduced income are partially responsible. Of course, there are important exceptions and some older persons have filled their spare time with creative activities.

Informal social participation is an important form of interaction among rural people of all ages. Among older persons it assumes added significance both because they have more free time at their disposal and because so many other avenues of social expression are closed or appear to be closed to them.

Visiting with friends enables an older person to share pleasant memories, to keep alive his current interests, and to reinforce his position as a member of the community. Spaulding has suggested that leisure-time activities affect the participants in three ways: self-realization, intensification of relationships, and differentiation.[65]

The amount of informal social participation that older persons in rural areas are able to maintain is relatively high compared to most of their other interpersonal free-time activities. In Casey County, Kentucky, 92 percent of the old people knew others quite well in the community and over 60 percent of them have either frequent or occasional visiting patterns.[66] Talking with friends ranked first among all leisure-time activities in the rural areas of New York.[67] Entertaining and being entertained by friends was an important activity for persons approaching old age in Vermont and did not noticeably decline through age 64.[68]

In Thurston County, Washington, 56 percent of the older persons had 20 or more friends in the same community and 68 percent had 20 or more friends living outside the community.[69] Informal visiting was mentioned as an activity by 64 percent of the older persons living in the open country.[70]

As old age approaches, the number of friends tends to diminish and the frequency of visits declines. Withdrawal from occupation-oriented activities, the departure of children, failing health, transportation difficulties, and the death of friends are among the reasons the quantity, if not the intensity, of informal social participation tends to decline.

In Almond, New York, 61 percent of the older persons saw friends less frequently than before.[71] Among the 49 older men interviewed by Samson and Mather only 2 had more friends and 17 had fewer friends after retirement. Over 70 percent of these men saw their friends less frequently in their later years.[72]

The conditions under which informal visiting takes place have not been the subject of investigation. References are made to home visits, backyard conversations, telephone calls, meetings at the store or post office, visits at weddings, funerals, auctions, and to many other occasions and places where older persons can get together. Religious groups, clubs, and other formal organizations provide an opportunity for informal visiting. It has been demonstrated, for example, that the one important function of the Townsend clubs was to provide a setting for informal conversation,[73] and the more recent Golden Age clubs have a similar purpose. When older persons relinquish their interest in formal associations and in community affairs, there is a corresponding decline in opportunities for informal social participation.

The informal social activities of persons living in rural areas usually decline with age. Their leisure time increasingly is used for the more passive, sedentary, and solitary activities such as listening to the radio or watching television. In general, older persons in rural areas tend to maintain those hobbies that were ardently pursued when they were younger. Leisure-time activities closely related to occupational interests also are popular. These include gardening, working around the house, and sewing. Visiting with friends and relatives is also maintained late in life.

CORRELATES OF COMMUNITY INVOLVEMENT

The withdrawal of older persons from community activities is not uniform. It varies from one section of the country to another and it is conditioned by both their personal attitudes and the social conditions under which they live. It is dangerous to generalize about the social participation of the older person because there are so many different correlates of community involvement.

Taietz and Larson have demonstrated that although participation in formal social organizations is inversely related to age, socioeconomic status and retirement status are even more important in explaining the low rates of participation among older persons in rural areas.[74] Several investigations have pointed out the impact of education, occupation, home ownership, size of dwelling, income, and other socioeconomic variations on the activities of older persons.

Older persons who live on farms in the open country usually have fewer community activities than those who live in rural nonfarm areas, although some exceptions occur. In Iowa the open-country aged exhibited less social participation;[75] in Vermont there was not much difference in balance between the elderly in the two residential categories,[76] and in Thurston County, Washington, older persons living in the open country ranked low in the extent of their participation in formal organizations and in church activities.[77] In the California study the extent of farming operations was positively related to both formal and informal social participation.[78]

As a rule older persons who received public assistance had more hours of free time but participated in fewer leisure-time activities than did the independent aged. In Thurston County, Washington, the public assistance clients devoted much of their time to such activities as sitting and thinking and working around the house.[79]

Mayo reported that the index of social participation was higher for Negro older persons than for white persons and that among the former there was greater fluctuation in social participation from one age group to another.[80] In Connecticut the native-born aged had significantly higher formal and informal social participation rates than did the foreign born.[81] The foreign-born aged in a California retirement community exhibited a bimodal distribution in both informal and formal social participation.[82]

A case-growing technique was employed in the California research to determine clusters of traits that were associated with the social participation of older persons. It was found that persons 65-69 years of age who were currently employed, well educated, in good health, and who had lived in the community for at least seven years tended to have high formal and informal participation scores.[83]

Social participation has also been examined as an independent variable. Several researchers have attempted to determine if adjustment in the later years is related to the degree of community involvement. Most research concerning urban populations shows a positive association between adjustment or morale and social participation. Albrecht, Britton, Scott, Burgess, Shanas, Cavan, Kutner, and Schmidt all indicated that the degree of social participation was related to the adjustment experienced by older persons.[84] Bernard Kutner has suggested that older persons may find an outlet for their feelings by increased participation, thus satisfying a fundamental need through sheer activity in community affairs.[85]

Morrison and Kristjanson pursued this possibility in some detail in their research entitled *Personal Adjustment Among Older Persons*. They concluded that there was no statistical significance between the personal and social activities of older persons and their adjustment but that high involvement was consistently associated with high adjustment.[86] The authors point out that their index of activities is based on the number of activities and that the intensity of participation in these activities was not measured.

COMMUNITY SERVICE

Public attention has been concentrated on meeting the immediate needs of older persons and ameliorating unfavorable circumstances that beset the older population. Largely overlooked have been the contributions that older people themselves can make to society. There is no reason to believe that civic competence and civic responsibilities cease when a person withdraws from the labor force. Indeed, just the opposite may be true. The need to be needed persists. Only the avenues of service are altered.

The goals and roles of man change as he passes from childhood and becomes an adult. They also change in the later years. In childhood the emphasis is on self. The emphasis in adulthood is on the family. But in the later years a new dimension enters. Now it is possible for him to subordinate family and self and to establish broader goals. He is in a favorable position to render service to the community. First of all, he has acquired the skills and wisdom that come with experience. His counsel and his participation can supply ingredients to the social, economic, and political life of the community that a young person cannot furnish.[87] Second, he has an abundance of free time, a commodity that most working people lack. Finally, he has a detachment that can come only after retirement when a person's livelihood cannot be threatened by what he says or does.

Older persons in rural areas have a special opportunity to engage in activities that render service to their communities. Many of the services in the rural community, such as libraries, civil defense, meals on wheels, and a telephone reassurance program, to mention only a few, do not require the full-time attention of a paid worker yet are sorely needed. The older person with skills along these lines can perform the job adequately on a part-time volunteer basis.

There is a vast reservoir of human resources to be found among the older population in rural areas. The task of involving older persons in most leisure-time activities now available in the community has not been an easy one. They have only limited interest in hobbies and recreational activities. Community service, on the other hand, affords a more satisfactory substitute for work than almost any other activity. It satisfies the work ethic and at the same time it is an area in which the older person can successfully compete with his junior.

The range of community service activities is broad. Sometimes older persons serve in an advisory capacity. McKain reported that in Paradise, California, older persons assumed leadership in such diverse community projects as a teenage center, an airport, a garbage disposal program, a motion picture premiere, a new high school, and a house-numbering project.[88] In other instances the older people in a rural area are action oriented and perform the services themselves. They engage in Red Cross projects, collect money for voluntary health programs, supervise athletic events, conduct classes in handicrafts, serve on planning and zoning boards, supervise youth centers, act as librarians, write community histories, serve as information centers, or visit nursing homes and hospitals.

Usually the person who was a leader in community affairs during his working years continues in his role when he retires. This suggests that the opportunity to render community service is related more to experience than to age. Taves and Hansen found that only a few older persons seem to want to assume leadership in community organizations but point out that the proportion who are interested may correspond to the proportion of persons of all ages who are community leaders.[89]

The political role of older persons is another important area of community involvement. According to Pressey and Kuhlen, voting and other forms of political behavior do not decline markedly after retirement.[90] Such decline as does occur is related more to poor health than to a lessening of interest in politics.

Research in Mississippi,[91] New York,[92] Pennsylvania,[93] and in a midwestern community indicates that over three-fourths of the older persons voted in either local or national elections or both. In the Mississippi community the proportion of older persons who voted increased after age 70 was reached. In a California community only 62 percent of persons over 65 voted in one election, but this compared favorably with the voting record of those 35-64 years of age (42 percent).[94] A detailed analysis of the voting behavior in this community revealed that whenever issues of particular interest to older persons appeared in an election the turnout of older voters was high.

A LOOK INTO THE FUTURE

"No other society has ever before known the mass extension of life and leisure time that is now upon us," Clark Tibbitts reminds us and then goes on to predict that it may take a generation or more before society will learn how to make use of this gift of time.[95] Nels Anderson refers to leisure as a "child not planned for,"[96] but the child is with us and plans must be formulated.

Coming generations of both rural and urban older persons will only faintly resemble older persons of today. They will be better educated and have larger incomes. More of them will be native born and more of them will enjoy good health. They will be more mobile. Their patterns of life will have more appropriate guidelines based on the successes and failures of the older population that preceded them.

The apparent withdrawal of older persons from community life in rural areas does not mean that this process is inevitable or nonreversible. Youmans concludes, "What older persons do now with their free time is not necessarily an indication of what they can do."[97] The disengagement we see around us may be society's present inability to provide a satisfactory substitute for work in the later years rather than an inherent disengagement process.[98] The older person probably abandons some activities in favor of others. It is important that his decisions represent a voluntary choice and are not forced upon him by his community.

Older persons, even in rural areas, are learning to accept and to respect retirement from gainful occupations. The role of the community in their lives is increasing just as their roles in the community are becoming more sharply outlined. It can be expected that community service will capture the imagination of growing numbers of the aged. This adventure will enrich the "second prime of life which we should discover, explore, and cherish."[99]

NOTES

[1] Otto von Mering and Frederick L. Weniger, "Social-Cultural Background of the Aging Individual," in James E. Birren (ed.), *Handbook of Aging and the Individual* (Chicago: University of Chicago Press, 1959), pp. 320-25.

[2] Carol Larson Stone and Walter L. Slocum, *A Look at Thurston County's Older People* (Washington Agricultural Experiment Station Bulletin 573; Pullman, Wash., May 1957), p. 26.

[3] Walter C. McKain, Jr., and Elmer D. Baldwin, *Old Age and Retirement in Rural Connecticut: 1. East Haddam: A Summer Resort Community* (Storrs Agricultural Experiment Station Bulletin 278; Storrs, Conn., June 1951), p. 39.

[4] Jere Hoar, "A Study of Free-Time Activities of 200 Aged Persons," *Sociology and Social Research*, 45 (Jan. 1961), 158.

[5] Wayne A. Fuller, Ray E. Wakeley, Walter A. Lunden, Pearl Swanson, and Elizabeth Willis, *Characteristics of Persons 60 Years of Age and Older in Linn County, Iowa* (Iowa Agriculture and Home Economics Experiment Station, Special Report 33; Ames, Iowa, June 1963), pp. 22-24.

[6] Judson T. Landis, "Attitudes and Adjustments of Aged Rural People in Iowa" (unpublished Ph.D. thesis, Louisiana State University, 1940).

[7] Walter C. McKain, "The Social Participation of Old People in a California Retirement Community" (unpublished Ph.D. thesis, Harvard University, 1947).

[8] A'Delbert P. Samson and William G. Mather, *Personal and Social Adjustments of 49 Retired Rural Men* (Pennsylvania Agricultural Experiment Station, Progress Report 19; Pennsylvania State College, Jan. 1950), p. 14.

[9] Stone and Slocum, *A Look at Thurston County's Older People*, p. 43.

[10] E. Grant Youmans, *Aging Patterns in a Rural and an Urban Area of Kentucky* (Agricultural Experiment Station Bulletin 681; Lexington, Ky., March 1963), p. 45.

[11] McKain and Baldwin, *Old Age and Retirement in Rural Connecticut*, p. 42.

[12] Hoar, "A Study of Free-Time Activities," p. 159.

[13] Marvin J. Taves and Gary D. Hansen, "Seventeen Hundred Elderly Citizens," in Arnold Rose (ed.), *Aging in Minnesota* (Minneapolis: University of Minnesota Press, 1963), p. 133.

[14] Fuller, *et al.*, *Characteristics of Persons 60 Years of Age*, p. 28.

[15] Ruth Albrecht, "The Social Roles of Old People," *Journal of Gerontology*, 6 (April 1951), 142.

[16] Selz C. Mayo, "Age Profiles in Social Participation in Rural Areas of Wake County, North Carolina," *Rural Sociology*, 15 (Sept. 1950), 246.

[17] Philip Taietz and Olaf F. Larson, "Social Participation in Old Age," *Rural Sociology*, 21 (Sept.-Dec. 1956), 233.

[18] Fuller, *et al.*, *Characteristics of Persons 60 Years of Age*, p. 27.

[19] Stone and Slocum, A Look at Thurston County's Older People, p. 43.

[20] Youmans, Aging Patterns, p. 45.

[21] McKain, "Social Participation of Old People," p. 55.

[22] Stone and Slocum, A Look at Thurston County's Older People, p. 48.

[23] Roland L. Warren, "Old Age in a Rural Township," in Age Is No Barrier, New York State Joint Legislative Committee on Problems of the Aging, Legislative Document No. 35 (Albany, N. Y., 1952), p. 156.

[24] McKain and Baldwin, Old Age and Retirement in Rural Connecticut, p. 42.

[25] Landis, "Attitudes and Adjustments of Aged Rural People in Iowa."

[26] Albrecht, "The Social Roles of Old People," p. 142.

[27] Von Mering and Weniger, "Social-Cultural Background of the Aging Individual," p. 323.

[28] Youmans, Aging Patterns, p. 45.

[29] Taves and Hansen, "Seventeen Hundred Elderly Citizens," p. 133.

[30] Fuller, et al., Characteristics of Persons 60 Years of Age, p. 30.

[31] Taietz and Larson, "Social Participation in Old Age," p. 233.

[32] Youmans, Aging Patterns, p. 47.

[33] Philip Taietz, Gordon F. Streib, and Milton L. Barron, Adjustment to Retirement in Rural New York State (Cornell Agricultural Experiment Station Bulletin 919; Ithaca, N. Y., Feb. 1956), p. 18.

[34] Stone and Slocum, A Look at Thurston County's Older People, p. 28.

[35] McKain and Baldwin, Old Age and Retirement in Rural Connecticut, p. 39.

[36] Youmans, Aging Patterns, p. 47.

[37] Marianne Muse, Preparations for Old Age by Rural Vermonters Aged 50-64 (Vermont Agricultural Experiment Station Bulletin 638; Burlington, Vt., Feb. 1964), p. 39.

[38] Ibid., p. 41.

[39] McKain and Baldwin, Old Age and Retirement in Rural Connecticut, p. 40.

[40] Stone and Slocum, A Look at Thurston County's Older People, p. 29.

[41] Marshall McLuhan, Understanding Media (New York: McGraw-Hill, 1964).

[42] Taietz, Streib, and Barron, Adjustment to Retirement, p. 18.

[43] McKain and Baldwin, Old Age and Retirement in Rural Connecticut, p. 39.

[44] Muse, Preparations for Old Age by Rural Vermonters, p. 38.

[45] "A Study of Free-Time Activities," p. 159.

[46] Preparations for Old Age by Rural Vermonters, p. 37.

[47] Stone and Slocum, A Look at Thurston County's Older People, p. 28.

[48] Taietz, Streib, and Barron, Adjustment to Retirement, p. 22.

[49] Youmans, Aging Patterns, p. 47; McKain and Baldwin, Old Age and Retirement in Rural Connecticut, p. 39.

[50] Warren, "Old Age in a Rural Township," p. 155.

[51] Fuller, et al., Characteristics of Persons 60 Years of Age, p. 26.

[52] Stone and Slocum, A Look at Thurston County's Older People, p. 27.

[53] Fuller, et al., Characteristics of Persons 60 Years of Age, p. 23.

[54] Youmans, Aging Patterns, p. 47.

[55] Stone and Slocum, *A Look at Thurston County's Older People*, p. 28.

[56] Taietz, Streib, and Barron, *Adjustment to Retirement*, p. 18.

[57] Muse, *Preparations for Old Age by Rural Vermonters*, p. 38.

[58] Youmans, *Aging Patterns*, p. 47.

[59] Stone and Slocum, *A Look at Thurston County's Older People*, p. 28.

[60] Youmans, *Aging Patterns*, p. 47.

[61] Stone and Slocum, *A Look at Thurston County's Older People*, p. 28.

[62] Taietz, Streib, and Barron, *Adjustment to Retirement*, p. 18.

[63] Muse, *Preparations for Old Age by Rural Vermonters*, p. 37.

[64] Irving Lorge and Jacob Tuckman, "The Best Years of Life: A Study in Ranking," *Journal of Psychology*, 34 (1952), 145.

[65] Irving A. Spaulding, "Perspective in Play, Recreation and Leisure," paper presented at Rural Sociology Society Annual Meeting, 1964.

[66] Youmans, *Aging Patterns*, p. 46.

[67] Taietz, Streib, and Barron, *Adjustment to Retirement*, p. 18.

[68] Muse, *Preparations for Old Age by Rural Vermonters*, pp. 38-39.

[69] Stone and Slocum, *A Look at Thurston County's Older People*, p. 39.

[70] *Ibid.*, p. 28.

[71] Warren, "Old Age in a Rural Township," p. 157.

[72] *Personal and Social Adjustments*, p. 10.

[73] McKain, "Social Participation of Old People," p. 59.

[74] "Social Participation in Old Age," p. 237. For a contrary viewpoint see Arnold W. Green, *Recreation, Leisure, and Politics* (New York: McGraw-Hill, 1964), p. 131.

[75] Fuller, *et al.*, *Characteristics of Persons 60 Years of Age*, p. 28.

[76] Muse, *Preparations for Old Age by Rural Vermonters*, pp. 39, 40.

[77] Stone and Slocum, *A Look at Thurston County's Older People*, p. 43.

[78] McKain, "Social Participation of Old People," p. 114.

[79] Stone and Slocum, *A Look at Thurston County's Older People*, p. 28.

[80] "Age Profiles in Social Participation," pp. 248-49.

[81] McKain and Baldwin, *Old Age and Retirement in Rural Connecticut*, p. 39.

[82] McKain, "Social Participation of Old People," p. 132.

[83] *Ibid.*, pp. 143-56.

[84] As reported in Denton E. Morrison and G. Albert Kristjanson, *Personal Adjustment Among Older Persons* (South Dakota Agricultural Experiment Station, Technical Bulletin 21; Brookings, S. D., June 1958), pp. 10-13.

[85] Bernard Kutner, D. Fanshel, A. M. Togo, and T. S. Langner, *Five Hundred Over Sixty* (New York: Russell Sage Foundation, 1956).

[86] P. 48.

[87] Leo W. Simmons, *The Role of the Aged in Primitive Society* (New Haven: Yale University Press, 1945).

[88] McKain, "Social Participation of Old People," p. 78.

[89] "Seventeen Hundred Elderly Citizens," p. 151.

[90] S. L. Pressey and R. G. Kuhlen, *Psychological Development Through The Life Span* (New York: Harper and Brothers, 1957).

[91] Hoar, "A Study of Free-Time Activities," p. 161.

[92] Warren, "Old Age in a Rural Township," p. 157.

[93] Samson and Mather, *Personal and Social Adjustments*, p. 15.

[94] McKain, "Social Participation of Old People," pp. 64-69.

[95] "Aging as a Modern Social Achievement," in Wilma Donahue, *et al.* (ed.), *Free Time* (Ann Arbor: University of Michigan Press, 1958), p. 27. The growth of leisure time is shown in a national time budget for the years 1900, 1950, and 2000. See Marian Clawson, "How Much Leisure, Now and in the Future," in James C. Charlesworth (ed.), *Leisure in America: Blessing or Curse* (Philadelphia: The American Academy of Political and Social Science, April, 1964), pp. 10-11.

[96] *Dimensions of Work* (New York: David McKay Company, 1964), pp. 90-105.

[97] *Aging Patterns*, p. 51.

[98] Robert W. Kleemeier, "Leisure and Disengagement in Retirement," *The Gerontologist*, 4 (Dec. 1964).

[99] Martin Gumpert, "A Second Prime of Life—After 70," *New York Times Magazine*, July 8, 1951, p. 14.

E. GRANT YOUMANS

Disengagement among
Older Rural and Urban Men

One of the current and more systematic explanations of human aging as social-psychological phenomena is found in "disengagement theory." As formulated by Cumming and Henry[1] and modified by Neugarten[2] and Williams and Wirths,[3] this theory suggests that human aging involves an inevitable withdrawal from interactions with others and that this withdrawal is associated with important changes in the goals, attitudes, orientations, and personality of the aging person. This theory conceives the aging person as being at the center of a network of social relationships and, as he ages, his social life space tends to constrict and he experiences a general curtailment of involvement in the social system, a process which is beneficial to the society and to the individual. Critics of disengagement theory, among them Kutner[4] and Rose,[5] maintain that the process of disengagement is not inevitable, that nonengagement in later life may be a continuation of lifelong patterns of social participation, that disengagement is not beneficial to the individual, and that sociocultural trends in American society serve to counteract the forces making for disengagement.

Such theoretical differences may, in part, be resolved by empirical data on specific populations of older people. This chapter presents data on disengagement among elderly men living in their respective communities. It focuses on disengagement in three major aspects of life: disengagement from economic activities, from family life, and from hobbies and community activities.

97

Data are presented relevant to three central questions: (*a*) What evidence exists of disengagement in these three areas of life? (*b*) What relationships exist between social disengagement and the men's inner, subjective life? (*c*) What influence does the type of community have on the disengagement process?

It is recognized that assessments of disengagement can be made best by long-term studies of the same persons. However, longitudinal investigations present many practical and financial problems which preclude their use by many social scientists. In the absence of the ideal, this chapter compares two age groups of men—those aged 60 to 64 and those aged 75 and over. Differences between these two age groups, it is theorized, reflect aspects of the disengagement process.

Data for comparisons are obtained from two samples of non-institutionalized elderly men—one from a rural county in Kentucky and the other from an urbanized area in the state.[6] Characteristics of the two samples are shown in Table 1. About one-

Table 1. Social Characteristics of Males Aged 60-64 and 75 and Over by Percentage in Casey County and Lexington, Kentucky, 1959

Characteristics	Casey County		Lexington	
	Aged 60-64 (N = 72)	Aged 75 and over (N = 102)	Aged 60-64 (N = 49)	Aged 75 and over (N = 57)
Color:				
White	100	100	71	84
Nonwhite	—	—	29	16
Religion:				
Protestant	67	75	88	77
Catholic	3	—	2	2
Other	4	3	6	2
No response	26	22	4	19
Education:				
0-4 grades	35	39	19	26
5-8 grades	46	47	33	25
9-12 grades	9	10	24	16
Some college	6	2	20	26
No response	4	2	4	7
(Median grade)	(5.3)	(5.1)	(7.4)	(6.8)
Residence:				
Farm	89	65	—	—
Village or town	8	25	—	—
Open country, not farm	3	10	—	—
Large city	—	—	100	100
(Median years lived in present community)	(56)	(68)	(35)	(39)

fifth of the urban men but none of the rural men were nonwhite. About three-quarters of the men were Protestant. In both rural and urban areas the older men had received slightly less formal education than the younger men. Most of the men in the rural county lived on farms and in both residential areas the men constituted stable populations.

ECONOMIC DISENGAGEMENT

For most men in American society, paid employment is the chief means of connecting them with the economic life of the community. A job gives a man something to do, defines a meaningful role for him, and offers opportunities to develop friendships and achieve recognition among his peers. A job also provides a man with an income, an important means of participating in economic and social life and in maintaining his status in the community.

Withdrawal from the major work role disconnects a man from economic life and from many meaningful activities. He may experience a severe loss in income, a declining level of living, a decrease in social standing in the community, a loss of something to do, a severance of bonds with others, and a loss of sense of purpose.

As shown in Table 2, disengagement from employment increased markedly with age among both rural and urban men. In the rural area, the proportions of older and younger men in the labor force were 29 and 87 percent, respectively. The predominant occupation in the rural county was farm operator. Three-quarters of the younger rural men but only one-quarter of the older rural men were active farm operators.

The urban men evidenced a similar pattern of disengagement from employment, although this disengagement appeared to be more sharply related to age among urban than among rural men. Only 18 percent of the older urban men but 76 percent of the younger urban men were in the labor force. The major occupations in the metropolitan center were professional, managerial, and factory work. About one-third of the younger urban men were engaged in professional and managerial work, compared with 9 percent of the older men. About one-third of the urban younger men were engaged in factory work, compared with 5 percent of the older urban men.

Table 2. Occupation and Income of Males Aged 60-64 and 75 and Over by
Percentage in Casey County and Lexington, Kentucky, 1959

Occupation and Income	Casey County		Lexington	
	Aged 60-64 (N = 72)	Aged 75 and over (N = 102)	Aged 60-64 (N = 49)	Aged 75 and over (N = 57)
Occupation:				
Professional and managerial	10	4	33	9
Clerical and sales	—	—	8	—
Factory work	1	1	33	5
Farm operator	74	24	—	2
Farm laborer	2	—	2	2
Retired	9	61	18	81
Unable to work	4	10	6	1
Income:				
$0- $499	20	35	2	13
$500- $999	25	39	8	24
$1,000-$1,999	26	14	10	17
$2,000-$2,999	14	4	22	14
$3,000-$4,999	6	4	31	9
$5,000 or over	6	1	27	11
No response	3	3	—	12
(Median)	($1,105)	($668)	($3,333)	($1,399)

Advances in age brought a sharp drop in annual income among both rural and urban men, but the relative decline was greater in the urban than in the rural area (see Table 1). Each respondent was shown a card listing ranges of income and asked to indicate the range of annual family income. In the rural area, the median annual income for the younger men was $1,105, almost double the median income of $668 for the older men. In the urban area, the median annual income of the younger men was more than twice that of the older men, $3,333 and $1,399, respectively.

The disengagement hypothesis suggests that withdrawal or severance from interactions with others may be associated with important changes in the subjective life of a person. The older men in this study were substantially more disengaged than the younger men from the economic life of the community. Thus, it might be expected that the older and younger men would differ in values and outlook. Streib has suggested that satisfactions with life may increase after retirement and that it is the compulsory form of retirement which may bring deleterious results.[7]

Data were not collected from the men in this study on whether their retirement was voluntary or compulsory. They were asked several questions about their subjective evaluations of their economic conditions. Although these evaluations do not assess the men's subjective reactions to all the losses connected with retirement or severance from a job, they do give an indication of their economic satisfactions or dissatisfactions.

One question was: "Do you have to go without things because you don't have enough money?" Responses to this question indicated that subjective economic deprivation decreased with the age of the men. Despite the markedly low incomes of the older men, they felt less deprived than did the younger men who reported substantially higher annual incomes. In the rural county, the proportions of older and younger men who said they had to go without things because they lacked money were 42 and 57 percent, respectively. In the metropolitan center the corresponding percentages were 32 and 45.

Another question assessing subjective reactions to their economic conditions was: "Do you have serious financial problems?" In both residential areas, marked differences were found between the older and the younger men. However, these differences did not coincide with reported incomes. It was the younger men with the higher incomes and not the older men with the lower incomes who emphasized their financial problems. For example, in the rural area the percentages of younger and older men who said they had serious financial problems were 40 and 21, respectively. In the city, the corresponding percentages were 39 and 21.

A final question concerning subjective evaluations of economic conditions was: "Do you feel you need more opportunities to work for pay or profit?" Affirmative responses to this question, it is inferred, reveal dissatisfaction with economic conditions. It might be expected that the older men, who were receiving slight benefits from the economic system, would reveal the greater dissatisfaction. In the rural area, the opposite was the case. One-quarter of the younger rural men said they wanted more opportunities to work for pay or profit, but only 6 percent of the older rural men gave this response. Among the city dwellers, approximately equal proportions of younger and older men said they needed more opportunities to work for pay (27 and 23 percent, respectively).

The marked difference between older and younger rural men

in the desire for more paid work and the lack of such a difference in the urban center suggest a number of interpretations. Perhaps in the rural county the older men tend to conform to the traditional role of the retired patriarch. The older rural man may have given up his expectation for economic betterment and may gracefully accept his present lot. Urban older men, in contrast, may not subscribe to such acceptance of a traditional role and may be motivated by a desire to obtain work and earn more money. Perhaps, also, there are very few opportunities in a rural community for men aged 75 and over to earn money, and the responses of the older rural men may realistically reflect this condition.

DISENGAGEMENT IN FAMILY LIFE

Satisfactory primary-group relationships are essential for emotional health and most people find this type of relationship in the family setting. For older persons, continued relationships with family members may constitute the most important aspect of their lives. Townsend has given evidence of the central role of family life to many old people.[8] Streib and Shanas point out that, in a rapidly changing world, kinship ties may assume different meanings to the individual but that the family becomes more and not less important.[9] Disengagement from or disruption or severance of family ties may have a critical bearing on the well-being of older people.

Family relationships are extremely complex and difficult to assess. Data were collected on the existing family structure of the men and on three aspects of family relationships that permit an assessment of disengagement: (a) visiting patterns, (b) helping relationships, and (c) subjective reactions of the men to some ideas about family acceptance of older persons.

Data on existing family structure are shown in Table 3. In both residential areas, there were no significant differences between the older men (aged 75 and over) and the younger men (aged 60 to 64) in the proportions who had living children and in the proportions who said they lived with one or more of their siblings. In both residential areas, significantly larger proportions of the older than younger men were widowed and not living with any of their children. In the rural area, a smaller proportion of older

Table 3. Family Structure of Males Aged 60-64 and 75 and Over by Percentage in Casey County and Lexington, Kentucky, 1959

Question	Response	Casey County		Lexington	
		Aged 60-64 (N = 72)	Aged 75 and over (N = 102)	Aged 60-64 (N = 49)	Aged 75 and over (N = 57)
Are you a widower?	Yes	5%	23*	10	35*
Do you have any children living?	No	1	2	2	7
Do you live with any of your children?	No	38	49*	41	58*
Do you have any brothers or sisters living?	No	3	15*	18	32
Do your live with any of your brothers or sisters?	No	86	78	71	58
Have any of your brothers or sisters died in the past 5 years?	Yes	19	28	18	35*

* P < 0.05, one-tailed test.

than younger men had brothers and sisters living, and in the urban area a significantly larger proportion of older than younger men reported they had lost brothers and sisters through death "in the past five years."

VISITING PATTERNS

An indication of disengagement may be found in the frequency of visiting between older people and their relatives. It is recognized that frequency of visiting may not reveal the intensity of the relationship. Data were obtained from the men on the frequency of visiting between themselves and their children and siblings who lived apart. It was expected that this visiting would depend largely upon the proximity of the children and siblings. Consequently, each respondent who had living children and living siblings was asked about the number who lived at varying distances—under 10 miles, 10 to 49 miles, 50 to 250 miles, and over 250 miles. Next, each respondent was asked how often he visited with any of his children or any of his siblings at each of these distances—daily, weekly, monthly, two to four times a year, once a year, or less often.

The data presented in Table 4 show rather slight evidence of disengagement from visiting with children who lived apart. The older men visited only slightly less often with their children than did the younger men. In the rural area, the difference in frequency of visiting between the older and younger men was not statistically significant. In the metropolitan center, the difference was statistically significant, but this difference was accounted for by the percentages who visited weekly. Whereas 29 percent of the younger urban men visited weekly with their children who lived apart, only 2 percent of the urban older men gave this

Table 4. Visiting Patterns with Children Living Apart Reported by Males Aged 60-64 and 75 and Over by Percentage in Casey County and Lexington, Kentucky, 1959*

Frequency of visiting	Casey County		Lexington	
	Aged 60-64 (N = 72)	Aged 75 and over (N = 102)	Aged 60-64 (N = 49)	Aged 75 and over (N = 57)
Daily	13	11	11	11
Weekly	22	18	29	2
Monthly	20	16	11	26
2, 3, 4 times a year	26	26	21	10
Yearly	11	14	17	13
Less often	6	14	9	15
No response	2	1	2	23
(Number of children)	(134)	(194)	(47)	(61)

* Rural $P > 0.05$; urban $P < 0.05$, "no response" categories excluded.

response. One hypothesis to explain this important difference might be found in the transportation facilities available. Weekly visiting with children probably requires the use of an automobile. Many of the younger men (aged 60 to 64) probably were licensed to drive automobiles and thus could make weekly visits to see their children. Many of the older men (aged 75 and over) may not have been able to drive a car and thus were dependent upon their children's coming to see them.

Extremely little evidence of disengagement was found in the visiting patterns existing between the respondents and their siblings who lived apart. As shown in Table 5, the men interviewed visited less often with their siblings than with their children.

Table 5. Visiting Patterns with Siblings Living Apart Reported by Males
Aged 60-64 and 75 and Over by Percentage in Casey County
and Lexington, Kentucky, 1959*

Frequency of visiting	Casey County		Lexington	
	Aged 60-64 (N = 72)	Aged 75 and over (N = 102)	Aged 60-64 (N = 49)	Aged 75 and over (N = 57)
Daily	2	3	—	2
Weekly	20	11	16	8
Monthly	13	17	13	21
2, 3, 4 times a year	23	19	31	17
Yearly	16	20	23	21
Less often	21	29	16	31
No response	5	1	1	—
(Number of siblings)	(131)	(137)	(61)	(48)

* Rural > 0.05; urban > 0.05; "no response" categories excluded.

Although the older men in both residential areas visited slightly less often with their siblings than did the younger men, the differences were not statistically significant.

HELPING RELATIONSHIPS

One inevitable form of disengagement occurs in American society as children grow up and leave their family of orientation. The aging parents are thus relieved of some of their responsibilities for their children. In some cultures adult children may venerate aged persons and seek them out to obtain advice and assistance. In American society this practice is rather uncommon. The findings presented in Table 6 give evidence of this among the samples in this study. The men were asked if any of their children came to them for advice. A substantially smaller proportion of older than younger men gave an affirmative answer to this question. In addition, a smaller proportion of older than younger men also reported they helped their children in some way. The marked difference between older and younger men, particularly in the proportions who reported that their children came to them for advice, indicates the loss of prestige, of power, and of authority experienced by many members of American society in old age.

Helping relationships between the men and their other relatives showed little deterioration with age. As shown in Table 6, negligible differences were found in both residential areas in

Table 6. Family Helping Relationships Reported by Males Aged 60-64 and 75 and Over by Percentage in Casey County and Lexington, Kentucky, 1959

Helping relationship	Casey County		Lexington	
	Aged 60-64 (N = 72)	Aged 75 and over (N = 102)	Aged 60-64 (N = 49)	Aged 75 and over (N = 57)
Do any of your children come to you for advice?				
Yes	44	21*	49	28*
No	46	66	24	39
No response	10	13	27	33
Do you help your children in any way?				
Yes	26	15*	29	18
No	64	70	42	53
No response	10	15	29	29
Do any relatives come to you for advice?				
Yes	7	2	18	18
No	68	67	67	60
No response	25	31	15	22
Do you help your brothers or sisters?				
Yes	3	2	—	1
No	86	77	78	61
No response	11	21	22	38

* P < 0.05, one-tailed test, "no response" categories excluded.

the proportions of older and younger men who said their relatives came to them for advice or who said they helped their brothers or sisters in some way.

FAMILY ACCEPTANCE

The disengagement hypothesis suggests that severance from institutional life in society is associated with changes in outlook and attitude. Since the older men in this study had experienced some disengagement in their family life, it is expected that these losses would be reflected in negative attitudes and possibly in feelings of rejection.

The men responded to two questions that probed their feelings of rejection by their families. They were asked if they agreed or disagreed with the following statements: "Most families like to have older people around" and "Older people are better off if they live with their children." Responses to these two questions indicated that feelings of family acceptance were positively related to age in the rural area. For example, the percentages of older and younger men in the rural area who agreed that families like to have older people around were 46 and 38, respectively. The percentages of older and younger rural men who agreed that older people are better off if they live with their children were 27 and 6, respectively. In the metropolitan center, the responses were in the opposite direction. The percentages of older and younger men in the city who agreed with the first question were 32 and 45, respectively, and the percentages who agreed with the second question were 11 and 27, respectively.

Two factors may explain the stronger feelings of family acceptance revealed by the older rural men. One is the greater prevalence of folk culture in the rural than in the urban area. Folk culture is characterized by emphasis on tradition and custom, on strong kinship ties and informal interpersonal relationships, and on feelings of solidarity and cohesion. In urban society, in contrast, emphasis is placed on rationality and efficiency, on calculated self-interest, and on critical and objective standards of behavior. These differing value orientations undoubtedly were more strongly held by the older than younger rural men, and thus probably influenced their notions about family acceptance.

A second factor may contribute to the stronger feeling of family acceptance on the part of the older rural men. This is the nature of housing conditions existing in some rural and urban areas of the United States. Urban housing conditions usually are not conducive to three-generation family living. The prevalence of apartment living and the smaller homes found in most urban centers virtually preclude taking in the older couple. Available evidence suggests that aged persons in American cities prefer to live close to but apart from their children.

DISENGAGEMENT IN LEISURE TIME ACTIVITIES

Nonwork activities such as hobbies and participation in various community organizations are important means for connecting individuals with society. For many older males in American society who have retired, leisure-time interests may serve as substitutes for work-centered activities. Decline in physical vigor and limited financial resources may cause many older men to disengage themselves from free-time activities, and this disengagement may be associated with negative attitudes and feelings about leisure time.

Data were obtained from the men in this study on four aspects of their leisure time interests and activities: (a) their participation in active and sedentary hobbies, (b) their participation in formal organizations in the community, (c) their involvement in informal social relationships, and (d) their attitudes and values related to leisure-time use.

HOBBIES

As shown in Table 7, very slight disengagement from active hobbies occurred with advances in the age of the men. In both residential areas, no statistically significant differences were found between younger and older men in their participation in active hobbies and pastimes.

The four most popular pastimes, in both residential areas, were gardening, visiting, hunting and fishing, and athletics and sports. Visiting was a more common activity in the rural county than in the metropolitan center, whereas athletics and sports were more popular in the city. In both residential areas, participation declined with age principally in hunting and fishing and in athletics and sports.

Significant differences were found between younger and older men in their participation in sedentary hobbies and pastimes. As shown in Table 7, disengagement from some sedentary activities occurred with advances in age, whereas in others there was increased participation. Negligible differences were found between younger and older men in the average numbers of their sedentary pastimes.

Neugarten points out that the process of disengagement is believed to be accompanied by a release from normative patterns of behavior and that this decrease in normative influences may contribute to the emergence of eccentric behavior in older people.[10] One form of behavior commonly observed among older people is the increased preoccupation with self. If this behavior

Table 7. Hobbies Participated in by Males Aged 60-64 and 75 and Over by Percentage in Casey County and Lexington, Kentucky, 1959

Hobbies	Casey County		Lexington	
	Aged 60-64 (N = 72)	Aged 75 and over (N = 102)	Aged 60-64 (N = 49)	Aged 75 and over (N = 57)
Active:*				
Gardening	35	22	24	30
Visiting	37	29	14	19
Hunting and fishing	33	16	31	9
Athletics and sports	18	12	39	18
Travel and rides	15	9	12	9
Handcrafts	3	4	10	11
Clubs and meetings	6	2	6	5
Odd jobs	—	6	6	4
Shopping	1	1	4	2
(Average per person)	(1.49)	(1.00)	(1.47)	(1.05)
Sedentary:**				
Television or radio	54	50	69	53
Reading	25	27	16	33
Sit and think	3	23	8	25
Cards	11	3	8	5
Writing letters	1	3	4	2
Sewing	—	1	4	2
Movies	1	—	6	—
Painting	3	3	—	—
(Average per person)	(0.99)	(1.10)	(1.16)	(1.19)

* Rural P > 0.05; urban P > 0.05.
** Rural P < 0.05; urban P < 0.05.

were evidenced among young or middle-aged persons, it might be considered abnormal or even deviant, but among older people it probably is accepted as a normal aspect of old age. Whether an increased inward orientation is a direct consequence of disengagement from meaningful interactions with others or whether it is based in the personality cannot be assessed from the data here. What the data show is that preoccupation with internal thoughts and feelings increased with the age of the men. As shown in Table 7, the only sedentary pastime which increased with the age of the men in the rural county was "sitting and thinking." Only 3 percent of the younger rural men said they sat and thought, but 23 percent of the older rural men said this was a pastime. In the urban center, the corresponding percentages were 8 and 25 percent, representing an increase with age comparable to the increase in reading as a pastime.

It might be expected that men who have disengaged themselves from gainful employment would spend large portions of their free time watching television or listening to radio programs. Williams and Wirths were convinced that watching television increased with age in their study of persons over age 50.[11] Watching television or listening to radio programs was the most popular pastime of the men in both residential areas of the study reported here, but this pastime had little relationship with the age of the men. In the rural area, about half of younger and older men reported they watched television or listened to the radio. In the metropolitan center, there was a slight decrease in this pastime with the age of the men. Access to or ownership of receiving sets was not a factor in participation in this activity. Almost all the men, regardless of age, had access to television or radio sets, although radio sets were more common than television sets in the rural county.

COMMUNITY ORGANIZATIONS

As shown in Table 8, very slight disengagement from participating in community organizations occurred with advances in the age of the men. In the rural area, a significant difference was found between younger and older men, and this difference was due principally to the smaller proportion of older than younger men who took part in farm organizations. In the urban center no significant difference was found between younger and older men in their participation in community organizations.

Table 8. Community Organizations Participated in by Males 60-64 and 75 and Over by Percentage in Casey County and Lexington, Kentucky, 1959*

Organization	Casey County		Lexington	
	Aged 60-64 (N = 72)	Aged 75 and over (N = 102)	Aged 60-64 (N = 49)	Aged 75 and over (N = 57)
Church	68	77	88	81
Sunday school	36	33	31	30
Clubs and lodges	10	10	33	25
Farm organizations	15	3	2	2
Labor unions	—	—	8	4
Veterans organizations	4	—	4	2
Other	—	—	8	5
(Average number per person)	(1.33)	(1.23)	(1.74)	(1.49)

* Rural P < 0.05; urban P > 0.05, one-tailed test.

It is commonly believed that aged persons are the backbone of religious organizations and that church attendance increases in the later years of life. Ideally, religious institutions can help older persons accept the inevitable losses that come with old age. Barron points out that there is some intensifying of inner religiosity in later life but little change of interest in the church. He adds that instead of a large-scale turning to religion in old age, most people persist in the religious patterns of their earlier years.[12] Among the predominantly Protestant men in this study, church-related activities were the most popular means of participating in the organized life of the community. However, participation in these organized activities varied very slightly with the age of the men. In both residential areas, approximately equal proportions of younger and older men engaged in church-related activities.

INFORMAL SOCIAL RELATIONSHIPS

Disengagement from informal social relationships was assessed by means of three questions. One question was: "Do you know people in the community real well?" Rural men revealed stronger feelings of attachment to others in the community than did the urban men. In the rural area these attachments remained constant with age, but in the metropolitan center they declined with advances in age. In the rural county, the proportions of younger and older men who said they knew people in the community real well were 94 and 90 percent, respectively. In the metropolitan center the corresponding percentages were 76 and 53.

A second question concerning informal social relationships in the community was worded: "Do you help your friends and neighbors in any way?" Responses to this question indicated that helping relationships were more common in the rural than in the metropolitan center. However, in both residential areas disengagement from or deterioration in these helping relationships increased with the age of the men. The percentages of younger and older rural men who said they helped friends and neighbors in some way were 74 and 44, respectively. In the metropolitan center, the corresponding percentages were 43 and 19.

A third question about informal social life was: "How often

do you visit with friends and neighbors—once a week, once a month, or less?" In both residential areas, substantial decline in visiting occurred with advancing age. Whereas 68 percent of the younger rural men said they visited friends and neighbors once a month or more often, only 45 percent of the older rural men gave this response. In the metropolitan center, the corresponding percentages were 67 and 38.

ATTITUDES ABOUT ACTIVITIES

Some of the attitudes and feelings of the men about leisure-time activities were revealed in their responses to four questions. In some cases, age was associated with negative attitudes or dissatisfactions; in other cases it was not. For example, unoccupied time appeared to be a burden with advances in age. Substantially more of the older than younger men reported that they found time "hanging heavily on their hands." They were asked if they agreed or disagreed with the statement, "I don't know what to do with my spare time." In the rural county, the proportions of younger and older men who agreed with the statement were 17 and 41 percent, respectively. In the metropolitan center, the corresponding percentages were 8 and 35.

However, only slight differences were found between older and younger men in their feelings about being useful. They were asked if they agreed or disagreed with the statement, "I feel my life could be more useful." In the rural area, the proportions of younger and older men who felt their lives could be more useful were 51 and 43 percent, respectively. In the urban center, the corresponding percentages were 39 and 30.

Old age is commonly associated with loss of physical vigor and this decline may have a bearing on disengagement from various activities. The men were asked if they had cut down on their activities because of their health. A large proportion of rural men acknowledged this reduction in activities but the decline was not associated with age in the rural area. About three-quarters of both younger and older men in the rural area said they had cut down on their activities because of their health. In the metropolitan center, in contrast, a much smaller proportion of the men said they had reduced their activities and the decline was associated with age. Only 27 percent of the younger urban men said they had cut down on their activities, but 46 percent of the older urban men gave this response.

These data suggest that older men living in an agrarian environment are more prone than those in an urban center to attribute a decline in activities to their health. The data also suggest that this "explanation" on the part of the men occurred at an earlier age in the rural than in the urban environment. Normal adult roles in an agrarian setting probably require more physical strength and stamina than those in a metropolitan center. With the normal decline in physical vigor which occurs with older age and the consequent inability to perform as well as in the past, the rural male probably is acutely aware of his physical limitations at an early age, and he may attribute those to declining health.

Since substantially more of the older than younger men in this study had relinquished their major work role, it might be expected that they would desire or have need for additional activities. They were asked: "Are there some activities you would like to take part in which you are not now doing?" Rather small proportions of the men responded in the affirmative and no statistically significant differences were found between the older and younger men, in either the rural or the urban area. The proportions of older and younger men in the rural county who expressed a desire for more activities were 35 and 24 percent, respectively. In the metropolitan center the corresponding percentages were 28 and 26.

CONCLUSIONS

This chapter has examined evidence of disengagement in two samples of elderly men in three areas of life: economic, family relationships, and leisure-time activities.

Objective economic disengagement increased markedly with age among the men. In both residential areas, the older men had markedly lower economic status than did the younger men, i.e., the older men were much less involved in work roles and had markedly smaller incomes. Decline in economic status occurred more sharply with age in the urban than in the rural area. Marked incongruities were found between objective and subjective indicators of economic disengagement. Despite their relatively low economic status, the older men felt less subjective economic deprivation than did the younger men, a finding which suggests that the older men had made substantial adaptations and adjustments to their economic conditions.

It is recognized that survey findings from two age groups must be viewed with caution. Differences in behavior and attitude between younger and older men may, in some cases, reflect generational phenomena rather than age changes. Perhaps the older men, during their life course, had internalized somewhat stronger economic values of frugality and parsimony. Perhaps the younger men had been oriented to a more expansive and demanding need for material wealth and possessions. These different value orientations, in turn, probably influenced their notions of economic deprivation in old age.

In both residential areas, the older men revealed only slightly more disengagement in family life than did the younger men; at the time of interview, the older men in both residential areas visited with their children and siblings only slightly less often than did the younger men. However, the older men in both residential areas appeared to have experienced loss in power and authority over their children, but there was no appreciable decline with age in the influence over siblings or other relatives. Urban men evidenced somewhat stronger feelings of rejection by their families than did the rural men, a finding which probably reflects the greater prevalence of folk culture in the rural area.

Extremely slight disengagement from leisure-time activities occurred with advances in the age of the men. In both residential areas, the older men were engaged in only slightly fewer active hobbies and in slightly fewer community organizations than were the younger men. Engagement in sedentary hobbies increased significantly with the age of the men, but the difference was accounted for principally by the increased proportions of rural and urban men who said they spent time in "sitting and thinking." This increased preoccupation with self with advances in age may reflect decreases in normative influences operating among older people in the United States. Watching television and listening to radio programs was the most popular pastime of the men, but participation in this sedentary activity bore slight relationship to the age of the respondent. The most popular of organized community activities in both residential areas were church related, and advances in age had little bearing on participation in them. Rural men revealed stronger informal attachments to other persons in the community than did the urban men, and these attachments declined somewhat with age in both residential areas. Older men, compared to younger men, evidenced greater dissatisfaction with unoccupied free time. However, despite this negative feeling, small proportions of older men indicated interest in taking up new leisure-time activities. The low rates of participation in community life on the part of the men living in rural Kentucky are consistent with the low rates of participation in other rural areas reported by McKain. This study supports the contention of Kutner that changes with advances in age are not necessarily degenerative or linear.[13] It adds support to the findings of Williams and Wirths that disengagement can occur in different aspects of a person's behavior and at different rates in these various aspects.[14]

NOTES

[1] Elaine Cumming and William E. Henry, *Growing Old* (New York: Basic Books, 1961).
[2] Bernice L. Neugarten, *et al.*, *Personality in Middle and Late Life* (New York: Atherton, 1964).
[3] Richard H. Williams and C. G. Wirths, *Lives Through the Year* (New York: Atherton, 1965).
[4] Bernard Kutner, "The Social Nature of Aging," *The Gerontologist*, 2 (March 1962), 5-8.
[5] Arnold M. Rose and Warren A. Peterson (eds.), *Older People and Their Social World* (Philadelphia: F. A. Davis, 1965).
[6] Data are obtained from a survey made jointly by the Human Resources Branch, Economic Development Division, Economic Research Service, U. S. Department of Agriculture, and the Agricultural Experiment Station, University of Kentucky. The interpretations and statements made are those of the author and not necessarily those of the U. S. Department of Agriculture or of the Kentucky Agricultural Experiment Station.

In 1959, men and women aged 60 and older in an area-probability sample of households in a rural Kentucky county and in a random sample of persons of comparable age in a Kentucky metropolitan area were interviewed in their homes. Institutionalized older persons were not included. The rural county, located in the southern Appalachian region and isolated from large urban centers, had a population of about 14,000 in 1960. The Lexington urbanized area had a population of about 112,000 persons in 1960. The rural sample included 72 men aged 60 to 64 and 102 men aged 75 and over. The urban sample included 49 men aged 60 to 64 and 57 men aged 75 and over. The oldest man interviewed was 96.

[7] G. F. Streib, "Morale of the Retired," *Social Problems*, 3 (1956), 270.

[8] Peter Townsend, *The Family Life of Old People* (Glencoe: The Free Press, 1957).

[9] Ethel Shanas and Gordon F. Streib (eds.), *Social Structure and the Family: Generational Relations* (New York: Prentice Hall, 1965).

[10] Neugarten, *et al.*, *Personality in Middle and Late Life.*

[11] *Lives Through the Year.*

[12] Milton L. Barron, *The Aging American* (New York: Thomas Y. Crowell, 1961).

[13] "The Social Nature of Aging."

[14] *Lives Through the Year.*

HENRY D. SHELDON

Distribution of
the Rural Aged Population

Any consideration of the older population living in the rural areas of the United States leads to an examination of the extent to which the age structure of this population merely reflects that of the population as a whole and of the extent to which its characteristics arise from its rural condition. In the following discussion, therefore, some attention is given to trends in the age structure in the United States as a whole and of the rural population as reported in census statistics.

The twentieth century has been marked both in the United States and in the countries of western Europe by a rapid increase in the proportion of persons at the upper age levels. In the United States, for example, the percentage of the population 65 years old and over more than doubled between 1900 and 1960. This increase has been the result of relative declines in fertility and mortality. As successive generations of women have passed through the childbearing period, they have contributed relatively fewer children to the next generation than their mothers did, and thus cumulatively the proportion of older persons has increased. This trend has been augmented to some degree by the relative decline in mortality, which has permitted a larger proportion of births to survive to the more advanced years. The post-World War II rise in fertility has served to dampen but not extinguish the increase in the concentration of older persons in our population.

DEFINITION OF URBAN AND RURAL
POPULATION

The distinction between urban and rural population is conceptually a primitive one. The urban population is that population living in cities and towns and the rural population is the population living outside cities and towns. To convert this simple definition into an operational one which can be used to count urban and rural population involves a number of complications.

SIZE OF URBAN AGGREGATES

The first of these complications arises in developing an answer to the question as to the size of an aggregation of population which qualifies it as a city or town. Since the census of 1910 the Bureau of the Census has defined an urban place as a place with a population of 2,500 inhabitants or more.[1] This criterion is purely arbitrary; in earlier censuses urban places had been defined as places of both 4,000 and 8,000 or more. For certain purposes in certain states the Bureau of Public Roads uses a lower limit of 5,000, and any human ecologist, if his attention were turned to this question could, through an examination of services and functions by size of place, develop a different cutting score based on "urban" functions. The criterion of 2,500 has become more or less universal simply by the weight of tradition and the huge volume of statistics based on it.

BOUNDARIES AND CORPORATE LIMITS

The second complication arises from the necessity of setting boundaries to a city or town before a count of population can be made. In the census definition of urban population, the major element is the population of *incorporated* places of 2,500 or more. The use of incorporated units automatically provides boundaries (corporate or city limits) and also provides population figures for legal entities defined as towns or cities. Incorporation in the great majority of cases is for the purpose of exercising municipal functions and incorporated areas can therefore be assumed to involve concentrations of population; but not all areas are incorporated for this purpose. In the last decade, dairy farmers in the Los Angeles milkshed banded together and incorporated their farms as a town to save them from real estate development. Likewise, as will be noted later, not all concentrations of population are to be found in incorporated areas.

NEW ENGLAND TOWNS

The third complication arises from the unique system of county subdivisions in the New England states and to a lesser degree in the Middle Atlantic states. New England counties are subdivided into "towns," but there are no incorporated places within towns. In other words, concentrations of population have no legal boundaries and the ideal typical New England town, like the Greek city-state, is characterized by a center of population concentration—a place in the ordinary sense of the word— and a sparsely settled hinterland. Some of the largest towns are incorporated officially as cities and thus fit into the classification of incorporated places. Other towns of 2,500 or more are classified as "urban under special rule" and a few county subdivisions elsewhere in the county are similarly classified. In the period between 1910 and 1940, in which the basic elements of the bureau's current urban definition evolved, the treatment of this problem varied and no really satisfactory solution was developed.

URBAN FRINGE AND UNINCORPORATED PLACES

In the 1940 census, the urban population was defined as the population of incorporated places of 2,500 or more and the population of county subdivisions urban under special rule. In planning for the 1950 census, it became clear that, if the urban population is regarded as the population living in densely settled, built-up areas, the 1940 definition of urban population was deficient in two respects: it failed to include the population of unincorporated places which to the naked eye, or in terms of a density criterion, could not be distinguished from incorporated places, and it failed to include similar territory on the outskirts of cities immediately outside their corporate limits.

To correct these deficiencies the bureau prior to the 1950 census identified and established boundaries for unincorporated places of 1,000 or more and delineated an urban fringe surrounding cities of 50,000 or more. This fringe area might be described loosely as suburban, although it is reasonably heterogeneous, including both incorporated places and built-up, unincorporated territory. The problem of New England towns was resolved by treating the concentrations of population within towns outside urban fringe areas as unincorporated places, and the built-up parts of towns adjacent to large cities as urban fringe. This solution was satisfactory from the point of view of producing a more consistent nationwide urban-rural classification but was not so regarded in New England.

The 1960 definition of urban-rural residence was essentially similar to that of 1950. Urban fringe was defined after the census was taken in terms of density criterion applied to small enumeration districts, rather than before the census was taken by inspection, and a category of urban towns and townships was added. This device had the advantage of preserving the identity of New England towns and Pennsylvania and New Jersey townships and, at the same time, of not materially increasing the urban total over what it would have been under the 1950 definition. Most of the population of these areas would have been included either in unincorporated places or as urban fringe.

CHARACTER OF CURRENT URBAN DEFINITION

Beginning then with a simple and apparently unequivocal classification, a reasonably complex and not completely satisfactory definition of the urban population has evolved as the simple definition has been applied to crude empirical demands of census taking. The definition represents a compromise among a number of factors—what would be ideally desirable, the nature of the raw materials to be classified, the climate of public opinion in which a census is taken, and the resources available. The wisdom of each of the component parts of the definition viewed in isolation may be open to question, but all too frequently the categorical resolution of one problem gives rise to a number of equally disturbing problems which then require resolution. In short, as long as certain groupings of the population cannot be discarded as irrational and irrelevant, a certain "patchwork" quality is bound to remain in the definition.

It is clear that the urban population, as defined in the 1960 census, is homogeneous only in terms of being the population of areas of relatively high density and that it is made up of highly diverse elements.

THE POPULATION OF RURAL AREAS

The rural population is a residual; that is, it is the population of the country after the various components of urban population have been removed. As such it might be assumed to be homogeneous; as will be noted later, however, it too is composed of several rather disparate parts.

OLDER POPULATION IN URBAN
AND RURAL AREAS

In 1960 the proportion of the population 65 years old and over in urban and rural areas was about the same—9.2 percent and 9.3 percent, respectively (Table 1). The highest percentage, 12.3 percent, occurred in villages of 1,000 to 2,500 in rural territory, and the lowest, 7.2 percent, in the urban fringe; that is, that part of the urban population which may loosely be designated as suburban and in which population growth in the previous decade had been rapid. With the possible exception of central cities of urbanized areas, the figures suggest that the proportion of the elderly population increases as size of place declines. Outside urbanized areas, for example, 9.9 percent of the population of places of 10,000 to 50,000 inhabitants were 65 years old and over, 11.0 percent of the population of places of 2,500 to 10,000, and 12.3 percent of the population of places of 1,000 to 2,500. Figures from the 1950 census, as well as the examination of 1960 listings for a number of states in 1960, suggest that, if age data for incorporated places under 1,000 had been tabulated, they would have shown a still higher percentage 65 and over than places of 1,000 to 2,500. If this is the case, it would suggest that the residual open-country rural population would have had a somewhat lower concentration of older persons than the figure shown in Table 1, 8.9 percent.

URBAN-RURAL DIFFERENCES IN THE NONWHITE POPULATION

Since the nonwhite population has been characterized by somewhat higher fertility and mortality than the total population, the concentration of older persons in the nonwhite population is somewhat less than in the total, 6.2 vs. 9.3 percent. Given this general difference in level, the pattern of distribution among the various urban and rural components is not essentially different from that of the total population. Among nonwhites the concentration of older persons is clearly greater in the rural than in the urban population, and the difference from large to small places is more sharply defined. The contrast between central cities of urbanized areas and their urban fringe is less marked in the nonwhite population than in the total, although in the same direction. The relatively small difference in the percentage 65 and over between central city and fringe in the nonwhite population as well as the lower percentage for central cities in contrast to smaller places reflects in large part the heavy migration of young adult nonwhites from the South into the central cities of urbanized areas of the North and West.

FARM-NONFARM DIFFERENCES IN THE PROPORTION OF OLDER PERSONS

As indicated earlier in this discussion, the concentration of older persons in villages of 1,000 to 2,500 was greater than in the balance of the rural population. If the rural population is split in another dimension—farm-nonfarm residence—it appears that in 1960 the proportion of older persons in the farm population (9.6 percent) was marginally greater than the proportion in the nonfarm population (9.2 percent).

This difference noted at the national level does not lend itself to a global interpretation, since the higher percentage of

Table 1. White and Nonwhite Population Aged 65 and Over and Total Population by Residence Areas for Conterminous United States, 1960

Areas	Total			White			Nonwhite		
	All ages (thousands)	65 and over		All ages (thousands)	65 and over		All ages (thousands)	65 and over	
		Thousands	Percent		Thousands	Percent		Thousands	Percent
Total	178,464	16,525	9.3	158,455	15,293	9.7	20,009	1,232	6.2
Urban	124,699	11,503	9.2	110,202	10,664	9.7	14,497	838	5.8
In urbanized areas	95,497	8,461	8.9	83,661	7,834	9.4	11,836	672	5.3
Central cities	57,681	5,724	9.9	47,547	5,182	10.9	10,134	542	5.4
Urban fringe	37,816	2,737	7.2	36,114	2,653	7.3	1,702	85	5.0
Outside urbanized areas	29,202	3,041	10.4	26,541	2,830	10.7	2,661	211	7.9
Places of 10,000 or more	16,034	1,586	9.9	14,478	1,470	10.2	1,556	117	7.5
Places of 2,500 to 10,000	13,168	1,455	11.0	12,063	1,360	11.3	1,105	94	8.5
Rural	53,765	5,023	9.3	48,253	4,628	9.6	5,512	394	7.2
Places of 1,000 to 2,500	6,440	792	12.3	5,973	751	12.6	468	41	8.9
Other rural	47,325	4,231	8.9	42,280	3,878	9.2	5,045	353	7.0
Rural nonfarm*	40,300	3,724	9.2	36,378	3,428	9.4	3,923	295	7.5
Rural farm*	13,465	1,299	9.6	11,875	1,200	10.1	1,590	99	6.2

* Rural nonfarm and rural farm data are based on 25-percent sample and adjusted to the 100-percent level.
Source: U. S. Bureau of the Census, *United States Census of Population: 1960*, Series PC(1)B (Washington, D. C., 1963), Vol. 1, Characteristics of the Population. Part I, U. S. Summary. Table 46.

older persons in the farm population is characteristic of only 27 of the 48 states in conterminous United States. In all of the states east of the Mississippi except Vermont, Wisconsin, Illinois, and Mississippi, the percentage 65 and over in the farm population exceeded that in the nonfarm population, and in all of the states west of the Mississippi the percentage in the nonfarm population exceeded that in farm population except in Oregon, California, Nevada, New Mexico, and Texas. Although the definition of farm population in 1950 was considerably less restrictive, the same general pattern of farm-nonfarm differences by state occurred, but at the national level the concentration of older persons was greater in the nonfarm than in the farm population. It seems reasonable to conclude that the combined effects of genuine changes in the age structure of the farm population and of the change in definition did not alter the basic regional patterns but perhaps gave greater weight to those states in which the percentage 65 and over in the farm population exceeded that in the nonfarm population.

CHANGES IN RURAL AGE STRUCTURE: 1950-1960

TOTAL RURAL

The change in the age structure of the rural population between two decennial censuses falls into two parts: Changes in the age structure of the population living in area classified as rural at the beginning of the decade, and at the end of the decade those resulting from the conversion of a part of this rural territory to urban—places of less than 2,500 at the earlier census which the later census showed to have attained a population of 2,500 or more, rural areas adjacent to cities of 50,000 or more at the beginning of the decade which, at the end of the decade had acquired a sufficient density to qualify them as a part of the urban fringe, rural areas annexed to cities of 2,500 or more, and so on.

Data from the Current Population Survey (CPS) permit some rough assessment of the effects of these two elements. In that survey, sample segments are identified as urban or rural in terms of the preceding census classifications. Such classification cannot be changed until another decennial census is taken because there is no feasible way, other than a census, of determining when an initial rural segment becomes urban. Thus at the end of a decade, when a new decennial census is being taken, the CPS provides an estimate of the population of the areas which were rural at the preceding census. A comparison of this estimate with the results of the current census gives some indication of the amount and character of the population converted by definition from rural to urban. Further, if we project the population at the beginning of the decade to the end, a comparison of this population with the CPS estimate gives some indication of the net effect of migration to and from the initial rural areas.

Table 2. Total Rural Population Aged 65 and Over, Observed and Expected, for Conterminous United States, 1950 and 1960

Year and type of area	Total (thousands)	65 and over	
		Thousands	Percentage of total
1950	54,230	4,443	8.2
1960:			
Expected*	65,779	5,685	8.6
Observed:			
1950 area (CPS)**	70,668	5,383	7.6
1960 area (1960 census)	53,765	5,023	9.3
Rural area converted to urban	16,903	360	2.1

* On the basis of census survival rates and fertility ratios adjusted to approximate the expected population implied by net migration derived from recorded births and deaths.
** Adjusted to include estimate of armed forces in rural areas.
Source: U. S. Bureau of the Census, *United States Census of Population: 1960* (Washington, D. C., 1961), Vol. I; U. S. Bureau of the Census, *United States Census of Population: 1950* (Washington, D. C., 1953), Vol. I; and U. S. Bureau of the Census, *Current Population Reports,* Series P-27, No. 28, April 17, 1961.

The results of such an analysis are presented in Table 2. In 1950, the rural population was about 54 million and the percentage 65 and over was 8.2. A rough projection of the 1950 rural population indicates a population in 1960 of about 66 million with a percentage 65 and over of about 8.6. Actually, the CPS figures indicate a population of about 71 million of which 7.6 percent were 65 and over. In short, there was a net inmigration of about 5 million in which the concentration of older persons was relatively low. The 1960 census figures indicate a population of 54 million, with 9.3 percent 65 years old and over. Therefore, it appears that the application of the urban definition to the 1960 census results converted a population of nearly 17 million from rural to urban. Only about 2 percent of this population fell in the age group 65 years old and over.

These figures suggest then that, in general, extensive in-migration tends to lower or dampen the concentration of older persons in a population. It was precisely these areas of rapid growth, rural in 1950, that were classified as urban at the end of the decade, and thus the concentration of older persons in the rural population increased at about the same rate as the total population.

COMPONENTS PARTS OF THE RURAL POPULATION

The rural population, like the urban, is by no means homogeneous. As already noted, it has a farm component and a nonfarm component, and in another dimension village and open-country components. It is also clear that a simple city-country dichotomy oversimplifies what is really a continuum ranging from the rural population living in the periphery of large cities to the rural population in open country which is reasonably remote from any urban area. Using counties as a unit of classification, it is possible to identify in a rough fashion three segments of this scale:

(a) *Rural population in metropolitan counties* is, to a large degree, oriented toward central cities in terms of employment and commutation, and if the urban fringe is primary suburban territory, then the rural area might be designated as secondary or quasi-suburban territory. It is the territory which will supply additions to the urban fringe in the next census.

(b) *Rural population in nonmetropolitan counties with some urban population* will include an element suburban to places of 2,500 to 50,000. This element is suburban in both the primary and secondary senses described in connection with the metropolitan counties, since urban fringe area has not been established for the smaller urban places. The relative size of this element varies, of course, from county to county and, generally speaking, the major element will be open-country rural.

(c) *Rural population in nonmetropolitan counties with no urban population* is relatively uncontaminated by urban contact and, as such, may be regarded as the quintessence of rurality. In 1960 there was a definite gradient in the percentage of the population 65 and over among these components, ranging from 7.6 percent for the metropolitan counties to 11.2 percent for the all-rural counties. This same gradient by type of family was apparent for villages of 1,000 to 2,500 and at a somewhat lower level for the residual rural population outside such places. It is clear, however, that although in terms of whole counties the concentration of older population increases as the proximity of the urban areas declines, open country does not represent the end of the scale as far as age structure is concerned. Rather, the city-suburb pattern of the urban population appears to carry over to the type-of-county classification—the concentration of older persons being higher in villages than in the open country in each class.

The explanation of this gradient by type of county relates in all likelihood to migration. The rural parts of metropolitan counties have been characterized by appreciable in-migration and high concentrations of adults in the childbearing ages. Although the data presented in Table 3 indicate little growth between 1950 and 1960, this is primarily because, as indicated by the general analysis of rural change, it is the rural balance of metropolitan counties from which additions to the urban fringe are largely drawn. Thus this population has the age structure of a rapidly growing population, but the increase has been siphoned off by conversion into urban population.

At the other extreme the all-rural counties were for the most part subjected to substantial out-migration during the decade 1950-60 and out-migration usually results in an increasing concentration of older persons in the population from which the out-migration occurs. Thus between 1950 and 1960 the population of all-rural counties declined by about 7 percent and the percent 65 and over increased by 2.3 percentage points.

The part-rural counties stand somewhere between the two extremes: their population remained at about the same level during the decade, which implies some out-migration and conversion to urban, and the percentage 65 and over increased by 1.3 points—not materially different from the corresponding increase for the country as a whole.

Table 3. Total and Rural Population Aged 65 and Over by Residence and Age for Conterminous United States, 1950 and 1960

Age and residence	Total			Places of 1,000 to 2,500: 1960 (thousands)	Other rural: 1960 (thousands)
	1960 (thousands)	1950 (thousands)	Percent change		
Total:	53,765	54,230	− 0.9	6,440	47,325
Metropolitan counties	13,641	13,474	1.2	1,322	12,319
Part-rural nonmetropolitan counties	31,664	31,687	− 0.1	3,589	28,074
All rural nonmetropolitan counties	8,460	9,069	− 6.7	1,529	6,932
Persons 65 years and over:	5,022	4,443	13.0	792	4,231
Metropolitan counties	1,032	1,000	3.1	132	900
Part-rural nonmetropolitan counties	3,043	2,638	15.4	440	2,604
All-rural nonmetropolitan counties	947	805	17.6	220	727
Percentage 65 years old and over:	9.3	8.2	1.1	12.3	8.9
Metropolitan counties	7.6	7.4	0.2	10.0	7.3
Part-rural nonmetropolitan counties	9.6	8.3	1.3	12.3	9.3
All-rural nonmetropoli tan counties	11.2	8.9	2.3	14.4	10.5

Source: U. S. Bureau of the Census, *United States Census of Population: 1960, Characteristics of the Population* (Washington, D. C., 1961), Vol. I; U. S. Bureau of the Census, *United States Census of Population: 1950, Characteristics of the Population* (Washington, D. C., 1953), Vol. II.

STATE DIFFERENCES, 1960

Among the states in 1960, the highest concentration of elderly persons in the rural population (12.0 to 13.1 percent 65 years old and over) was found in Missouri, Kansas, Nebraska, and Oklahoma (Table 4). One factor affecting this regional distribution is the greater practice of formal retirement to towns in the Midwest and West. Those having the lowest concentrations

—ranging between 5.8 and 6.9 percent—were Arizona, New Mexico, Nevada, South Carolina, Utah, and North Carolina. In general the level for the rural population of each state tends to reflect the level of the total population of the state (r = .86), which in turn reflects its demographic history in the lifetime of the current population.

The states with high concentrations of elderly persons are those in which the fertility level has been relatively moderate and from which there has been a consistent pattern of out-migration in the better part of the twentieth century. Those with low concentrations have been states with high fertility or, as in the case of Nevada, have had an extremely heavy recent in-migration of young adults.

The increase in the concentration of older persons from metropolitan rural to all-rural counties appeared for all except five states—Rhode Island, North Carolina, North Dakota, Arizona, and Oregon. The format used in this analysis is not well adapted to Rhode Island, which has only five counties, none of which is all rural.

In North Carolina and North Dakota, the concentration of older persons in the rural metropolitan population exceeded that in the part-rural counties. In North Carolina, the higher percentage 65 and over in the Asheville State Metropolitan Statistical Area (SMSA), a retirement area, (10.0 as compared with a range of from 5.7 to 6.9 percent for the other SMSA's of the state) appears to account for the deviation. In North Dakota, the one metropolitan county is Cass County, a part of the Fargo-Moorehead SMSA. It is doubtful whether the Fargo-Moorehead urban complex is large enough to support a flourishing quasi-suburban development.

In Arizona, the gradient is in reverse direction. Apache County—the single all-rural county—is inhabited largely by Navaho Indians and the high fertility and mortality of this group keeps the concentration of older persons down. On the other hand, the rural population of the Phoenix and Tucson SMSA's (Maricopa and Pima counties) is spotted with rural places and census county divisions with relatively high concentrations of older persons, suggesting that the level has been raised by special facilities and developments for retired older persons.

In Oregon the percentage 65 and over in the all-rural counties

Table 4. Persons Aged 65 and Over as Percentage of Total Rural Population by Residence Areas for Conterminous United States, 1950 and 1960

Division and state	Total		Metropolitan counties		Part-rural nonmetropolitan counties		All-rural nonmetropolitan counties	
	1960	1950	1960	1950	1960	1950	1960	1950
United States, total	9.3	8.2	7.6	7.4	9.6	8.3	11.2	8.9
New England:								
Maine	10.9	10.6	9.5	10.3	10.7	10.2	14.3	14.4
New Hampshire	11.6	11.9	10.8	11.6	11.5	11.8	15.1	13.5
Vermont	11.0	10.5	—	—	10.9	10.3	11.9	11.2
Massachusetts	9.2	9.9	8.7	9.7	12.4	12.0	17.4	13.7
Rhode Island	8.5	7.9	9.0	8.6	8.0	7.2	—	—
Connecticut	8.4	9.2	7.3	8.8	9.5	9.6	—	—
Middle Atlantic:								
New York	9.8	10.4	8.6	9.6	10.7	11.1	13.4	11.5
New Jersey	9.4	9.1	8.7	8.6	10.1	9.6	—	—
Pennsylvania	9.2	8.5	8.7	8.0	9.7	8.8	11.7	10.6
East North Central:								
Ohio	9.0	9.6	7.5	7.7	9.7	10.5	14.0	12.9
Indiana	10.0	10.0	7.3	7.6	10.4	10.5	12.2	11.3
Illinois	11.1	10.1	7.8	7.8	12.5	11.1	14.4	11.9
Michigan	9.0	8.9	6.9	7.3	9.7	9.7	12.5	10.7
Wisconsin	10.8	9.3	8.8	8.4	10.8	9.3	13.8	10.9
West North Central:								
Minnesota	10.6	8.8	8.0	6.4	10.4	9.3	12.6	9.5
Iowa	11.7	10.2	8.9	9.0	11.4	9.9	14.3	12.0
Missouri	13.1	11.5	8.3	9.0	13.2	11.3	15.1	13.0
North Dakota	9.5	7.8	10.2	7.2	8.8	8.3	9.8	7.5
South Dakota	10.8	8.3	9.7	8.9	10.2	8.3	11.3	8.3
Nebraska	12.6	10.0	8.0	8.8	11.8	9.7	14.2	10.6
Kansas	12.8	11.1	6.7	8.9	12.8	11.0	15.0	11.8

South Atlantic:								
Delaware	8.0	8.8	6.7	7.0	8.5	9.6	—	—
Maryland	7.8	7.6	6.5	6.8	8.7	8.3	9.0	8.3
District of Columbia								
Virginia	8.1	6.9	5.6	5.3	7.5	6.6	9.1	7.6
West Virginia	8.7	6.5	7.2	5.8	8.4	6.1	11.0	8.4
North Carolina	6.9	5.6	6.7	5.6	6.5	5.3	8.7	6.7
South Carolina	6.2	5.5	5.6	5.7	6.3	5.4	7.7	6.6
Georgia	7.7	6.5	5.3	5.3	8.0	6.5	8.6	7.1
Florida	9.2	7.6	6.7	6.6	10.3	8.1	10.9	8.0
East South Central:								
Kentucky	9.4	7.6	6.3	7.1	9.0	7.1	10.8	8.5
Tennessee	9.1	7.4	6.9	6.2	9.4	7.6	10.1	7.5
Alabama	8.8	6.9	7.1	6.1	9.1	7.0	9.6	7.7
Mississippi	9.1	7.1	8.3	6.8	8.8	6.9	9.9	7.7
West South Central:								
Arkansas	11.0	7.6	9.2	7.4	10.5	7.3	13.7	8.8
Louisiana	8.6	6.9	6.1	6.4	8.0	6.7	9.9	8.2
Oklahoma	12.0	8.9	7.9	7.0	12.4	9.1	14.4	10.2
Texas	10.4	7.7	7.8	6.1	10.9	8.0	12.8	9.2
Mountain:								
Montana	9.4	8.1	5.7	5.6	7.9	7.4	11.8	9.4
Idaho	7.9	6.6	—	—	7.7	6.5	8.5	6.9
Wyoming	7.3	5.8	—	—	6.6	5.3	8.8	7.1
Colorado	8.6	7.1	5.6	6.5	9.0	7.2	10.3	7.4
New Mexico	5.9	4.8	4.1	3.4	5.4	4.8	8.1	5.5
Arizona	5.8	5.1	6.2	4.9	5.8	5.5	4.4	4.1
Utah	6.5	5.5	4.5	4.7	6.9	5.4	8.1	6.4
Nevada	6.2	7.0	4.1	4.7	6.2	6.7	9.5	9.9
Pacific:								
Washington	8.8	8.2	7.7	8.2	9.4	8.1	10.4	9.1
Oregon	8.9	7.3	8.9	7.4	9.0	7.3	8.4	7.1
California	8.2	7.2	7.0	6.7	9.0	7.6	13.6	11.7

Source: U. S. Bureau of the Census, *United States Census of Population: 1960* (Washington, D. C., 1961), Vol. I, and *United States Census of Population: 1950* (Washington, D. C., 1953), Vol. II.

is lower than that of the part-rural counties. The all-rural counties are concentrated in eastern Oregon and in general those characterized by large-scale wheat farming. Data on net migration indicate a higher net out-migration rate for persons 65 and over than for the population under 65 years. This situation suggests the hypothesis that the expected increase in concentration of older persons in these counties is blunted by out-migration of retired wheat farmers to other places—among them Arizona.

CHANGES IN PERCENTAGE 65 AND OVER, 1950-60

Although the proportion of older persons increased generally in the total rural population between 1950 and 1960, this increase was not characteristic of the various segments of the rural population in all states. In nearly one-half of the 45 states with metropolitan counties, the percentage 65 and over decreased, and similar decreases in the rural population of part-rural counties occurred in seven states. For the all-rural counties there were declines in the concentration of older persons in only two states—Maine and Nevada.

The percentage 65 and over in the total rural population decreased in seven states—New Hampshire, Massachusetts, Connecticut, New York, Delaware, Ohio, and Nevada. In all of these states except Massachusetts, the decrease occurred in the rural population of both metropolitan and part-rural counties. With the exception of Nevada, a special case of heavy and pervasive net in-migration, the remaining states are located in or adjacent to the large metropolitan agglomeration of the East Coast. The heavy weighting of metropolitan rural population with its low concentration of older persons, and with some suggestion of the extension of this pattern to the part-rural counties, would seem to account for the decline in the proportion of older persons. The evidence in support of this hypothesis, however, is not completely convincing. Ohio is marginal to the East Coast metropolitan belt and Rhode Island and New Jersey, the states which are the basis of the hypothesis under consideration, would be expected to display a decline in the percentage 65 and over in the rural population, actually had increases between 1950 and 1960.

NET MIGRATION AND CHANGES IN AGE STRUCTURE

An analysis in terms of net migration would be extremely useful in the examination of changes in the age structure of the rural population. Unfortunately, one of the necessary conditions of such analysis is an identical area at the beginning and end of the migration period, and thus the method cannot be used in connection with the rural population of metropolitan and part-rural counties because at the end of the period, parts of the rural area have been converted to urban. In the case of the all-rural counties of 1960, such an analysis is possible.[2]

The general assumption, which is implicit in some of the foregoing discussion, is that normally, or in the modal case, the concentration of older persons among migrants is lower than it is in their population of origin or destination. It follows then that out-migration will tend to increase the proportion of older persons and in-migration decrease this proportion. The lower proportion of older persons among migrants is more frequently observed than any other relationship to the parent or receiving population, but occasionally the reverse is true and occasionally there are net out-movements of older persons combined with net in-movements of younger persons or vice versa.

More specifically, the age structure at the beginning of the decade and births and deaths during the decade imply the age structure to be expected at the end of the decade in the absence of migration. If the concentration of older persons among migrants is lower than in the expected proportion the concentration in the actual or observed population will be higher than in the expected population in the case of out-migration and lower in the case of in-migration.

The data for Arkansas illustrate the usual effect of out-migration. For the entire state there was an out-migration of 432,463 between 1950 and 1960. The percentage 65 and over among net out-migrants was 1.0. The expected percentage 65 and over was 8.9 and the observed percentage was 10.9. The effect of out-migration was to increase the percentage 65 and over by 2.0 points.

The data for Nevada illustrate the usual effects of in-migration. During the decade there were 86,134 net in-migrants, of whom 3.1 percent were 65 years old and over. The expected

Table 5. Population Aged 65 and Over, Observed and Expected, in All-rural Counties by Percentage in Conterminous United States, 1950 and 1960

Division and state	1960		1950 Observed[3]	Percentage-point increase			Net migration rate[7]
	Observed[1]	Expected[2]		1950 to 1960[4]	From natural increase[5]	From net migration[6]	
United States, total	11.2	9.7	8.9	2.3	0.8	1.5	−18.2
New England:							
Maine	14.3	13.2	14.4	−0.1	−1.2	1.1	− 9.5
New Hampshire	15.1	14.0	13.5	1.6	0.5	1.1	− 5.7
Vermont	11.9	11.1	11.2	0.7	−0.1	0.8	−14.3
Massachusetts	17.4	13.6	13.7	3.7	−0.1	3.8	− 3.2
Rhode Island	—	—	—	—	—	—	—
Connecticut	—	—	—	—	—	—	—
Middle Atlantic:							
New York	13.4	12.5	11.5	1.9	1.0	0.9	4.3
New Jersey	—	—	—	—	—	—	—
Pennsylvania	11.7	11.2	10.6	1.1	0.6	0.5	− 7.8
East North Central:							
Ohio	14.0	12.7	12.9	1.1	−0.2	1.3	−11.8
Indiana	12.2	11.9	11.3	0.9	0.6	0.3	− 8.1
Illinois	14.4	12.7	11.9	2.5	0.8	1.7	−19.0
Michigan	12.5	11.4	10.7	1.8	0.7	1.1	− 5.7
Wisconsin	13.8	12.2	10.9	2.9	1.3	1.6	−14.2
West North Central:							
Minnesota	12.6	11.0	9.5	3.1	1.5	1.6	−16.4
Iowa	14.3	13.0	12.0	2.3	1.0	1.3	−15.7
Missouri	15.1	14.0	13.0	2.1	1.0	1.1	− 8.8
North Dakota	9.8	8.7	7.5	2.3	1.2	1.1	−23.8
South Dakota	11.3	9.8	8.3	3.0	1.5	1.5	−21.9
Nebraska	14.2	12.0	10.6	3.6	1.4	2.2	−21.0
Kansas	15.0	12.8	11.8	3.2	1.0	2.2	−18.0
South Atlantic:							
Delaware	—	—	—	—	—	—	—

	[1]	[2]	[3]	[4]	[5]	[6]	[7]
Maryland	9.0	8.6	8.3	0.7	0.3	0.4	− 1.2
District of Columbia	—	—	—	—	—	—	—
Virginia	9.1	8.3	7.6	1.5	0.7	0.8	−11.8
West Virginia	11.0	8.8	8.4	2.6	0.4	2.2	−24.4
North Carolina	8.7	7.5	6.7	2.0	0.8	1.2	−18.1
South Carolina	7.7	7.0	6.6	1.1	0.4	0.7	−22.1
Georgia	8.6	7.6	7.1	1.5	0.5	1.0	−20.0
Florida	10.9	8.7	8.0	2.9	0.7	2.2	−16.1
East South Central							
Kentucky	10.8	8.9	8.5	2.3	0.4	1.9	−21.4
Tennessee	10.1	8.2	7.5	2.6	0.7	1.9	−22.5
Alabama	9.6	8.0	7.7	1.9	0.3	1.6	−24.5
Mississippi	9.9	7.9	7.7	2.2	0.2	2.0	−25.2
West South Central:							
Arkansas	13.7	10.2	8.8	4.9	1.4	3.5	−29.0
Louisiana	9.9	8.7	8.2	1.7	0.5	1.2	−17.0
Oklahoma	14.4	11.4	10.2	4.2	1.2	3.0	−26.3
Texas	12.8	10.6	9.2	3.6	1.4	2.2	−19.9
Mountain:							
Montana	11.8	11.2	9.4	2.4	1.8	0.6	−14.7
Idaho	8.5	8.2	6.9	1.6	1.3	0.3	−17.0
Wyoming	8.8	8.3	7.1	1.7	1.2	0.5	−17.1
Colorado	10.3	8.9	7.4	2.9	1.5	1.4	−24.8
New Mexico	8.1	6.6	5.5	2.6	1.1	1.5	−27.9
Arizona	4.4	4.3	4.1	0.3	0.2	0.1	−21.4
Utah	8.1	7.2	6.4	1.7	0.8	0.9	−22.4
Nevada	9.5	11.5	9.9	−0.4	1.6	−2.0	5.7
Pacific:							
Washington	10.4	10.8	9.1	1.3	1.7	−0.4	− 7.1
Oregon	8.4	8.6	7.1	1.3	1.5	−0.2	−14.1
California	13.6	13.7	11.7	1.9	2.0	−0.1	11.5

[1] 1960 census.   [2] If no migration.   [3] 1950 census.

[4] Observed 1960 minus observed 1950.

[5] Expected 1960 minus observed 1950.

[6] Observed 1960 minus expected 1960.

[7] Net migration as percentage of expected population.

Source: U. S. Bureau of the Census, *United States Census of Population: 1960* (Washington, D. C., 1961), Vol. I and *United States Census of Population: 1950* (Washington, D. C., 1953), Vol. II; U. S. Department of Agriculture, Economic Research Service, *Population-Migration Report* (Washington, D. C., 1965), Vol. I.

percentage 65 and over was 7.8 and the observed 6.4, a reduction of 1.4 percentage points. Florida, a retirement state, however, did not conform to normal expectation. A net in-migration of 1,616,790, in which the percentage 65 and over was 15.8, increased the expected percentage, 8.9, by 2.3 points to 11.2 percent in the observed population. In Connecticut a net in-migration of 238,627 of persons under 65 years and over and a net out-migration of 4,418 of persons 65 years old and over decreased the expected percentage 65 and over by 1.2 points.

Data indicating the effects of net migration on the proportion of older persons in the completely rural counties are presented in Table 5. The difference between the observed percentage, 1950 and 1960, is of course the percentage point change in the proportion of older persons. The difference between the percentage observed in 1950 and that expected in 1960 indicates that part of the total change is attributable to age structure in 1950 and natural increase. The difference between the observed and expected 1960 percentage indicate the remaining part attributable to net migration.

The total United States figures for all-rural counties indicate a net out-migration which contributed 1.5 percentage points, or roughly two-thirds of the total increase in the percentage 65 and over, 2.3 percentage points. In 42 of the 44 states with all-rural counties, there was out-migration from these counties ranging from —1.2 percent for Maryland to —29.0 percent for Arkansas. Of the 42 states characterized by out-migration from all-rural counties, the out-migration made a positive contribution to the increase in the percentage 65 and over in 40 states. In the exceptions, Oregon and Washington, the proportion of older persons among net out-migrants was higher than in the expected population and thus, contrary to normal expectation, out-migration lowered the concentration of older persons. In Nevada and California, net in-migration with a proportion of older persons lower than that in the expected population reduced, in conformity to normal expectation, this proportion.

NET MIGRATION AND AGE STRUCTURE IN PLACES OF
1,000 TO 2,500

It has already been noted that the concentration of older persons in places of 1,000 to 2,500 was, in both 1960 and 1950, greater than in the surrounding rural territory, and that this relationship existed in all three segments of the rural population —in metropolitan counties, in part-rural counties, and in all-rural counties. An examination of state figures indicates that this relationship is characteristic of most states. Since in the completely rural counties the typical increase in the proportion of older persons attributable to net migration is a matter of relatively lower out-migration rates among persons 65 and over than among persons under 65, the question arises as to whether village

Table 6. Expected and Observed Population and Net Migration by Age in Places of 1,000 to 2,500 in All-rural Counties in Nebraska and Georgia, 1960*

Characteristic	Total	Places of 1,000 to 2,500	Other rural
NEBRASKA			
Expected population			
Total	364,426	78,622	285,804
Under 65 years	320,599	67,327	253,272
65 years and over	43,827	11,295	32,532
(Percent)	(12.0)	(14.4)	(11.4)
Observed population			
Total	287,783	69,616	218,167
Under 65 years	246,807	55,251	191,556
65 years and over	40,976	14,365	26,611
(Percent)	(14.2)	(20.6)	(12.2)
Net migration			
Total	− 76,643	− 9,006	− 67,637
Under 65 years	− 73,792	−12,076	− 61,716
65 years and over	− 2,851	+ 3,070	− 5,921
GEORGIA			
Expected population			
Total	626,833	92,401	534,432
Under 65 years	579,037	84,832	494,205
65 years and over	47,796	7,569	40,227
(Percent)	(7.6)	(8.2)	(7.5)
Observed population			
Total	501,206	87,213	413,993
Under 65 years	457,984	78,395	379,589
65 years and over	43,222	8,818	34,404
(Percent)	(8.6)	(10.1)	(8.3)
Net migration			
Total	−125,627	− 5,188	−120,439
Under 65 years	−121,053	− 6,437	−114,616
65 years and over	− 4,574	+ 1,249	− 5,823

* Net migration for places of 1,000 to 2,500 in 1960 is computed on the basis of census survival rates and fertility ratios adjusted to approximate total net migration derived from recorded births and deaths. Survival rates for the white population were used for Nebraska, and age-specific weighted averages of white and nonwhite survival rates were used for Georgia.

Source: U. S. Bureau of the Census, *United States Census of Population: 1960* (Washington, D. C., 1961), Vol. I; *United States Census of Population: 1950* (Washington, D. C., 1953), Vol. II; and U. S. Department of Agriculture, Economic Research Service, *Population-Migration Report* (Washington, D. C., 1965), Vol. I.

population is subject to this process in a more acute form or whether indeed, as observation suggests, villages serve as retirement centers for the surrounding rural population.

In order to obtain explicit evidence relating to this question, appropriate statistics were compiled for 1950 and 1960 for places in Nebraska and Georgia which in 1960 had a population of 1,000 to 2,500 and estimates of net migration were computed. The estimates were then combined with the standard Department of Agriculture figures for the all-rural counties. The results are presented in Table 6.

These data confirm the assumption that in Nebraska and Georgia places of 1,000 to 2,500 do serve as retirement centers for the surrounding rural population. In both states, although there was an overall net out-migration from these places, there was an appreciable net in-migration of persons 65 and over. In the total population of the all-rural counties, the concentration of older persons was increased by a greater relative out-migration of persons under 65 years old than of those 65 and over, but within these counties the shift of older persons from the surrounding rural population to the villages served to augment the increase in these areas and dampen the increase in the surrounding rural areas. Although the all-rural counties of Nebraska and Georgia are in no sense a sample of all completely rural counties, the findings are certainly suggestive with respect to the generally observed differences between villages and the surrounding rural territory in the concentration of older persons.

FUTURE PROSPECTS

Any speculation as to future trends in the age structure of the rural population involves consideration both of possible trends in the development of the rural population and of trends in the age structure of the population of the country as a whole.

FUTURE TRENDS IN THE RURAL POPULATION

Because at the end of each decade areas formerly rural are converted into urban territory, ordinary methods of population projections are not applicable to either the urban or the rural population. Although superficially this conversion appears to have a certain arbitrary quality, it does reflect real changes, illustrated most dramatically in the past two decades by the conversion of potato fields and orange groves to housing developments.

Some examination of past trends, however, may throw some light on what may be expected in the future. In 1900, about two-thirds of the population of the country would have lived in non-metropolitan counties under the current definition of SMSA's and one-third in metropolitan counties (Table 7). By 1960, not quite two-thirds lived in metropolitan counties and slightly more than

Table 7. Population In and Outside Standard Metropolitan Statistical Areas, Urban and Rural, for Conterminous United States, 1960 and 1900

Area	Population (thousands)		Percent distribution	
	1960	1900*	1960	1900
Total	178,464	75,995	100.0	100.0
In SMSA's	112,385	24,009	63.0	31.6
Urban	88,188	19,749	49.4	26.0
Rural	24,197	4,259	13.6	5.6
Places of 1,000 to 2,500	1,366	495	0.8	0.7
Other rural	22,831	3,764	12.8	4.9
Outside SMSA's	66,079	51,986	37.0	68.4
Urban	24,344	10,411	13.6	13.7
Rural	41,736	41,575	23.4	54.7
Places of 1,000 to 2,500	4,193	2,803	2.3	3.7
Other rural	37,542	38,772	21.1	51.0

* Statistics based on previous urban-rural definition. The 1900 population of SMSA's is the 1900 population of the 1950 SMSA's which in 1900 had a population of 50,000 or more in their principal central city.
Source: U. S. Bureau of the Census, *United States Census of Population: 1960* (Washington, D. C., 1961), Vol. I, and *United States Census of Population: 1900* (Washington, D. C., 1901), Vol. I, Pt. 1.

one-third remained in the nonmetropolitan counties. The gain in metropolitan population was largely at the expense of the open-country rural population; the urban population and the population of places of 1,000 to 2,500 in nonmetropolitan counties constituted about the same proportion of the total population in 1960 as they did in 1900, but the proportion in "other rural" dropped from 51.0 percent to 21.0 percent, a loss of 30 percentage points, roughly equivalent to the percentage point gain in the population of metropolitan counties.

This shift in the distribution of population has had the same general character as that of the increase in urban population. The population in the metropolitan counties of 1900 has, of course, grown, and decade by decade as cities in nonmetropolitan counties attained a population of 50,000 or more they became metropolitan counties. In turn as metropolitan counties, the rural parts are, through population growth, the areas most likely to be converted to urban.

In the absence of any very convincing evidence to the contrary, it seems not unreasonable to assume that at least for the next few decades the trend observed in the first part of this century will continue. The population of metropolitan areas will grow at the expense of the population of all-rural counties. The population of part-rural counties will hold its own or perhaps decline somewhat, as the rapidly growing counties become metropolitan. As to the rural population per se, it seems probable that in metropolitan counties it may increase, but only in a very modest way, since areas of really rapid growth will be siphoned off into the urban population. The rural population of part-rural counties may grow as its quasi-suburban component increases, but again this growth must be balanced against the loss of the most rapidly growing parts to metropolitan areas. The all-rural counties would continue to lose population unless this trend is reversed by massive development programs.

FUTURE TRENDS IN AGE STRUCTURE

For the total population of the United States, current projections of the population indicate that in the next several decades the percentage of the population 65 years old and over, which increased from 4.1 in 1900 to 9.3 in 1960, will tend to level off.[3] Projection A, which assumes the highest fertility level and most rapid rate of growth, indicates a percentage 65 and over of 9.3 in 1975 and 9.1 in 1985. Projection D, which assumes the lowest fertility level and rates of growth, shows corresponding percentages of 9.9 and 10.4. It would appear then that the concentration of older persons in the total population is not likely to exceed by any substantial amount a figure of approximately 10 percent.

Future changes in the concentration of older persons in the total rural population would seem, in all probability, to parallel those in the total population and thus be relatively small. With continued out-migration from all-rural counties, an appreciable increase in the population of older persons may be expected. To the extent that rural population of part-rural counties becomes increasingly suburban, the percentage 65 and over will remain relatively low.

Against this general background, however, consideration should be given to the effects of mobility associated with retirement. Evidence has been cited which suggests that the high concentration of older persons in the village population arises in part from the in-migration of older persons and the data for all-rural counties in Oregon and Washington indicate a reduction in the expected proportion of older persons as the result of relatively high out-migration. The results of in-migration of older persons are also apparent in rural enclaves in the Phoenix SMSA. An examination of the county data on net migration indicate a relatively heavy in-migration of older persons not only to Florida but in certain counties in other states—for example, in Cape May County, New Jersey, about 25 percent of the net in-migrants were 65 years old and over in 1960 and the corresponding percentage for Barnstable County, Massachusetts, was about 16. If instances of this type represent the beginning of a trend, then it is possible that the next several decades may witness the multiplication of senior-citizen enclaves and retirement communities in various parts of the country. It remains an open question, however, whether such enclaves and retirement communities will be rural or urban. As in the case of the rural population in metropolitan counties, rapid growth will increase the probability of their conversion from rural to urban territory.

CONCLUSIONS

In 1960 the concentration of older persons in the rural population was not materially different from that in the urban population. There were, however, appreciable differences among the various segments of the rural population. The proportion of older persons tends to increase from a relatively low level in the quasi-suburban rural population of metropolitan counties, through the rural population of part-rural counties, to a relatively high level in all-rural counties. With almost complete uniformity the summary state data showed a higher concentration of older population in places of 1,000 to 2,500 than in the surrounding rural population in each of the three types of counties. If the decade 1950-60 can be taken as representative, the increases in the concentration of older persons, and by inference its high level, in all-rural counties seem in general to be the result of out-migration. Because population growth results in the conversion of rapidly growing rural areas to urban, and statistics describing these changes are not normally available, precise projections of the rural population are not feasible. For the remaining years of the twentieth century, population projections suggest a leveling off of the relative growth of the older population and, in terms of current data, there is little evidence to suggest that the age structure of the rural population and its component parts will be essentially different from that observed in 1960.

NOTES

[1] For a discussion of the historical development of the definition of the urban population, see U. S. Bureau of the Census, *Current Population Reports*, Series P-23, No. 1, August 5, 1949, by Leon E. Truesdell.

[2] This analysis is based on data presented in: U. S. Department of Agriculture, Economic Research Services, *Population— Migration Report—Net Migration of the Population 1950-60 by age, sex, and color*, Vol. I, prepared in cooperation with the Research Foundation, Oklahoma State University, and the Area Redevelopment Administration, U. S. Department of Commerce, Washington, D. C., 1965.

The data in Table 5 on the expected population are derived by subtracting the published Economic Research Service estimates of net migration from the 1960 population. These estimates of net migration were computed by the use of census survival rates but were controlled to a net migration total derived from recorded births and deaths. This procedure insures a precise estimate of net migration, but it implies an expected population which in both size and structure reflects the effects of net migration on natural increase. In the case of in-migration it reflects the effects of births and deaths to in-migrants and in the case of out-migration it fails to reflect births and deaths to members of the initial population who left the area.

The use of survival rates and fertility rates in relation to the initial population would of course produce an expected population completely free from the effects of migration, and the implied net migration would reflect not only the result of the actual movement but also the side effects on natural increase. The differences in the results of the application of these two approaches in general appear to be small. In the interests of consistency, however, the estimates of expected population of net migration presented in Tables 2 and 6, which in the absence of data on recorded births and deaths were prepared on the basis of census survival rates and fertility ratio, were adjusted to approximate a total net migration derived from recorded births and deaths.

[3] U. S. Bureau of the Census, *Current Population Reports*, Series P-25, No. 325, January 25, 1966.

JUANITA M. KREPS

Economic Status
of the Rural Aged

In recent years public attention has been focused on various economically disadvantaged groups. The flood of statistics rising from the poverty programs have shown that certain characteristics such as occupation, age, sex, education, regional location, and color are related to income level. Attempts have been made to isolate the influence of single factors on economic status. In analyzing the extent to which low incomes are associated with these characteristics, one author concluded that such debilitating socioeconomic factors are not necessarily at the core of poverty:

> Aging is not a cause of poverty, nor is being non-white a cause of poverty, nor is living in the south a cause of poverty. . . . There is some unidentified agent which can produce poverty. Whether the carrier of this agent will in fact be poor is highly dependent upon whether he also possesses one or more of the poverty-linked characteristics.
> A second point to be made about the socio-economic characteristics of the poor . . . is that they are clearly inter-related. A very large proportion of the poor have more than one debilitating socio-economic characteristic. Southern, non-white and farm operator are poverty-linked characteristics often found together. Sixty-five percent of the aged poor have some other poverty-linked characteristics. . . .[1]

This chapter deals with the aged population, whose median income is significantly lower than that of younger persons and families, more specifically with the aged in rural areas, where incomes are in turn lower than the incomes of the urban population. The combination of old age and rural residence makes the rural aged one of the lowest income groups in the United States. The lower educational level of the older population is a part of the explanation of the aged's low-income position, and the fact that the rural older persons have even less education than the urban aged further accentuates their problems.

CURRENT ECONOMIC POSITION

Of the many indexes of levels of living, money income is the most commonly used. Some economists and sociologists raised the question of oversimplification when an annual money income of $3,000 was taken as the dividing line between poverty- and non-poverty-level families. However, that figure continues to be widely used in discussions of public policy. Any other dollar figure would probably have been equally untenable if taken as the sole indicator of economic well-being. Much more reliance can be placed on a series of indexes such as the ones used by Cowhig, described below.[2] It is nevertheless of some importance to indicate the money incomes of the rural elderly and to compare these incomes with the incomes of both the urban aged and the younger rural population.

INCOME LEVELS

The 1963 Survey of the Aged, which provides detailed data on the money incomes of older families and persons, gives the 1962 median income for older married couples as $2,875, and the median for older nonmarried persons as $1,130 ($1,365 for unmarried men and $1,015 for unmarried women).[3] In the case of both the families and single persons, the median was about half that of the younger counterpart. The data in Table 1 show that about one-third of the aged unmarried persons received $810 or less and that about one-third of the aged couples received $2,200 or less. Standardizing for family size (which averaged 3.9 persons in younger and 2.5 persons in older families), the 1962 median in-

Table 1. Percentage Distribution of Income for Households Which Include Persons Aged 65 and Over by Marital Status in the United States, 1962

Income	Married couples*	Widowed, single, and divorced persons		
		Total	Men	Women
(Number in thousands)				
(Total)	(5,445)	(8,731)	(2,402)	(6,329)
(Reporting income)	(4,719)	(7,709)	(2,173)	(5,536)
Less than $1,000	5	43	31	49
$1,000 - $1,499	10	22	25	21
$1,500 - $1,999	14	13	12	13
$2,000 - $2,499	13	8	11	7
$2,500 - $2,999	12	4	5	3
$3,000 - $3,999	15	4	6	3
$4,000 - $4,999	11	2	3	1
$5,000 - $9,999	15	4	6	3
$10,000 and over	5	**	1	**
(Median income)	($2,875)	($1,130)	($1,365)	($1,015)

* With at least 1 member aged 65 or over.
** Less than 0.5 percent.
Source: Social Security Bulletin, 27, No. 3 (March 1964), 8.

come for older families was found to be about seven-tenths that of younger families.[4]

Since the 1963 survey does not give income by place of residence, it is necessary to use earlier data from the 1960 census when making rural-urban comparisons. Median incomes, summarized in Table 2, are tabulated by 10-year age spans, so the comparison afforded is that of the aged's median with that for all age groups, rather than the preferred comparison of the median for the 65 and over with that of the 64 and under. Even so, the differences in media are striking: from a high of $5,911, the me-

Table 2. Median Income of Families and Unrelated Individuals in the United States Aged 65 or Over and Total by Place of Residence, 1960

Place of residence	Families		Unrelated individuals	
	Total	With head aged 65 or over	Total	Aged 65 or over
(Total number in thousands)	(43,435)	(6,200)	(10,900)	(3,653)
Urban	$5,911	$3,382	$1,992	$1,176
Rural nonfarm	5,620	2,352	1,150	840
Rural farm	2,875	2,294	875	*
(Number in thousands)	(3,490)	(623)	(372)	(146)

* Median not shown where base is less than 200,000.
Source: U. S. Bureau of the Census, *Current Population Reports, Consumer Income,* Series P-60, No. 37, January 17, 1962, p. 27.

dian for all urban families, the figure falls to $3,382 for urban older families; from a median income of $5,620 for all rural non-farm families to a median of $2,352 for rural nonfarm older families; from a median income of $2,875 for all rural farm families to a median of $2,294 for older rural farm families. Thus, the older urban family's median was about 57 percent of the median for all urban families, whereas the rural nonfarm older family had 42 percent and the rural farm older family 85 percent of the median for their respective groups.

When the comparison is made not between the aged and the total population within the place-of-residence grouping, but between the median income of the aged family in the rural areas and that of the aged family in urban areas, the following percentages appear: Rural farm older families have a median income of about 98 percent of the median for rural nonfarm older families and of about 68 percent of the median for urban older families. The urban older family receives a median money income $1,030 higher than that of the rural nonfarm, and $1,088 higher than that of the rural farm family with head aged 65 or over. A Census Bureau classification of families into farm and nonfarm (the latter including urban and rural nonfarm) shows the following median money incomes:

	Head under 65 years	Head 65 years and over
All families	$5,905	$2,897
Nonfarm	6,091	2,989
Farm	3,058	2,294

The farm-nonfarm difference in median for the older families is $795, giving the nonfarm group a median income about one-third higher than that of the older farm group. In the earlier comparison of the median for older rural families with that of older urban families, the differential of $1,030 gave the urban group a median 43 percent greater than the rural nonfarm families. One further comparison indicates the proportions of the rural and urban populations with incomes under $3,000, $2,000, and $1,000. Table 3, in summary, notes that 64 percent of the rural older families (as compared with 41 percent of the urban older families) had 1959 money incomes of less than $3,000; 46 percent and 17 percent, respectively, received under $2,000. The proportion of aged unrelated individuals whose incomes

Table 3. Percentage Distribution of Income for Aged Families and Unrelated Individuals by Rural and Urban Residence in the United States, 1959

Income interval	Families with head 65 and over		Unrelated individuals 65 and over	
	Rural	Urban	Rural	Urban
(Number in thousands)	(598)	(4,067)	(907)	(2,846)
Under $1,000	18.6	8.1	63.5	45.4
Under $2,000	46.4	17.1	85.7	74.2
Under $3,000	63.7	41.0	92.6	84.7
$3,000 and over	36.3	59.0	7.4	15.3

Source: U. S. Bureau of the Census, *United States Census of Population: 1960, Sources and Structure of Family Income,* PC(2)-4C (Washington, D. C., 1963), Tables 3 and 6.

are under $2,000 is very high for both groups: 86 percent for the rural and 74 percent for the urban persons, with 64 percent and 45 percent, respectively, of these groups receiving under $1,000 of money income.

Census data reveal significant differences in family incomes by region of the country. These differences reflect degrees of industrialization in the various regions and hence the extent to which farming continues to be a major source of income. Median family income in the South, for example, was $4,467, or about four-fifths of the amount ($5,663) received by all families in the nation. Older husband-wife families in the South had a median income ($2,335) about three-fourths that of older husband-wife families for the nation ($3,052). Although rural-urban income data by age and region are not given by the census, the above comparisons do give some rough indication of the differential that exists between the median income for the nation as a whole and that for a region that is still heavily agricultural. It should be noted that a significant income differential exists for both young and old families.[5]

INDEXES OF LEVELS OF LIVING

The older rural family's lower money income may be offset to some extent by cost-of-living differences and by the ability of rural nonfarm people, and particularly the rural farm group, to supplement money income with food produced by the family.

In an attempt to develop a measure of poverty that makes allowance for differences in family size and composition, and in farm-nonfarm residence, a recent study by Mollie Orshansky provides some basis for comparing the status of the two groups, making allowance for the lesser needs of the farm families for cash income. On the assumption that a farm family needed 40 percent less net cash than a nonfarm family of the same size and composition, the incidence of poverty as measured by the usual $3,000 income level, and by the author's index, were as follows: for farm families, 43 percent were poor by the $3,000 standard and 15 percent were poor by the economy-level index (for nonfarm families, the proportions were 17 percent and 15 percent). Among families headed by persons aged 65 and over, 45 percent were poor by the $3,000 standard, and 24 percent by the economy-level index. Finally, of the two-person families, 30 percent were below the $3,000 income level but only 16 percent below the economy-level income.[6]

Money income comparisons need always to be complemented by other indexes of economic well-being, and it is especially important to find other measures when urban-rural (particularly urban-rural farm) comparisons are being made. Comparable measures of level of living for the urban and rural populations have recently been developed, with the household taken as the unit of analysis.[7] These measures, available from census data, are: (a) availability of an automobile, (b) availability of a telephone, (c) hot and cold water piped inside the home, (d) dwelling units in sound condition, (e) a summary measure based on the proportion of all households having items (a) through (d), and (f) housing units with 1.01 or more persons per room. Summarizing the findings for all age groups, the author finds only minor differences between rural and urban households in their ownership of automobiles and in the proportion of homes with more than one person per room. On the basis of the other indexes, however, urban families fared better, with particularly marked differences appearing in the proportion of families having hot piped water inside the residence and the proportion having homes in sound condition. The proportion of homes reporting all of the first four items varied from 73 percent in urban to 44 percent in rural farm residences.

These measures provide a basis for comparing the economic status of the rural and urban households headed by employed males and throw some light on the status of the aged among the two groups. Among households headed by males aged 55 and over, the proportion having all the first four items, as compared with all households in the sample, is as follows:

	Head 14 years and over	Head 55 years and over
Total	69	66
Urban	73	70
Rural nonfarm	60	58
Rural farm	44	46

A higher proportion of households headed by males aged 35-54 had each item than was the case for households headed by either younger or older men. On the basis of other census reports the author concluded that in 1960 about three-fourths of all non-farm households headed by men aged 60 or over were in houses in sound condition with all plumbing facilities. By contrast, less than half the older farm families were similarly housed.

It is important to note that the four measures of levels of living in the Cowhig study rank only those urban and rural households that are headed by employed males, with the older group starting at age 55. The decline in level of living, as measured by median income, is quite pronounced for both rural and urban men after age 65, even when they continue working. The 1960 census data show the following median incomes for older urban and rural males who worked in 1959.

Age group	Urban	Rural
65-69	$4,158	$2,234
70-74	3,349	1,831
75 and over	3,149	1,695

One further indicator of the comparative economic status of the rural aged is provided by the census data showing ownership of durables. All five durables (television set, freezer, air conditioner, washer, and dryer) were owned by less than 1 percent of all rural and urban older families. Of the families headed by persons aged 64 and under, about 2 percent owned all durables. The proportions of families with none of these appliances were as follows: older rural families, 8.4 percent; older urban families, 4.9 percent; all younger families, 3.4 percent (Table 4).[8]

Table 4. Percentage of Families Owning Home Appliances by Age of Head of Household and Place of Residence in the United States, 1960

Ownership	Aged 65 and over			Aged 64 and under			All families
	Total	Rural	Urban	Total	Rural	Urban	
With all appliances*	0.82	0.67	0.90	1.97	1.69	2.09	1.82
With no appliances	6.11	8.43	4.98	3.40	4.84	2.82	3.77

* Appliances include TV, freezer, air conditioner, washer, and dryer.
Source: Calculated from the 1960 census.

CONSUMPTION PATTERNS

Consumer expenditure data for families in urban and rural nonfarm areas are now available from the Bureau of Labor Statistics survey.[9] On the basis of Tables 5 and 6, certain conclusions can be drawn as to the consumption patterns of these two groups, as well as to the behavior of families in and outside of Standard Metropolitan Statistical Areas (SMSA's).

Attention should be drawn first to the 1961 money income after taxes for the three groups: $5,957 for urban, $6,220 for families inside, and $4,150 for families outside SMSA's. Of the rural nonfarm population, approximately one-fourth resided in the SMSA's, where incomes were more than $2,000 (or about 50 percent) higher than were the incomes of families outside the SMSA's. Expenditure patterns reflected this wide difference in income, the families living near large urban centers spending about one and a half times as much as the other rural nonfarm families. For the three basic living expenses, both groups used an average of 53 percent of their total consumption expenditure, but SMSA families spent a larger proportion for shelter and a smaller proportion for food and beverages, whereas families outside the metropolitan areas devoted a higher percentage to automobile purchases and operation. Having much higher incomes, the metropolitan families not only spent more dollars for each item, they also made larger gifts and contributions, saved more, and spent larger amounts for personal insurance, including payments into social security and other retirement funds.

The consumption pattern of the SMSA families resembled more closely the pattern set by urban families than that of rural families outside SMSA's. This similarity of urban and rural nonfarm

Table 5. Average Annual Expenditures, Income, and Savings of All Rural Nonfarm Families and Single Consumers, United States, 1961

Item	Average per family			Percentage of expenditures for current consumption		
	Total rural nonfarm	Inside SMSA's	Outside SMSA's	Total rural nonfarm	Inside SMSA's	Outside SMSA's
Expenditures for current consumption	$4,296	$5,657	$3,806	100.0	100.0	100.0
Food and beverages	1,133	1,429	1,026	26.3	25.2	27.1
Tobacco	85	100	80	2.0	1.8	2.1
Housing, total	1,189	1,660	1,018	27.7	29.2	26.7
Shelter, fuel, light, refrigeration, and water	727	1,039	613	16.9	18.3	16.1
Household operations	222	308	191	5.2	5.4	5.0
House furnishings and equipment	240	313	214	5.6	5.5	5.6
Clothing, materials, services	408	547	358	9.5	9.7	9.4
Personal care	123	158	111	2.9	2.8	2.9
Medical care	297	384	266	6.9	6.8	7.0
Recreation	165	231	141	3.8	4.1	3.7
Reading and education	68	95	58	1.6	1.7	1.5
Automobile purchase and operation	700	858	643	16.3	15.2	16.9
Other transportation	37	62	28	.9	1.1	.7
Other expenditures	91	133	77	2.1	2.4	2.0
Gifts and contributions	221	300	193	—	—	—
Personal insurance	241	360	199	—	—	—
Money income before taxes	5,168	6,973	4,516	—	—	—
Money income after taxes	4,700	6,220	4,150	—	—	—
Other money receipts	76	86	72	—	—	—
Net change in assets and liabilities*	+176	+220	+161	—	—	—
Account balancing difference**	−158	−213	−136	—	—	—

Number of families in sample	2,285	608	1,677
Estimated number of families in universe (in thousands)	11,663	3,095	8,569
Average family size	3.5	3.6	3.4
Percent nonwhite families	6	5	7
Percent homeowners	67	71	65
Percent auto owners	82	89	80

* The algebraic sum of increases and decreases in assets and liabilities. Net increases in assets or decreases in liabilities represent a net saving (+) during the year. Net decreases in assets or increases in liabilities represent a deficit (−) or net dissaving.

** A statistical measure of the net reporting discrepancy of the receipts and disbursements accounts. In this table, the balancing difference is obtained by subtracting current consumption expenditures, gifts and contributions, personal insurance, and the net change in assets and liabilities from the sum of money income after taxes and other money receipts. If reported receipts are less than disbursements (including savings or dissavings), the balancing difference is negative (−).

Source: U. S. Department of Labor, Bureau of Labor Statistics, Consumer Expenditure and Income (Washington, D. C., 1965), Rural Nonfarm Areas in the United States, 1961, p. 2.

Table 6. Average Annual Expenditures, Income, and Savings of All Urban Families and Single Consumers, United States, 1961 and 1960-61

Item	Average per family: 1961	Percentage of expenditures for current consumption: 1960–61
Expenditures for current consumption	$5,381	100.0
Food	1,306	24.3
Tobacco	93	1.8
Alcoholic beverages	87	1.7
Housing, total	1,585	29.4
Shelter, fuel, light, refrigeration, and water	997	18.4
Household operations	317	5.9
House furnishings and equipment	271	5.1
Clothing, materials, services	563	10.4
Personal care	156	2.9
Medical care	362	6.6
Recreation	218	4.0
Reading and education	109	2.0
Automobile purchase and operation	690	13.0
Other transportation	92	1.7
Other expenditures	120	2.2
Gifts and contributions	298	—
Personal insurance	323	—
Money income before taxes	6,756	—
Money income after taxes	5,957	—
Other money receipts	93	—
Net change in assets and liabilities*	219	—
Account balancing difference**	−171	—
Number of families in sample	4,879	
Estimated number of families in universe (in thousands)	40,131	
Average family size	3.1	
Percent nonwhite families	13	
Percent homeowners	54	
Percent auto owners	73	

  * See note 1, Table 5.
 ** See note 2, Table 5.
Source: U. S. Department of Labor, Bureau of Labor Statistics, *Consumer Expenditures and Income* (Washington, D. C., 1964), Urban United States, 1960-61, p. 2.

SMSA families is to be expected, given the comparability of incomes of the two groups. One major difference occurs in the case of automobile expenditures, which rose in 1961 to 13 percent of total expenditures for urban families but continued to be a higher proportion (15.2 percent) of the metropolitan family's total expenditure and a much higher percentage (16.9) of the nonmetropolitan family's expenditures. Comparison of the consumption pattern of the rural farm population with that of the urban and rural nonfarm must await tabulation of consumer data on the rural farm families. However, it seems likely that the lower incomes of rural farm families (as well as some similarity of living arrangements and costs) will reveal similarities between this group and the rural nonfarm families outside the SMSA's, with the consumer expenditures of both these groups being markedly different from the urban and rural nonfarm SMSA families.

Consumer expenditure tabulations by age do not permit comparison of the expenditures of older urban and rural nonfarm SMSA families, on one hand, with those of older rural nonfarm families outside SMSA's and older rural farm families, on the other. Table 7 summarizes the data on family characteristics and income and expenditures for all urban and rural nonfarm families, and for families headed by persons 65-74, and 75 and over, by these two places of residence. Again, there are marked differences between the average money income of the rural nonfarm aged ($2,846 for families headed by 65-74-year-olds and $2,003 for families with head aged 75 and over), and the urban aged ($3,903 for the 65-74 age group and $3,013 for the 75 and over age group), and between the incomes of the rural nonfarm aged and the total rural nonfarm population ($2,846 and $2,003 as compared with $4,700). Family size, too, varies significantly: 3.5 persons for all families, but only 1.9 and 1.8 for the older families. The average number of full-time earners is less favorable for the rural nonfarm elderly, and the educational level of the very old rural family head is lower. Home and automobile ownership is much more frequent among the rural nonfarm young and old families.

Analysis of expenditures for current consumption by the two groups reveals first, the overriding factor of difference in totals. The urban families spent over a thousand dollars more per year on current consumption than the rural nonfarm family; the urban family with head aged 65-74 spent about $900 more, and the very old urban family over a thousand dollars more than the respective older rural nonfarm families. A further separation of the older rural nonfarm families into those in and those outside SMSA's and data on the older rural farm families' expenditures would reveal even wider differences in current consumption totals. Some offset is afforded by the higher proportion of home and automobile ownership among the rural nonfarm people. However, it should be noted that housing costs nevertheless constitute almost one-third of the older nonfarm family's total con-

Table 7. Family Characteristics, Expenditures, Income, and Savings by Age of Family Head Urban and Rural Non-farm Families and Single Consumers, 1960 and 1961

Item	Urban families (1960)			Rural nonfarm families (1961)		
	All	Head aged 65-74	Head aged 75 and over	All	Head aged 65-74	Head aged 75 and over
Family characteristics:						
Average family size	3.1	1.8	1.7	3.5	1.9	1.8
Net change in assets and liabilities	$152	$130	-$42	$176	$45	$81
Average number of full-time earners	.8	.3	.2	.7	.2	.1
Average age of head	47	69	80	50	69	80
Years of schooling of head	10	8	8	9	8	7
Percent homeowners, all year	52	58	59	67	78	75
Percent auto owners, end of year	72	47	28	82	63	42
Income, expenditures and savings:						
Total receipts	$7,646	$4,781	$3,937	$6,414	$3,986	$2,972
Money income after taxes	5,829	3,903	3,013	4,700	2,846	2,003
Other money receipts	73	32	42	76	21	108
Decrease in assets	876	734	828	831	1,030	822
Increase in liabilities	868	112	54	807	89	39
Account balancing difference	-244	-63	-82	-158	-14	57
Total disbursements	7,890	4,844	4,019	6,572	4,000	2,915
Increase in assets	1,366	799	728	1,334	1,008	891
Decrease in liabilities	530	177	112	480	156	50
Personal insurance	324	144	70	241	81	36
Gifts and contributions	302	316	272	221	249	117
Expenditures for current consumption	5,368	3,408	2,837	4,296	2,506	1,821
Percentage distribution:						
Expenditures for current consumption	100.0	100.0	100.0	100.0	100.0	100.0
Food, total	24.4	26.8	26.9	25.2	25.4	30.3
Tobacco	1.8	1.5	0.9	2.0	1.6	1.4
Alcoholic beverages	1.8	1.5	0.8	1.2	1.0	1.2
Housing, total	29.7	32.0	36.5	27.7	31.7	32.8

Fuel, light, refrigeration, water	4.5	5.7	6.7	6.4	9.6	11.4
Household operations	6.0	6.8	8.6	5.2	5.9	5.8
House furnishings and equipment	5.2	3.4	3.0	5.6	5.1	4.8
Other housing expense	14.0	16.1	18.2	10.5	11.1	10.8
Clothing, clothing materials, services	10.2	8.0	6.7	9.5	6.7	5.0
Personal care	2.8	2.9	2.7	2.9	2.6	2.5
Medical care	6.4	9.1	10.9	6.9	10.4	11.4
Recreation	4.0	2.7	2.1	3.8	2.8	1.9
Reading	0.9	1.1	1.2	0.8	1.0	1.0
Education	1.1	0.6	0.3	0.8	0.2	—
Transportation	14.7	11.4	8.1	17.1	13.8	9.4
Other expenditures	2.2	2.4	2.9	2.1	2.8	3.1

Source: U. S. Department of Labor, Bureau of Labor Statistics, *Consumer Expenditures and Income* (Washington, D. C., 1964), Urban United States, 1960-61, Table 3-B, and Rural Nonfarm Areas in the United States, 1961, Table 3.

sumption expenditure, and that the ownership of an automobile means that the rural nonfarm elderly are spending a larger percentage of their income for transportation than are the urban aged. Finally, it is evident that the big difference in medical costs is not primarily a rural-urban difference but an age-related difference, although rural nonfarm families in general actually use a slightly larger proportion of their lower incomes for medical care than do the urban families.

From an earlier detailed study of consumption patterns of the aged in 1950,[10] the author concluded that differences in consumer behavior between young and old families could be largely explained by differences in incomes. A similarly complete analysis of the 1960 survey data would indicate whether there is evidence of any age-related patterns of consumption, holding income constant, in the present era. The results of the 1960 survey of the rural farm population will also throw further light on comparative patterns. For any very low-income group, the amount of discretionary income is of course extremely small, and expenditures are of necessity concentrated heavily on basic needs. Some variation in the use of money income may be discernible, however, in the case of farm families who supply some of their own food.

ECONOMIC TRENDS AND THE RURAL AGED

Differences in the levels of living of the rural in comparison with the urban population are many-faceted, and the special case of the rural aged can be explained only within the context of overall economic trends. Of particular import are the changes in farm output per man-hour and the related decline in the significance of agriculture as a source of employment. Paralleling these developments, there have been important shifts in the composition of employment in rural areas, with consequent impact on the rural population's incomes and consumption patterns.[11]

CHANGES IN FARM OUTPUT AND EMPLOYMENT

In the current concern with technological improvements, and especially with the effect of automation on employment, surprisingly little attention has been given to the rapid rise in output per man-hour in the agricultural sector of the economy. The slowing down of job opportunities in this sector assumes increased importance in the present era, when job opportunities in the nonagricultural sector are not growing fast enough to absorb the new entrants to the labor force. Movement of workers out of farming into manufacturing, service industries, etc., has thus not been sufficiently rapid, and the failure of out-migration from farms to bring farm and nonfarm incomes more nearly into equality must be explained partly in terms of the overall unemployment rates of the post-World War II period.

In the past half-century, man-hours of labor used for farm work have declined from 32.5 billion to 8.8 billion, or a decrease in a 1957-59-based index of 129 points—from 212 in 1910 to 83 in 1963.[12] The past two and a half decades, moreover, have brought most of this decline: from 20.6 billion hours, or an index of 194, in 1939, man-hours fell to 8.8 billion, or an index of 83, in 1963. This decline of almost 60 percent in man-hours used for farm work was made possible by an almost fourfold increase in farm output per man-hour; from a 1939 index of 35, the figure rose to 135 in 1963, on the 1957-59 base.[13] Farm output, even with the greatly reduced number of hours worked, rose by almost two-thirds (from an index of 68 to one of 112) in the same period.[14] The net effect of these changes was to enable an agricultural worker to supply farm products to almost three times as many people (30.7 persons) in 1963 as he supplied in 1940 (10.7 persons).[15] Total farm employment consequently dropped from 11 million in 1940 to 6.5 million in 1963, according to the U. S. Department of Agriculture's concept of total farm employment ("farm operators, unpaid family workers, and hired workers"). By the Labor Department's classification, there were 5.4 million persons employed as farmers, farm managers, laborers, and foremen in 1960.

A longer-run view of agricultural and nonagricultural employment reveals the slow increase of farm workers during the second half of the nineteenth century. By contrast, the nonagricultural labor force increased sixfold between 1860 and 1910. In the 1910-63 period, agricultural employment declined, the rate of decline being more rapid in recent years, while nonagricultural employment rose to about two and one-half times its 1910 level.[16] Between 1960 and 1963 agricultural employment fell 13.5 percent, and an annual decline of 2 to 3 percent is expected during the next few years. By 1975, less than 1 out of 20 American workers will be farmers, as compared with the 1963 ratio of 1 in 15.[17]

SHIFTS IN OCCUPATIONAL STRUCTURE

The accelerated decline in farm employment is but one aspect of economywide changes in labor-force composition made possible (and necessary) primarily by improvements in technology after the Second World War. In broader terms, the postwar years have seen much faster rises in employment in the service-producing than in the goods-producing industries. Employment by occupational group shifted heavily in the direction of service workers, clerical and kindred workers, and professional, technical, and kindred workers. All of these trends are expected to continue.

Although the absolute and relative size of the rural farm segment is declining, the total rural population is expected to remain above 50 million for some time. Thus the nonfarm component of the rural population will rise, and the rural component as a proportion of the total population will decline, possibly from the 1960 proportion of 30 percent to a 1980 figure of 20 percent. In discussing the implications of these changes, one author has pointed out that the occupational and industrial attachments of rural nonfarm workers have traditionally been more like those of the urban than those of the farm population. With the technological advances in agriculture in recent years and the decline in farm employment, as well as the decrease in importance of industries which have traditionally employed rural persons (mining, for example), the occupational distinctions between urban and rural workers are diminishing. Adjustments still need to be made, however, involving "half or more of the farms and the people on those farms with units that are too small to provide a minimum adequate living from agriculture."[18]

Viewed in its occupational context, the adjustment can properly be considered as one requiring movement away from small or unproductive farms. When the particular position of the aged rural farmer is under consideration, however, this movement is complicated by factors such as the reduced mobility associated with age, the lower education and skill levels of older persons and their scant job opportunities elsewhere, and by strong attachments to the place of residence because of home ownership, and the like.

THE RURAL FARM AND NONFARM AGED

Agriculture's decline in importance has been of special significance to the aged because, in the past, few restrictions have been placed on the older man's continuance in a farm job. In other industrial sectors, the opportunity to continue working past the usual retirement age has been more and more limited since World War II. It is clear, therefore, that the trend toward fewer and larger, more efficiently run farms has reduced one source of employment for older men, and farming cannot be expected to assume any great importance in the older man's future job prospects.

But neither, apparently, can any other industrial sector. The movement toward compulsory retirement, particularly early retirement, is an outgrowth of persistent unemployment. In an effort to find jobs for middle-aged and younger men who typically have heavier family obligations than men aged 65 and over, the job needs of older men have understandably received less attention. The slightly more than 1 in 4 labor-force participation rate for older men (as compared with 2 in 3 at the beginning of the century) thus reflects in part a shift from agriculture. But in the past two decades it reflects also strong efforts to reduce the number of jobseekers. All the evidence points toward a continued emphasis on early retirement.

To the extent that this movement prevails, the income position of the rural and urban elderly will depend more and more upon public and private pensions and less and less on earned income. For future consideration, an important distinction must therefore be made between those who approach retirement with full social security benefits and some supplement in the form of a private pension or annuity, and those whose employment record does not entitle them to full benefits and who have no private pension or other claims. Since earnings are likely to provide a declining proportion of the aged's incomes, differences between retirement incomes of the rural farm, the rural nonfarm, and the urban elderly will probably be reduced.

Since the retiree's benefit is to some extent wage related, and since the earnings of rural workers tend to be somewhat lower than those of urban workers, the rural worker may less frequently qualify for the maximum benefit. Moreover, his lower earnings will probably mean that he has accumulated less in savings and insurance. It is difficult to generalize about the relative significance of private pension funds for the urban and rural nonfarm retirees except to say that private pension claims are correlated directly with job stability and earnings during working life. There is no opportunity for the older farm group to gain such coverage as farmers, though there may be some cases in which an earlier industrial job has given the farmer a private pension claim. The number of workers qualifying for private pensions is still a small proportion of the total;[19] this source of income, particularly for the lower-income workers, should therefore not be exaggerated.

As social security benefits become a larger proportion of the aged's total income, the smaller will be the income differential between the rural and the urban aged. The differential will not disappear entirely, so long as the earnings of urban workers remain higher. The same narrowing of differentials occurs in case of the aged white and the aged Negro's benefits.[20] In the long run, therefore, the problem is likely to be one of insuring that the program of income maintenance for all the aged is substantially raised along with the attempts to improve the lot of particularly disadvantaged segments of the elderly population.

IMPLICATIONS FOR THE RURAL AGED

The very poor among the aged can be identified by any one of several characteristics. Extremely low money incomes often accrue to the very old among the aged who are not able to work and who are not covered by social security benefits. As Table 8 reveals, the median income of the younger group (aged 62-64) and the older (aged 73 and over) are approximately the same for beneficiary couples and nonmarried men. Incomes of the nonmarried women retired workers in the younger group are slightly higher, and the median for widowed women substantially higher than that of the older group of women. Incomes of the beneficiaries aged 65-72 are higher in the case of both married couples

Table 8. Median Income by Age and Beneficiary Status of Household Units Aged 62 and Over in the United States, 1962

Age	Married couples*		Nonmarried men		Nonmarried women		
	OASDI beneficiaries	Non-beneficiaries	OASDI beneficiaries	Non-beneficiaries	Retired OASDI beneficiaries**	Widowed OASDI beneficiaries	Non-beneficiaries
62-64	$2,470	$5,900	$1,265	$2,685	$1,220	$1,350	$2,205
65-72	2,900	4,750	1,610	2,000	1,455	1,285	855
73 and over	2,430	1,680	1,260	860	1,120	960	720

* With at least 1 member aged 62 or over.
** The retired women receive benefits based on their own wage record.
Source: Lenore A. Epstein, "Income of the Aged in 1962," *Social Security Bulletin,* 27, No. 3; (March 1964), 17.

and nonmarried men, reflecting, first, the failure of the men aged 62-64 to find jobs and their willingness to accept a reduced benefit; second, the reduced earning capacities of the older men. In the case of the nonbeneficiaries, incomes are higher for the younger couples and single persons, since their earnings are generally higher.[21]

Low incomes accrue to older unattached individuals, who are often widows receiving some small OASDI benefit plus a welfare payment, or to those who are living altogether on welfare funds. The median income for aged single women in 1962 was $1,015; the median for aged unmarried men was $1,365. The aged nonwhite family or individual has a much lower income than the

Table 9. Summary and Ranking of Subgroups of Families with Heads Aged 65 and Over, 1959

Subgroup and rank	Number (in thousands)	Median income	Percentage with income of less than:	
			$2,000	$3,000
Ranking by number of families				
1. Urban-white, husband-wife	2,938	$3,782	23.6	40.4
2. Rural-white, husband-wife	1,505	2,344	43.6	62.2
3. Urban-white, female head	625	4,196	24.6	36.6
4. Rural-white, female head	218	2,330	45.5	58.9
5. Urban-white, other male head	213	5,187	17.5	28.3
6. Urban-nonwhite, husband-wife	209	2,338	44.0	61.5
7. Rural-nonwhite, husband-wife	126	1,369	73.4	85.5
8. Rural-white, other male head	109	2,753	38.6	53.7
9. Urban-nonwhite, female head	82	1,923	52.0	67.1
10. Rural-nonwhite, female head	41	1,091	76.0	87.2
11. Urban-nonwhite, other male head	23	2,718	38.2	54.6
12. Rural-nonwhite, other male head	15	1,502	65.7	78.9
Ranking by size of income				
1. Urban-white, other male head	213	$5,187	17.5	28.3
2. Urban-white, female head	625	4,196	24.6	36.6
3. Urban-white, husband-wife	2,938	3,782	23.6	40.4
4. Rural-white, other male head	109	2,753	38.6	53.7
5. Urban-nonwhite, other male head	23	2,718	38.2	54.6
6. Rural-white, husband-wife	1,505	2,344	43.6	62.2
7. Urban-nonwhite, husband-wife	209	2,338	44.0	61.5
8. Rural-white, female head	218	2,330	45.5	58.9
9. Urban-nonwhite, female head	82	1,923	52.0	67.1
10. Rural-nonwhite, other male head	15	1,502	65.7	78.9
11. Rural-nonwhite, husband-wife	126	1,369	73.4	85.5
12. Rural-nonwhite, female head	41	1,091	76.0	87.2

Source: Prepared by the Department of Health, Education and Welfare, Office of Aging, from tabulations of the 1960 census of population.

white family or single person; the family headed by an aged woman has a lower income than the family headed by an aged man. Finally, as the data presented earlier clearly demonstrate, the rural aged have lower incomes than the urban aged. Table 9 indicates the 1959 median incomes for aged families classified as to color, sex of family head, and place of residence; Table 10 shows similar data for aged single persons.

Lower living costs and a somewhat higher proportion of home-owners among the rural aged, plus the ability of the farm segment of this group to grow a part of the family's food provide some offset to the much lower money incomes of the rural aged, although it is very difficult to estimate the value of these offsets. There is evidence that some farmers with low incomes are using their farms as a form of partial retirement. More than one-fourth of the operators of farms with gross sales of $2,500 or less were aged 65 or over. But even after allowance is made for housing and food grown (the 1959 census of agriculture reported that part-time farmers made $178 from the sale of farm products, and

Table 10. Summary and Ranking of Subgroups of Unrelated Individuals Aged 65 and Over, 1959

Subgroup and rank	Number (*in thousands*)	Median income	Percentage with income of less than	
			$1,000	$2,000
Ranking by number of persons				
1. Urban-white, female	1,858	$1,043	48.8	76.6
2. Urban-white, male	752	1,558	31.3	64.8
3. Rural-white, female	526	738	67.7	87.9
4. Rural-white, male	308	992	50.4	79.1
5. Urban-nonwhite, female	140	695	71.9	92.7
6. Urban-nonwhite, male	101	958	52.2	80.6
7. Rural-nonwhite, female	40	548	91.3	98.4
8. Rural-nonwhite, male	33	651	76.9	93.5
Ranking by size of income				
1. Urban-white, male	752	$1,558	31.3	64.8
2. Urban-white, female	1,858	1,043	48.8	76.6
3. Rural-white, male	308	992	50.4	79.1
4. Urban-nonwhite, male	101	958	52.2	80.6
5. Rural-white, female	526	738	67.7	89.9
6. Urban-nonwhite, female	140	695	71.9	92.7
7. Rural-nonwhite, male	33	651	76.9	93.5
8. Rural-nonwhite, female	40	548	91.3	98.4

Source: Prepared by the Department of Health, Education and Welfare, Office of Aging, from tabulations of the 1960 census of population.

that food produced and eaten on the farm and an allowance for rental value of the farm totaled $431), the added income of part-time farmers is low.[22] Since the average age of the farm operator in 1962 was 50, and since there will be fewer farmers as the present older operators (who are more often operating the small farms) retire or die, the rural aged will be predominantly the rural nonfarm group.

The economic plight of the rural aged as a group will be somewhat improved (or at least less disadvantaged in comparison to the urban aged) as the lower-income-farm component diminishes in size. The fate of the rural nonfarm elderly is dependent on the same set of forces that dictate the future welfare of the urban aged, i.e., the extent of improvement in public and private pensions. It is unrealistic to expect significant improvements in job opportunities for older persons, barring an extreme change in labor market conditions such as a wartime situation might produce. It seems very likely, therefore, that in general the retirement incomes of the two groups will move closer together, just as occupational patterns already have done.

Job opportunities for those persons below retirement age continue to be the most significant single factor determining retirement income. Given a stable employment record with sufficient earnings to insure a maximum OASDI benefit, the retiree can usually acquire some savings and other assets. By contrast, the family head who cannot find employment during his late fifties and early sixties is prone to take an early retirement at a reduced benefit. The combined disadvantages of a lowered monthly benefit which must now support him for a longer period, plus the inability to save for retirement or qualify for a private pension, conspire against an adequate income in old age. Insofar as employment opportunities are better in urban than in rural areas, income of the rural retirees will continue to mirror this disadvantage, just as the earnings of the younger rural population will reflect their relatively disadvantaged position.

NOTES

[1] Eugene Smolensky, "The Past and Present Poor," an unpublished paper prepared for the United States Chamber of Commerce Task Force on Economic Growth and Opportunity, 1963, pp. 22-23.

2 James D. Cowhig, "Urban and Rural Levels of Living: 1960," Economic Research Service United States Department of Agriculture; Agricultural Economic Report No. 79, Washington, D. C., July 1965.

3 Lenora A. Epstein, "Incomes of the Aged in 1962: First Findings of the 1963 Survey of the Aged," *Social Security Bulletin,* 27 No. 3. (March 1964), 3-35.

4 Bureau of the Census, *Current Population Reports, Consumer Income,* Series P-60, No. 37, January 17, 1962, pp. 6-7.

5 The following table shows differentials for other types of families:

Median Income of Families by Region and Age of Head and
Type of Family, 1960

Region	Head 65 and over			All families (including 65 and over)			
	Husband-wife families	Other male-head families	Female-head families	Husband-wife families	Other male-head families	Female-head families	All families
North	$3,451	$4,696	$4,051	$6,274	$5,580	$3,649	$6,034
South	2,335	2,476	2,108	4,791	3,360	2,067	4,467
West	3,461	4,174	3,849	6,646	5,742	3,400	6,374
Total U. S.	3,052	3,950	3,330	5,901	5,025	3,041	5,663

Source: U. S. Bureau of the Census

6 Mollie Orshansky, "Counting the Poor: Another Look at the Poverty Profile," *Social Security Bulletin,* Vol. 28 (Jan. 1965), pp. 3-29.

7 Cowhig, "Urban and Rural Levels of Living," p. 5. Data for this study were derived from the 1-in-1,000 sample of tabulations from the 1960 Census of Population and Housing and thus refer to the 36 million households headed by males employed in the civilian labor force. The author notes that although limiting his analysis to this group of households provides comparability, it also results in a more favorable picture than would result if data on unrelated individuals and households headed by women were included.

8 Note that the proportion of urban older families having none of these durables is about two-thirds that of rural older families and that the proportion of all younger families having none of the appliances is slightly more than one-half the proportion of all older families who lack all the appliances.

9 Consumer expenditure data are not yet available for farm families.

10 Sidney Goldstein, *Consumption Patterns of the Aged* (Philadelphia: University of Pennsylvania Press, 1960). See also Jean A. Crockett, "Older People as Consumers," in Harold L. Orbach and Clark Tibbitts, *Aging and the Economy* (Ann Arbor: University of Michigan Press, 1963), pp. 127-45.

11 See Louis J. Ducoff, "Occupations and Levels of Living," in *Yearbook of Agriculture,* U. S. Department of Agriculture (Washington, D. C., 1963), pp. 19-25.

[12] U. S. Department of Agriculture, *Changes in Farm Production and Efficiency*, Statistical Bulletin No. 233 (Washington, D. C., July 1964), Table 15, p. 33.

[13] *Ibid.*, Table 21, p. 42.

[14] *Ibid.*, Table 2, p. 9.

[15] *Ibid.*, Table 22, p. 44.

[16] Ducoff, "Occupations and Levels of Living," p. 19.

[17] U. S. Department of Labor, *Manpower Report of the President* (Washington, D. C., 1964), pp. 89 and 244. The figures are: from 5.4 million, or 8.1 percent of total 1960 employment, to 3.9 million, or 4.5 percent in 1975, or a decline of 28 percent in the 15-year period.

[18] Ducoff, "Occupations and Levels of Living," p. 24.

[19] According to a recent estimate made by the National Bureau for Economic Research, approximately 25 to 30 percent of the older persons will be receiving private pensions by 1979. Joseph Krislov, "Employee-Benefit Plans, 1954-62," *Social Security Bulletin*, 27, No. 4 (April 1964), 16-20.

[20] See Mollie Orshansky, "The Aged Negro and His Income," *Social Security Bulletin*, 27 (Feb. 1964), 3-13.

[21] For a fuller explanation of age differences in income, see Lenora A. Epstein, "Income of the Aged in 1962," *Social Security Bulletin*, 27, No. 3 (March 1964), 16-22.

[22] U. S. Department of Labor, *Manpower Report of the President*, p. 87.

JAMES E. MONTGOMERY

Housing of
the Rural Aged

In considering the housing of older rural people it is important
to bear in mind that the rural aged population is not homogeneous. There are major differences in age, sex, race, health, education, marital status, socioeconomic status, occupation, type of
household, type of housing, type of residential area, and region
of the country. As a result there are no typical rural senior citizens. They include the Navajo, the Negro, the Appalachian subsistence farmer, the Wyoming cowboy, the Alabama plantation
patriarch, the Wisconsin dairy farmer, the coal miner in rural
Pennsylvania, the up-state New York merchant villager, the industrial factory worker who once commuted to the job, and the
retired teacher in Illinois who hoped to escape the traffic and
taxes of the big city. Since housing needs are influenced by these
differences, there is no one solution to the housing problems of
the rural aged.

What, then do the rural aged have in common? Perhaps these
are the main common denominators: a) They live in areas of low
density. b) They are usually somewhat removed from the mainstream of American life as represented by the laboratory, the library, the legislature, the Congress, the union hall, the concert
center, the art gallery, the legitimate theater, and Madison Avenue. c) Their incomes vary sharply, but on the whole they have
less to spend for, and get less in, housing, medical care, clothing,

transportation, recreation, and the like. *d*) Finally, they are now outnumbered by more than three to one by an urban-oriented society.

HISTORICAL PRACTICES AND DEVELOPMENT

It is often said that you can't teach an old dog new tricks and that the aged are set in their ways. Be that as it may, no generation in America or very likely in any part of the world has lived through and adjusted to as many major changes as those presently 65 and over. They have lived through two major wars and a depression. They have seen and been affected by medical advances, the dynamic labor movement, mechanization of agriculture, developments in genetics, the coming of the automobile and airplane, urbanization and industrialization, a shorter work week, retirement at 65, social security benefits, civil rights legislation, and Medicare. These and other changes have weakened the influence of rural people both at the national and at the grassroots level. For example, in 1960 the dominant occupation of rural residents was "blue collar" (34.4 percent) rather than farmers and farm managers (14.3 percent). In fact, in 1960 professional and managerial occupations included slightly more persons than did the category of farmers and farm managers.[1]

Along with these changes have come modifications in living arrangements and housing. Formerly the rural aged (primarily farm people) fended for themselves as long as health permitted. The concept of retirement was all but foreign to rural residents. At the risk of overstepping the bounds of fact, one might suggest the following typologies of the ways in which the problems of the rural aged were met.

In the case of "respectable" or "substantial" persons, older persons, farmers and villagers, mastered their own housing destinies until death of a spouse or illness forced a dissolution of the household. At that point a married son or daughter would move in with the aged parent(s) or the latter would move in with the son or daughter. Although many young people moved westward, usually one or more continued to live near their parents. These older persons died in their own home or in that of their kin—not in a nursing home or hospital. In a way living and dying was a private family affair. Spinsters, often not so "substantial" economically, found a home with relatives where their hands found many uses.

Largely as a result of a paternalistic orientation, many plantation owners, larger farm operators, and mill and mine operators felt keenly their responsibility for assisting "their faithful" poor aged people. Therefore, they often provided for them housing, fuel, groceries, and perhaps a modicum of medical care. Ultimately many of these persons were also assisted by their children. Most of these aged persons lived out their days among relatives and in a familiar environment. But the threat of having to end their days in the county poorhouse was probably often in the forefront of their thinking.

During the nineteenth century the county-supported poorhouse or almshouse was the common means in most of the states for providing for the care of the destitute. As an illustration, in 1846 Michigan enacted a law which specified that any person " 'blind, old, lame, sick or decrepit, or in any way disabled or enfeebled so as to be unable to maintain himself,' if he became a public charge, was cared for in the county poorhouse."[2] These institutions were for the young as well as for the old: the blind, the deaf, the deformed, and the incurably ill. In commenting on Michigan poorhouses established under the law of 1846, Bruce and Eickhoff wrote: "The poorhouses were soon filled with various groups, representing many types of misfortune, but all failing to be selfmaintaining. . . . It was estimated, in 1873, that of an average poorhouse population of fifteen hundred persons two hundred and fifty were insane, one hundred and twenty-five were idiots, forty were blind, twenty were mute, and about three hundred were epileptic or had deformities or chronic diseases."[3]

The median income of rural families is much lower than that of their urban counterparts. Nevertheless, there has been a gradual strengthening of the economic position of the rural aged. At least the poorhouse is now largely history. Nonfarm opportunities have presented more alternatives to farming than was the case until well into the twentieth century. The combining of farm and non-farm work has increased the income of many rural people. But perhaps the most significant factor that has increased the economic independence of the rural aged was the Social Security Act of 1935. In 1951 farm laborers were given coverage and self-employed farmers in 1955. In 1962, four million self-employed farmers and farm laborers living in the fifty states and the Virgin

Islands were covered by social security. Also, a large but unknown number of part-time farmers and rural nonfarm persons are currently covered by social security. The Old Age Assistance program (OAA) instituted by the Social Security Act and implemented jointly by the federal and state governments has done much to close the doors of poorhouses and to enable older persons, rural and urban, to remain in their own homes until health forces a change in living arrangements.

An examination of the literature on care of the aged reveals that many efforts were made to assist the needy aged long before the Social Security Act was passed in 1935. There had been a growing disdain of poorhouses and increasing efforts to find other solutions. Religious, fraternal, philanthropic as well as state and municipal activities not only assisted the poor aged but, equally important, the leaders of these programs and activities created a climate of opinion in which sweeping reform could occur. By 1930, Montana, Wisconsin, California, and New York had passed laws which assisted the poor, including the poor aged. But until the economic debacle of the 1930's, many persons held that the children—not state or municipal governments, much less the federal government—had a moral duty to take care of their aged parents. In 1930, Rubinow observed: "A very extensive method of meeting the old age problems still remains within the power of the family group. In fact, this is frequently put forth as the only normal ethical and socially desirable method of handling the problems of the aged, so much so that any suggestions as to the broad social policies for many years were rejected by serious students on the ground that it might interfere with this more ethical method of family provision."[4]

Early reforms in the care of the aged usually were directed at the nonrural aged. In fact, there seems always to have been a lag in measures to aid rural senior citizens. Indeed, as will become apparent later, reforms, housing and otherwise, by and large reach rural areas only after they have functioned for several years in urban areas. For example, settlement houses, pension laws, and building codes did not originate in rural areas, nor did such housing improvements as central heating, modern plumbing, and electricity. Recently, however, the lines of demarcation between rural and urban have become blurred and less distinct.

In 1967 the housing needs of the rural aged are vastly different from what they were a generation ago. On the whole they are less acute than they once were. Nevertheless, many changes remain to be effected if the rural aged are to live in dignity and are to share in the fruits of an affluent society.

What, one may ask, are the antecedents of the deprivations, housing and otherwise, that are experienced daily by so many older rural people? The following are among the principal ones: (a) isolation from kin and others, (b) greatly limited incomes, (c) ill health, (d) negative stereotypes of the aged, (e) a relatively roleless and insignificant position in society, and (f) social and residential mobility of younger persons.

FACTORS AFFECTING HOUSING NEEDS

Health greatly affects one's ability to remain independent in one's own household. Older persons are ill more often than younger persons, are ill for a longer number of days, are hospitalized more often, and recover more slowly. There is considerable evidence that older rural persons have poorer health than older urban people. In commenting on a recent study conducted by the Public Health Service, Johnston stated that "more than half of all rural farm people over 65 reported some degree of activity-limitation from a chronic condition, compared with less than 40 percent of the urban and 46 percent of the rural nonfarm people of that age."[5]

Age and sex have relevance to housing needs. In 1960, 35 percent of the rural nonfarm and almost 31 percent of the rural farm population aged 65 and over were 75 years of age or older. For the combined rural categories, there were more than a quarter-million persons 85 and over. There were proportionately more females than males in each 5-year age interval from 65 to 85 and over for the rural nonfarm population. On the other hand, for the rural farm population the sex ratio was in favor of males except for the category 85 and over. In contemplating the housing needs of the rural aged it is especially significant that in 1960 there were more than three-fourths of a million persons 80 years old or older, considerably more than half of whom were females.

Still another variable materially affecting the housing needs of the aged is marital status. Today more than half of all women in the United States 65 years old and over are without husbands.

For the rural population 65 and over, 72.0 percent of the males were married and 18.4 percent were widowers; comparable figures for females were 44.6 percent and 47.9 percent. But, of course, as age advances widowhood becomes all the more prevalent. For example, in 1960, 50.8 percent of rural nonfarm males aged 85 and over were widowers, compared with 55.2 percent of rural farm males in this age category. But for females the figures for rural nonfarm and rural farm were 82.2 percent and 85.3 percent. These figures emphasize the point that housing for the aged means something quite different from suitable shelter for aged couples who enjoy reasonably good health. As age advances, housing becomes a problem of providing a compatible and functional physical and social environment of very old females.

The large majority of the 5.5 million rural persons 65 and over live in private households, usually their own. In 1960 the composition of all rural households that were headed by a person 65 or over was as follows: of the households having two or more persons, 44.8 percent consisted of a male head, a wife, and no nonrelatives; 26.5 had some other male head; and 8.1 percent were headed by a female. The remaining 20.6 percent were one-person households. The total number of rural households headed by a person 65 or over in 1960 was 3,527,369.[6]

It is of interest to note that a fifth of all older rural persons lived alone. The 1960 census data are inadequate in regard to a detailed account of the types of living arrangements of the rural aged, but perhaps no more than 5 percent live in an institutional setting. This percentage includes primarily the very aged who are beset by chronic disease or senility.

These variables—health, age, sex, race, marital status, and types of households—are important determinants of housing needs. Also, an interplay between these and other factors result in striking differences in styles of life among the rural aged. There are as many patterns of living to be found among this segment of the population as among any other 5.5 million Americans. Such vast variations in the styles of life evidenced by a retired Iowa farmer and a former vegetable picker in California suggest the folly of generalizing about the way older rural people live. If there is a common denominator of the styles of life of rural senior citizens, it is that most of them no longer play a productive economic role.

CURRENT HOUSING CONDITIONS

The quality of housing occupied by contemporary older persons, urban and rural, is inferior to that of other segments of the population. Older persons usually live in larger, older dwellings that frequently lack plumbing facilities and are in need of repairs. In 1960, only 46 percent of all rural farm households headed by a person 65 years of age or older occupied dwellings that were sound and had all plumbing facilities. Comparable percentages for the rural nonfarm and urban dwellings were 52 and 70, respectively. For all rural dwellings occupied by households having a head 65 years old or older, 623,806 (22.5 percent) were deteriorating or dilapidated. An additional 745,623 (26.9 percent) lacked some facilities or were without piped water (but not dilapidated). In short, approximately half of all dwelling units headed by an older rural person were deficient in one way or another (Table 1). Concealed in these brief statistics are many livable dwellings in a good state of repair. They perhaps also conceal such realities as inadequate water supplies, outdoor

Table 1. Percentage Distribution of Housing Conditions for Households Headed by Persons Aged 65 and Over by Place of Residence, in the United States, 1960

Housing condition	Urban	Rural nonfarm	Rural farm
Sound			
With all plumbing facilities	70.0	52.0	46.0
Lacking some facilities,			
with piped water	9.1	8.9	9.6
Deteriorating			
With all plumbing			
facilities	8.1	7.7	7.5
Lacking some facilities,			
with piped water	7.5	5.9	5.5
Sound or deteriorating,			
no piped water	.0	16.0	23.4
Dilapidated	5.3	9.5	8.0
Total	100.0	100.0	100.0
(Total number)	(9,244,944)	(2,067,351)	(700,791)

Source: U. S. Bureau of the Census, *United States Census of Housing: 1960, Rural Housing* (Washington, D. C., 1963), Vol VI, and *United States Census of Population: 1960, United States Summary,* Final Report (Washington, D. C., 1963)

privies, inadequate storage, poor heating and lighting, broken window panes, peeling paint, broken floors, sagging roofs, and a lack of safety precautions. This is often the case despite the fact that the older a person becomes the larger proportion of each day he spends in his housing environment. Also, older persons have less energy, are more prone to have accidents, are sick more often, recover more slowly from illness, have poorer vision, and require higher temperatures than younger persons. In the yearning to remain independent in their own households as long as possible, housing has a crucial role to play. But in 1965 relatively few older rural persons lived in houses that have been "aged proofed."

HOME OWNERSHIP

In 1960 approximately 62 percent of all nonfarm families in the United States owned their homes. But the rate of homeownership among the aged rural population was much higher. For all rural nonfarm dwellings occupied in 1960 by a household head 65 years old or older, 78.8 percent were owner occupied; the comparable percentage for rural farm was higher still, 88.4 percent. This high percentage of homeownership should render the problem of securing loans for improving housing much easier.

Data are not available for the age of the dwellings occupied by older rural persons. But the age of all dwellings, regardless of age of head of household, is revealing. The percentages of dwellings owner-occupied which were built in 1939 or earlier for urban, rural nonfarm, and rural farm were 48.0, 46.8, and 74.2, respectively. The percentages for renter-occupied dwellings were: urban 69.9 percent, rural nonfarm 59.3, and rural farm 81.0.[7]

SATISFACTION WITH HOUSING

A consideration of the characteristics of the housing of the rural aged raises the question: How satisfied are these older persons with their present locations and their dwellings, and what are their aspirations for the future? The following review of a number of recent studies will provide a partial answer to this question.

Evidence suggests that many older rural citizens have lived in the same neighborhoods and houses for a relatively long time. A study by Beyer and Wahl of a sample of nonfarm and rural farm persons 65 and over in 15 counties in central New York showed that 84 percent of the older farm respondents had lived in their present neighborhoods 20 years or longer.[8] A 1962 survey of 510 older persons in a small community in central Pennsylvania revealed that 61 percent of the respondents had lived in their present neighborhoods 25 years or longer and 55 percent had lived in their present dwellings for 25 years or longer.[9] The census data also show that older persons, regardless of type of community, are less mobile than any other sector of the population.

Older rural people, on the whole, seem to be relatively well satisfied with both their neighborhoods and houses. A study of retired Kansas farmers conducted in 1961 by Agan and Anderson revealed satisfaction with present arrangements. In commenting on attitudes toward locations, the researchers stated: "Most in the open country preferred to stay there, as they enjoyed activities associated with farming. The men, particularly, wanted to continue maintaining jobs around the farm and feared there would be nothing for them to do in town. The women, to a greater extent than men, would like to have been in town, partly for more social activities, and for more comfortable homes."[10]

Older rural people appear to be more nearly satisfied with their housing than younger persons. For example, a study of 212 rural homeowners (usually housewives were interviewed) in Oklahoma revealed that 37 percent of respondents under 45 years of age were satisfied with their dwellings compared to 58 percent of those 55 years old and over. The older the respondent the greater was the probability that she would be well satisfied with the following housing features: dining area, kitchen in general, number of bedrooms, bedroom storage, bathroom facilities, general storage, and traffic patterns. In this Oklahoma study age was found to be more sensitive as an independent variable than were socioeconomic status, family life cycle, and types of occupation.[11] In the study of the aged in a small Pennsylvania community referred to earlier, 76 percent of the respondents liked their dwellings "very well" and an additional 20 percent liked them "fairly well." Corresponding figures for their neighborhoods were 78 percent and 18 percent, respectively.

Available studies are virtually unanimous in stating that a large majority of older rural people are quite well satisfied with the places where they have lived for quite a long number of years.

As they approach a time in life when dependence on others is beginning to increase, the younger aged guard their independence almost fanatically. It may well be that this deeply felt desire to remain independent is a major reason why so many older persons express satisfactions with the housing *status quo;* they can ill afford to admit to themselves that change, which one way or another might erode their independence, is desirable. This desire to remain independent may pose a dilemma in that inevitably many older persons will end their days dependent upon others— in their own homes with nursing service, in the homes of relatives, in homes for the aged, in nursing homes, or in hospitals.

HOME IMPROVEMENTS

Indications are that most persons past 65 make few improvements in their housing. Cowles and Sweeney, in a study of rural housing in Wisconsin, stated:

> It was noticeable that special provisions for an elderly person had been made in relatively few dwellings. . . . Failure to make special preparations for good housing suitable for elderly people stems from several causes. In many cases, it was felt that no particular adaptation for the needs of the aged would be necessary since what is good housing for young people is also good for older. Another feeling, especially noticeable in the very old, was that their present level of comfort was what they had become accustomed to, and any lack of convenience was accepted as part of the disabilities which one expects in life. A further cause was that they would be leaving the farm sometime, perhaps fairly soon, and it was not worth while to improve the house at this state. The cost of any considerable housing improvement was also a deterent.[12]

In the Oklahoma study, to which earlier reference was made, it was found that relatively few older persons had made housing improvements in the recent past and that few contemplated improvements in the future. Moreover, respondents included in the Pennsylvania study revealed that they had made few adjustments in housing as they grew older. Almost three-fourths of them lived in houses having two or more stories. In 90 percent of the cases the bathroom was located on the same level as the bedroom, but in more than a third of the cases the living room and the bathroom were on different floors. Almost 90 percent of the dwellings were reached by means of steps or stairs.

The Kansas study also indicated that although many houses were undesirable for the older farmers, very few would consider moving. It was found that 88 percent of the men and 82 percent of the women climbed stairs at least two or three times a month; 42 percent of them climbed stairs daily.[13]

LOCATION OF HOME

Retirement villages and mobile homes to the contrary, research findings clearly indicate that the large majority of older rural persons want to remain where they are as long as possible—in the same community, neighborhood, and house.

Nygren and Sutker who recently conducted depth interviews with a small sample of the rural elderly in Oklahoma found, as have other researchers, a particularly strong desire to remain independent and in their own households as long as possible. The interviewers asked the respondents what they would do in the event they had to move from their present dwellings. The following four alternatives were stated to the respondents: live with married son on a nearby farm, move to a small house in a village in the county in which their children lived, move to a development for the aged in a nearby state, or move to a church-supported home near their children. The arrangement most often preferred was to live in a village near their children, and the least preferred was to move in with adult children.[14]

In this connection Beyer and Wahl found that more than half of the older farm respondents who were able to care for themselves thought that the best living arrangement for them was to live by themselves but near relatives, and almost a third of them thought living by themselves away from relatives was the best solution. Only 5 percent of the respondents aged 65 to 69 years indicated that they thought the most satisfactory plan would be to live with relatives, but 19 percent of the persons 80 years old and older gave this reply. These older farm persons were also asked to indicate the best living arrangement for older persons unable to care for themselves. In descending order of preference the responses were "own homes with nursing care," slightly more than half; "with their families," almost a fourth; and "nursing home," about a fourth.

In regard to the preferences of older persons indicated in the central New York study, Beyer and Wahl concluded:

> In general, responses to the question about living situations for the aged unable to care for themselves are in line with what is possible for the various groups. The more that income and living arrangements allow a choice for independence, the greater is this choice. It was found that couples, farmers, home owners, those living in their own households, and those with higher incomes would prefer to be in their own homes with nursing care. The aged with families to depend on tend to turn to them. Those who favored having the aged live with their families included those already living with children, those with low incomes, those in poor health, and those who were older. Others saw nursing homes in the realm of possibility. Those who favored nursing homes included renters and widowed, single women and men living alone or with non-relatives.[15]

EFFORTS TO IMPROVE HOUSING

In the nineteenth century various religious and philanthropic organizations attempted to improve the lot of the aged, but the majority of measures taken to provide more suitable housing for older persons date from the Depression of the 1930's. Usually, efforts exerted on behalf of the aged in general have had beneficial effects on the rural aged. Some of the measures that have materially affected the housing of the aged were not at all concerned with housing per se. Perhaps no one congressional act has done more to enable older persons to remain independent in their own homes than has the Social Security Act of 1935 through its OASDI and OAA programs. The National Housing Act of 1934, which enabled many persons to buy houses and have them paid for by the time the occupants reached age 65, and provisions for insuring home improvement loans have made for a better inventory of housing in the United States. Indirectly, also, the Serviceman's Adjustment Act of 1944 (GI Bill of Rights) and the decennial census of housing which began in 1940 have had salutory effects on the housing of the aged, urban and rural.

It should be stated that theoretically the measures designed by the federal government to assist the aged with their housing needs apply to rural as well as to urban people. However, for various reasons, several of the programs which assist the urban aged do not, in reality, reach the rural aged.

THE NATIONAL HOUSING ACT

There are more than a half-dozen programs either authorized by the National Housing Act of 1934 or by subsequent amendments to it which assist with the housing of the aged. For example, sections 203, 213, 231, 221(d)(3), and 203(K) are especially relevant here. Section 203 of the National Housing Act insures mortgages on single-family houses found in suburban developments, including housing in many retirement communities. Section 213 authorizes mortgagee insurance for housing cooperatives. Under section 231 of the National Housing Act as amended by the Housing Act of 1959, the Farmers Home Administration assists nonprofit organizations (religious, fraternal, labor, or a governmental agency) and profit-motivated sponsors. Long-term loans are insured by FHA at an interest rate of 5¼ percent plus ½ percent for insurance premiums. A study of 156 developments in 1963 revealed that 105 were "congregate" (that is, the projects provided accommodations for room and board, meals being provided in common dining rooms) and 51 were housekeeping units. Of the developments, 8 percent were located in small communities, 29 percent in the suburbs, and 63 percent in downtown or residential areas of cities. Approximately 75 percent of the occupants were women.[16]

Section 221(d)(3) of the National Housing Act, amended by the Housing Act of 1961, provides financing at an interest rate of 3⅛ percent for the construction or improvement of rented housing for families displaced by governmental programs and for other low-income families. Section 203(K) of the National Housing Act, as amended by the Housing Act of 1961, authorized the FHA to insure loans used by individuals outside of urban areas for the rehabilitation of single or multiunit dwellings. The allowable interest rate is 5¼ percent plus ½ percent for insurance premiums.[17]

In addition to these programs under FHA, the Community

Facilities Administration, a constituent agency of the Housing and Home Finance Agency, makes direct loans for the construction of housing facilities for the aged. Under Section 202 of the Housing Act of 1959 the CFA makes direct loans for the provision of rental housing for persons 62 years old or older whose incomes do not exceed $4,800 for a couple or $4,000 for an individual. Projects can be sponsored only by private nonprofit organizations —religious, civic, fraternal, labor groups, and the like. Terms of the loans are 50 years at an interest rate of 3⅝ percent. Unlike many of the units provided by FHA's 231 program, each dwelling unit financed by CFA's 202 program is required to include housekeeping facilities.[18]

The activities of the Public Housing Administration and of the Farmers Home Administration have direct bearing upon the housing of the rural aged. For all practical purposes, the Housing Act of 1937 initiated America's federally subsidized low-rent housing. In the early days of PHA, activities were largely confined to families with children who lived in larger cities. But over the past 25 years emphasis on the housing of the elderly has greatly increased, and projects were started in many small cities, towns, and even villages. At the end of 1963, 1,502 local housing authorities operated public housing in 2,044 "places." Enabling legislation permitting public housing has been enacted in each of the 50 states, Puerto Rico, and the Virgin Islands, except Oklahoma, Utah, and Wyoming. However, to date South Dakota and Iowa have not established any local housing authorities.

HOUSING PROJECTS

As of December 31, 1963 there were 539,000 occupied public housing units and, of these, 135,000 or 25 percent were occupied by persons 62 years of age or older. Since 1960 housing facilities have been specifically designed for the aged. Another development in public housing for the aged is an experimental policy to provide facilities for congregate living. In August of 1963 construction was started on a congregate housing project on an Indian reservation in South Dakota. Meanwhile by the end of 1963 applicants for congregate public housing had been received from Georgia, Kansas, Nebraska, and the Virgin Islands.

At present there are many small rural communities that participate in the Public Housing Program. As an example, the Northwest Florida Regional Housing Authority is cited. That authority currently operates public housing in 11 small communities ranging in population (1960) from 849 to 2,805 and located in eight counties. The number of low-rent units ranges from 6 in the town of Malone to 58 in Jasper. In three of the villages facilities serve whites only, in one Negroes only, and in the remaining seven both races are assisted. In the 11 rural communities are 192 low-rent units of which 61 or almost one-third are occupied by persons 62 years old or older.

The Public Housing Administration also assists Indians with their housing. In 1963 some 76,000 reservation Indian families occupied approximately 50,000 dwelling units of which 45,000 were judged to be substandard. Obviously, almost all reservation Indians are rural. At the close of 1963 PHA was assisting in providing 3,641 housing units on 50 Indian reservations in 17 states. Of the total, 270 were to be specifically designed for older Indians.

In considering the role of public housing in regard to the housing of the aged, it is important to note that in 1962 and 1963 about half of all units placed under contract were specifically designed for the elderly. Future commitments of the PHA are expected to continue to be designed for the aged. Important as the relatively small number of accommodations for the elderly is, perhaps of greater significance is the fact that a workable model for providing specially designed facilities for the aged is emerging. Until the beginning of the PHA program rarely did a low-income family occupy an architecturally planned environment for them; rarer still did older low-income families live in housing that had been designed for their needs. On this point the *Seventeenth Annual Report of the Housing and Home Finance Agency* commented:

> Low-rent public housing, specially designed for the elderly, seeks as do other programs for the elderly, to extend their years of independence and usefulness to the community by enabling them to exercise fully their mental and physical capabilities. Special design features of housing for the elderly include such items as nonskid floors, waist-high electric outlets, levers instead of knobs on doors and faucets, and kitchens and baths planned for safety and convenience, easy access to all areas of the dwelling and, where desirable

and feasible, means of sounding an outside alarm in case of need. Community facilities receive particular attention in planning for their needs.[19]

FARMERS HOME ADMINISTRATION

Another significant program having direct implications upon the housing of the rural elderly is the Farmers Home Administration (FHA), of the U. S. Department of Agriculture. Under this agency are three programs which serve the rural elderly, namely, mortgage insurance on rental multifamily accommodations, direct loans for rental housing for the rural elderly, and financial assistance to older rural individuals.

Under section 515(b) of the Housing Act of 1949, as amended by the Senior Citizens Housing Act of 1962, FHA insures mortgages used in constructing new or rehabilitating existing multifamily rental housing for rural persons 62 years of age or older. Such facilities must be located in communities having a population under 2,500. This type of mortgage insurance can be secured by an individual, partnership, corporation, or trust acceptable to the secretary of agriculture, or by nonprofit sponsors. These mortgages involve repayment over a maximum period of 40 years, can equal 100 percent of the appraised value or cost of the project, and bear an interest rate of 5¾ percent. No income limitation is placed on the occupants of such units. Facilities so provided are of the housekeeping type.

Through section 515(a) of the Housing Act of 1949, amended by the act of 1962, direct loans are made by FHA to nonprofit organizations, including consumer cooperatives. Loans are to be repaid over a period up to 50 years at an interest rate of 3¾ percent. Dwelling units built under section 515(a) are available to rural persons 62 and over who can afford to pay rent somewhat higher than those required in public housing developments but less than that paid by persons occupying comparable privately provided housing. Income limits are established locally and usually range between $4,500 and $6,000. Facilities are for housekeeping rather than for congregate living.

As an example of how a small community may assist senior citizens in cooperating with the FHA's 515(a) program, a brief account is given of recent efforts of Oak Grove, Missouri, which has a population of some 1,100 persons, a hundred or so of whom lived in inadequate housing. In 1964 some twenty local leaders, representing all major sectors of community life, formed a non-profit association for the purpose of building 20 new apartments for older Oak Grove citizens. The association borrowed $108,000 from the Farmers Home Administration with which to build six one-story apartment buildings and a seventh one to serve as a community center. These structures, designed by an architect, were built on a one-acre lot which is attractively planted with shrubs and grass. Each apartment contains a kitchen, bathroom, and living and dining areas. The occupants pay a monthly rent ranging from $35 to $40. More than twice as many persons have applied for admission to the project as can be accommodated. This project and similar ones reach few people, but the act making it possible will enable hundreds of small communities to improve the housing environment of their aging populations.

The third program of the Farmers Home Administration, section 501 of the Housing Act of 1959, amended by the Senior Citizens Housing Act of 1962, assists older rural persons in the construction of new houses and in buying and rehabilitating existing ones. FHA makes direct loans to older persons and requires a co-signer if their income indicates an inability to repay the loan. These loans are to be repaid over a period of 33 years at an interest rate of 4 percent and can equal up to 100 percent of the improved value of the property. Since these loans extend over a period of 33 years, obviously many of the beneficiaries will be deceased before the loans are repaid. In defense of this long-term repayment period, an official in the program remarked, "We don't bury the house with the man."

From 1949 until 1964, the Farmers Home Administration was authorized to make outright home improvement grants to rural home owners ineligible for other types of assistance. These grants were used widely in 1963, when this activity was terminated by the Congress, for such improvements as re-roofing, winterproofing, repairing siding, providing an adequate water supply, and the like. This FHA action was not exclusively for the rural aged, but it was frequently used by the elderly.

These various housing programs operated by the federal government provide the means by which many older rural persons can secure more nearly adequate housing. Thus far, it would seem, only modest changes have been realized. However, many of the programs actually are less than 10 years old. Therefore, more time will have to pass before a sound appraisal can be made. Yet the indications are that they ultimately will go a long way toward meeting the housing needs of the aged who are reasonably well. With the exception of the Federal Housing Administration's "Sec. 321" program which assists with congregate accommodations, as well as with housekeeping units, most of the federal programs viewed thus far are largely or entirely concerned with providing housing for independent living.

PRIVATE PROGRAMS

Housing for the aged sponsored by the federal government is by no means the only manifestation of interest in the housing problems of the aged. Private individuals and organizations and nonprofit bodies are engaged in a variety of activities that affect the housing of many older persons. During the last fifteen years or so there has been a rapid growth in retirement communities. According to the National Council on the Aging, in 1965 there were 557 such developments in 41 states. Moreover, there were an additional 269 projects in progress. Until recently, retirement villages were largely found in the areas of the country having mild winters, particularly in Florida and California. But more recently this phenomenon of building entire villages and even cities for the aged has occurred in other parts of the country, especially in New York and New Jersey. Currently there are 34 completed developments in New York and 15 in New Jersey. Few retirement villages are found beyond the reaches of State Metropolitan Statistical Areas, and fewer still are found in strictly rural areas, though occasionally a retired farm couple from Minnesota or Iowa and a retired teacher from a small Indiana village may find their way to Leisure World in Arizona.

In a recent Senate report the following observations were made concerning such "new-towns" for the aged:

> These communities cater to the younger retirees usually having age limits beginning in the fifties and offering housing in a self-contained community tailored to a particular concept of retirement life. While it is probably true, as many witnesses have told the sub-committee, that most people desire to remain in their home communities after retirement

to be near family and friends and to maintain contact with normal community life, it is apparent that a sufficiently large number at any point in time are attracted to a retirement community setting to constitute a very substantial market for this type of development. . . .

Much of the growth of retirement communities has occurred apart from the programs specifically directed to senior citizens housing. Some have been developed without recourse to any Federal program, but most and certainly the largest of these developments have been financed under sections 203 and 213 of the National Housing Act.[20]

In view of the fact that most older rural persons prefer to continue living in or near their home communities and that most retirement villages are near larger cities, one doubts that many of the rural aged will move to retirement communities.

CHURCH-RELATED HOUSING

In addition to the housing activities of private enterprise resulting in retirement communities and trailer or mobile home parks (Florida has more than 1,700 trailer parks available to rural and urban people), religious denominations are increasing their efforts to provide more and better congregate housing facilities for the aged. Churches became active in the latter half of the eighteenth century in assisting with congregate care for the destitute and to a considerable degree took over the functions of almshouses prevalent during the eighteenth century. In the nineteenth century various religious and philanthropic groups established many homes for the poor aged. Since the Methodist Episcopal Church established the first Protestant home for the aged in New York City in 1850, it has been especially active in helping to meet the needs of the aged. In 1965 the Methodist Church sponsored retirement homes located in 41 states and the District of Columbia. Although these homes make no distinction in accepting an urban or a rural person, the large majority of them are located in or near cities. Most of these Methodist homes provide congregate living accommodations which vary in many ways.

For example, on the Pacific Coast is a home requiring entrance fees ranging from $8,000 to $18,000 for which the organization provides lifetime care, including medical. In Ohio the church sponsors a home which is supported by the residents, by pension and relief checks, and by contributions. One does not need to be a Methodist to be admitted, and a person with money is categorically refused admission. And the Methodist church operates a home for the aged at Milwaukee, Wisconsin, which permits lump-sum payments for life care or monthly payments of $150 for single persons and $200 for a couple.

The following are some of the major characteristics of homes for the aged sponsored by various religious denominations and fraternal organizations: (a) They provide a long-term care for persons whose median age is perhaps 75 to 80. (b) They usually provide congregate care. (c) They usually sponsor various activities, therapeutic and social, for the residents. (d) They normally accept men and women, married or single. (e) They charge a "founder's fee," a "founder's fee" plus a monthly payment, or a monthly payment only. (f) The homes agree to provide living arrangements, food, nursing, medical care, and so on, for the life of the person. (g) They try to provide a positive and cheerful attitude toward life. (h) The designs of newer homes are likely to be functional and aesthetically pleasing.

WESLEY MANOR

Wesley Manor Village is operated by the Methodist church and is located nine miles south of Jacksonville, Florida. This facility was completed in 1964 with the financial assistance of the Federal Housing Administration. In a brochure issued by the church, prospective applicants are advised: "In your retirement years you can have comfort and complete security in beautiful surroundings. Freedom from drudgery of everyday living. Medical and nursing care should you become ill. Recreational facilities and hobbies at hand. The companionship of those your own age. The knowledge that your spouse will be well cared for in the event of your passing. If you desire these features you can find them all in Wesley Manor!"

Wesley Manor has apartments to accommodate 296 residents which are located in 11 buildings. The development is an excellent example of good contemporary architecture and was cited in 1964 by the FHA for being outstanding in design. Areas are well lighted and furnished. Meals are served in a large dining room that commands a view of the Jurlington River, a tributary of the St. Johns River. In some of the apartments are pullman kitchens. This setting provides facilities for a large variety of hobbies and other activities—games, crafts, painting, study, concert, drama, and the like. In each of the 11 buildings is a well-equipped family-type lounge with a family-size kitchen.

To be accepted one must be at least 62 years of age and in reasonably good health. For those who need it after being accepted in the home, 24-hour nursing care is provided. Single persons as well as married couples are admitted. An admission fee of $1,500 for a single person and $2,000 for a married couple is charged. Monthly fees for single persons range from $275 to $445 and from $450 to $615 for couples. These fees cover the costs of "three meals a day and all medical services, except the Wesley Manor will not assume the cost of treating pre-existing medical conditions of the residents, nor will Wesley Manor assume the cost of maintenance drugs prescribed and in use before admission, nor over the counter drugs (patent medicine) desired by the resident. Wesley Manor does not pay for dental care, the purchase of glasses or hearing aids." The organization reserves the right to increase fees in the event of an increase in the "Federal Cost of Living Index" and taxes, providing the residents' financial status would allow such increases.[21]

This model home for older persons undoubtedly provides a most favorable setting for those who are well enough physically and able financially to be admitted. But, of course, other types of arrangements will have to serve the needs of the vast majority of older persons—those ill and impoverished and unwilling to leave their relatives and familiar environment for a setting such as Wesley Manor. Yet, only the existence of many different kinds of facilities will meet the needs of *all* older persons.

CONCLUSION

Many older rural people encounter relatively great isolation. For a number of decades many younger persons have left farms, hamlets, and villages for town and cities. Better educational opportunities as well as different kinds of jobs have meant that styles of lives of younger persons are quite different from their parents.

However, with improved means of transportation, one doubts that isolation from one's kin is as great as it is often said to be. This does not mean, nevertheless, that older rural people live with their children to the degree that they once did.

But there are other forms of isolation which these older persons suffer. In twentieth-century America the city is the dominant ecological unit. Medical care, recreation opportunities, visiting welfare workers, employment, and cultural assets generally are found there. Rural villages, as idealized refuges for many rural senior citizens, are losing ground. As a result of shifts of population and services from the rural areas, many communities have lost their economic base.[22] This decline is occurring at a time when local nursing homes, physicians, and small hospitals are increasingly needed.

When one considers the decline of the rural farm population, the mobility of younger age groups, the paucity of rural services generally, one can but conclude that the older rural people will encounter many problems less common to those who live in larger communities. This, of course, does not imply that older rural couples in relatively good health may not continue greatly to enjoy a rural setting.

There are some 1.9 million aged couples in the United States whose incomes are less than $2,500 a year and 5.7 million older individuals whose annual incomes are less than $1,800. In commenting on the relationship between housing and economic status, Alleger stated, "The *real housing* problem of the rural aged is one of limited financial resources. Healthy and still active older persons with adequate incomes and savings experience no housing problems except those common to their communities."[23]

Despite the limited economic resources available to most older rural persons, the majority of them manage to remain in their own homes, inadequate as many are, until death of a spouse or until ill health forces them to live with their children, in a nursing home, or, rarely, in a home for the aged. The Social Security Act sounded the death knell of the poorhouse, but many older rural people are compelled to rely upon relatives, charities, or the government to see them through their final days. The prospects of a program of medical care under social security and of a better educated and a more financially able older citizen tomorrow present a brighter picture for the future.

A third major problem which older persons face, regardless of where they live, is health. As was noted earlier, on the average older persons are ill far more often than younger persons, require hospitalization more often, and recover more slowly. This is the case despite the fact that they are least able to pay for needed medical care. Housing can affect health and a person's ability to remain independent though in poor health. For example, an arthritic wife might be able to continue light housekeeping only if she were able to live in a one-story house or apartment that had modern facilities and labor-saving devices.

In all probability, more changes have occurred in the lives of today's older persons than in the lives of any other older generation of Americans. Modifications in housing, in varying degrees, have mirrored these changes. By the 1930's the results of efforts to foster reforms began to bear fruit. The Social Security Act was the first major breakthrough. Since then many other public programs, usually federal or federal and state, have provided a variety of avenues through which help reaches the rural aged. Half or more of such programs have been in operation too short a period of time to have accomplished a great deal. However, they have gained experience and have provided a structure that increasingly will improve the living arrangements of older persons.

It is recognized that more efforts to meet the needs of the aged are required today than ever before because of the rapidly growing number of older people and because of a growing conviction that the aged deserve more consideration than they have received in the past. The following are some of the major steps that should be taken if all older people are to be adequately and satisfactorily housed.

Individuals and policy-makers need to develop and carry out long-range plans calculated to assure that people will reach retirement age with reasonable financial resources and the best health possible. Also, plans should be made for housing before the onset of old age. For example, it may be that federal agencies should extend their efforts to assist persons 62 years old to include those aged 50 to 62. Many persons in their sixties seem to be unwilling to make desirable adjustments in their housing.

Small communities should develop a comprehensive plan for assisting the aged with their housing needs. Such plans should be designed to help older persons to cope with their shelter needs as they pass from independence to dependence. This would require housing that would prolong the capability to remain independent as long as possible, congregate housing for those unable to continue living independently, nursing homes for longtime care, and a hospital for emergencies and more serious illnesses. Despite the fact that numerous studies indicate that most older rural people want to live in their communities as long as possible, many villages and small towns are completely devoid of congregate housing, nursing homes, homes for the aged, and hospitals.

As a result of default and indifference on the part of private organizations and individuals, the federal government may be forced to be all things to all people. Yet a framework already exists through which private and public effort can be coordinated. For example, the federal government will insure mortgages on a variety of housing facilities sponsored by business groups. At the same time, nonprofit organizations can secure loans for a variety of housing facilities for the rural aged. Churches and other nonprofit groups have a better opportunity than ever before to take the initiative in providing homes, nursing homes, and other facilities for the aged. Effort needs to be made to assure a greater degree of coordination of the efforts being made by federal agencies, profit-motivated groups, nonprofit organizations, and individuals.

There is genuine need for research concerning where and how older rural people live. Four conditions underscore the importance of research in this area. First, thus far only limited studies have been made of the housing needs of the rural aged, and usually those that have been done have been descriptive; second, government programs are being operated largely without the benefit of research; third, the rural aged are not homogeneous enough to be considered as a group; fourth, the characteristics of older rural persons is changing very rapidly.

The following are areas in which research is most needed: (a) How the housing needs of the rural Negro are being met. (b) The variations in housing aspirations of older rural persons of differing socioeconomic status. (c) How housing and a series of related home services might reduce the demands for nursing home and hospital care. (d) The extent to which persons would make housing improvements if federal programs reduced the minimum age limit from 62 to 50. (e) The extent to which older rural persons would use and benefit by professional counseling service if it were available. (f) The incidence of social and residential mobility among various categories of older rural people.

Within the last two decades relatively few studies of the housing of the rural aged, regardless of their nature, have been made. To the writer's knowledge no comprehensive research projects on the housing of rural senior citizens have been completed. The ACTION (The American Council to Improve Our Neighborhoods) series of books contains much information on urban housing issues, and the publications of the Commission on Race and Housing present many findings on urban and suburban problems relating to racial housing. But where, one may ask, are comparable volumes on the housing of almost a third of the nation—the rural population, including the aged? Moreover, statistics on rural housing are few since often federal agencies issue reports on "nonfarm" phenomena.

In speculating about the reasons for these oversights or exclusions, one wonders if representatives of rural people at the national level press less vigorously for their constituents than do those representing urban and suburban people. If this speculation should prove correct, this would be a paradox because the older rural people of today, by and large, are the end products of an agrarian system that once molded the tenor of the nation. Yet the new and bold programs of the federal government in the 1960's could go far in removing many of the factors that cause rural life to be placed on the lower end of so many scales of comparison.

NOTES

[1] Howard L. Hill and Frank H. Maier, "The Farm Family in Transition," in *A Place to Live, The Yearbook of Agriculture, 1963* (Washington, D. C.: Government Printing Office, 1964), p. 168.

[2] Isabel Campbell Bruce and Edith Eickhoff, *The Michigan Poor Law* (Chicago: The University of Chicago Press, 1936), p. 74.

[3] *Ibid.*, p. 76.

[4] I. M. Rubinow (ed.), *The Care of the Aged*, Proceedings of the Deutsch Foundation Conference 1930 (Chicago: The University of Chicago Press, 1931), p. 8.

[5] Helen L. Johnston, "Health Trends in Rural America," in *A Place to Live*, p. 191.

[6] Bureau of the Census, *Census of Housing*, Vol. VI, *Rural Housing, 1960* (Washington, D. C., 1963), Table 1.

[7] Glenn H. Beyer, *Housing and Society* (New York: The Macmillan Company, 1965), p. 412.

194   OLDER RURAL AMERICANS

⁸ Glenn H. Beyer and Sylvia G. Wahl, *The Elderly and Their Housing* (Cornell University Agricultural Experiment Station, Bulletin 989; Ithaca, N. Y., 1963), p. 31.

⁹ James E. Montgomery, *Social Characteristics of the Aged in a Small Pennsylvania Community* (Research Publication 233; University Park, Pa.: Pennsylvania State University, 1965).

¹⁰ Tessie Agan and Elinor M. Anderson, *Housing the Rural Aged in Kansas* (Kansas State University Agricultural Experiment Station, Bulletin 427; Manhattan, Kan., 1961), p. 13.

¹¹ James E. Montgomery, Maie Nygren, and Sara S. Sutker, *Rural Housing in Garfield County, Oklahoma* (Oklahoma State University Publications, Vol. 56; Stillwater, Okla., 1959), pp. 21-23.

¹² May L. Cowles and Clara G. Sweeney, *Housing Rural Aged People in Wisconsin* (University of Wisconsin Agricultural Experiment Station, Bulletin 536; Madison, Wis., 1959), p. 18.

¹³ Agan and Anderson, *Housing the Rural Aged in Kansas*, pp. 13-20.

¹⁴ Maie Nygren and Sara S. Sutker, "A Report on the Study 'Toward Recommendations Becoming Realities in Housing for the Rural Aged,'" unpublished paper presented at the Oklahoma Home Economics Association Annual Meeting, Oklahoma City, March 14, 1964.

¹⁵ Beyer and Wahl, *The Elderly and Their Housing*, p. 19.

¹⁶ Federal Housing Administration, *Some Facts about FHA Housing for the Elderly Projects and People* (Washington, D. C., 1964), No. 372, pp. 1-3.

¹⁷ U. S. Senate, *Developments in Aging 1956 to 1963*, Report No. 8, 88th Congress, 1st Session (Washington, D. C., 1963), pp. 106-107.

¹⁸ *The Seventeenth Annual Report Housing and Home Finance Agency* (Washington, D. C., 1964), p. 363.

¹⁹ *Ibid.*, p. 285.

²⁰ U. S. Senate, *Developments in Aging 1963 and 1964*, Report No. 124, 89th Congress, 1st Session (Washington, D. C., 1965), pp. 37-38.

²¹ Publicity materials distributed by Wesley Manor, 1965, Jacksonville, Fla.

²² Dwight A. Nesmith, "The Small Rural Town," in *A Place to Live*, p. 184.

²³ Daniel E. Alleger, "Older Rural People," in *A Place to Live*, p. 54.

BERT L. ELLENBOGEN

Health Status of
the Rural Aged

The growth of medical knowledge, the diffusion of medical technology, and the expansion and specialization of health care in the
United States have had a profound impact on the health of the
nation. Between 1900 and 1960 the crude death rate dramatically
declined, almost all major communicable diseases sharply decreased, and life expectancy at birth increased from 47.3 to 64.7
years.[1]
Despite progress in health care, many segments of the population lack adequate health services. Among these groups are older
persons, who by their nature are subject to physical incapacities.
Research has shown that the limited financial resources of many
of the aged restrict the medical care they seek and obtain.[2] This
may be particularly true of those residing in rural areas, where
economic resources generally are less than in urban areas. In addition, the inadequacy of their medical care may also be explained, in part, by the fact that many older persons in rural areas
of the nation express rather strong beliefs in the efficacy of folk
medicine. The self-administered nostrum, the potion, the all-
purpose salve, along with the use of the "healer," the midwife,
and other prescientific medical personnel, although present in
both city and country, are more common in the latter environment.[3]
Little systematic attention, however, has been given to the
health behavior of the rural aged.[4] This lack of concern may have

been influenced by the traditional belief that the natural advantages of the rural setting offer a more healthful way of life. Whatever the case, health surveys in selected areas of the nation have shown that despite the natural advantages of rural life, in many respects rural people in the United States are less healthy than their urban counterparts.[5]

In presenting the following data on the health conditions of older persons living in rural areas of the United States, wherever possible, comparisons are made with the urban aged. The task is complicated by several difficulties: a lack of statistics on certain key items such as causes of death and types of acute conditions; an absence of information on certain control variables; a lack of comparable definitions of rural and urban areas; and the changes in reporting procedures which have taken place in recent years.

PHYSICAL HEALTH

Mortality rates are commonly used as an index of the health status of populations. Data for nonmetropolitan counties in the nation in 1960 indicate the precipitous increase in mortality for men and women aged 65 and over, but the rate is lower for women than for men (Table 1). Data for nonmetropolitan areas of New York state in 1960 showed that mortality rates varied with the size of the locality. For persons aged 65 to 74, mortality rates were higher in the larger localities (10,000 inhabitants and over) but for those 75 years and over, the mortality rates were higher in the smaller localities (under 10,000 population, Table 2).

Acute conditions (those ailments of less than three months'

Table 1. Mortality Rates per 1,000 Population for Adults Aged 25 and Over in Nonmetropolitan Counties by Sex in the United States, 1960

Sex	25-44 years	45-64 years	65-74 years	75 years and over
Both	2.4	11.1	36.0	104.6
Male	2.9	14.4	46.0	116.5
Female	1.8	7.9	26.9	94.1

Source: Adapted from: U. S. Department of Health, Education, and Welfare, *Vital Statistics of the U. S.: 1960,* Vol. I, *Natality,* Table 5-6, p. 5-19 and Vol. II, *Mortality,* Part B, Table 9-4, p. 9-87 (Washington, D. C., 1962)

Table 2. Mortality Rates per 1,000 Population in Nonmetropolitan Areas of New York State by Age and Sex, 1960

Sex and age	All nonmetropolitan areas	Localities with 10,000 inhabitants and over	Localities under 10,000 inhabitants
Males			
25-44 years	2.5	2.9	2.4
45-64 years	15.1	17.3	14.4
65-74 years	49.5	53.9	47.9
75 years and over	131.3	129.5	131.9
Females			
25-44 years	1.4	1.5	1.3
45-64 years	8.0	8.4	7.9
65-74 years	30.3	31.2	29.9
75 years and over	103.7	100.3	105.1

Source: Unpublished data provided by Office of Biostatistics, State of New York Department of Health, 1965.

duration requiring medical attention and restricting activity) provide another index of the physical status of the aged. In nonmetropolitan counties of the nation in 1963-64, persons 65 years and over were less prone to have acute conditions than the younger age groups, particularly those 25 to 44 years of age. However, the incidence of acute conditions was greater among farm than nonfarm dwellers among the aged groups (Table 3).

Table 3. Incidence of Acute Conditions in Standard Nonmetropolitan Counties by Place of Residence and Age in the United States, 1963-64

Age	Number of acute conditions per 100 persons per year		
	Nonmetropolitan counties	Nonfarm	Farm
25-44 years	177.2	184.1	140.8
45-64 years	145.9	141.2	164.7
65 years and over	117.4	115.9	125.1

Source: Adapted from: National Center for Health Statistics, *Vital Statistics, Data from National Health Survey, Acute Condition: Incidence and Associated Disability,* Series 10, No. 15 (Washington, D. C., 1965), Table 11, p. 22.

Injuries, one specific type of acute condition, tend to decline with age for rural residents. Individuals 25 to 44 years of age have an injury rate of 244.3 per 1,000 population per year as compared with a rate of 206.2 for those aged 65 and over. The rate of accidents is higher for farm than nonfarm persons under 65 years but higher for nonfarm than farm residents 65 years and over

(Table 4). When accidents do occur, older persons pay a higher social cost than do younger age groups. Rural people aged 65 and over had restricted activity and bed disability rates substantially higher than did persons under age 65, a pattern which maintained for farm and nonfarm dwellers, 1959-61 (Table 5).

Table 4. Number of Rural Adults Aged 25 and Over Injured per Year by Age and Residence in the United States, 1959-61

Age	Number of persons injured per year per 1,000 population		
	Rural	Nonfarm	Farm
25-44 years	244.3	233.8	275.9
45-64 years	227.7	220.3	241.4
65 years and over	206.2	208.2	202.5

Source: Adapted from health statistics from the U. S. National Health Survey: U. S. Department of Health, Education, and Welfare, *Persons Injured*, Series B, No. 37 (Washington, D. C., 1963), Table 18, p. 29.

A traditional view of illness and accidents may contribute to underreporting on the part of the aged. The aged may interpret physical discomfort and restricted activity as an inherent part of aging and thus may be more disinclined than younger individuals to report physical complaints when queried. Although this possibility cannot be discounted, it is highly questionable that it

Table 5. Social Cost of Injuries to Rural Adults Aged 25 and Over by Age and Residence in the United States, 1959-61

Residence and age	Restricted activity (number of days per 100 population per year)	Bed disability (days of bed disability per 100 persons per year)
Rural		
25-44 years	262.4	63.8
45-64 years	442.8	109.2
65 years and over	768.8	210.9
Nonfarm		
25-44 years	258.9	62.4
45-64 years	401.2	109.7
65 years and over	834.2	227.0
Farm		
25-44 years	273.2	68.1
45-64 years	519.0	108.3
65 years and over	650.6	181.7

Source: Adapted from health statistics from the U. S. National Health Survey: U. S. Department of Health, Education, and Welfare, *Persons Injured*, Series B, No. 40 (Washington, D. C., 1963), Table 1, p. 10 and Table 2, p. 11.

is a significant factor in explaining the difference in the incidence of acute conditions between older and younger age groups. A more likely explanation is in the selective process of illness with aging. That is, certain acute conditions may be experienced by the aged at an earlier period in life and immunities toward these conditions may have been built up or the condition may have been treated in such a way that recurrence is not likely. In addition, withdrawal from the occupational setting may result in the older person's being less exposed to certain dangerous conditions.

Health studies have consistently found that chronic illness and impairments are related to aging. Data from the National Health Survey for 1957-59 give evidence of this trend among rural adults. By age 65, eight out of every ten rural individuals reported a chronic condition, and the proportion was slightly greater for farm than nonfarm residents (Table 6). Rates of selected chronic conditions and impairments for rural persons aged 45 and over, 1957 and 1959, are shown in Table 7. With the exception of diabetes and asthma and hay fever, the prevalence of chronic conditions increases markedly with age. The most sa-

Table 6. Percentage of Persons Aged 45 and Over with Chronic Conditions and/or Impairments by Age and Residence in the United States, 1957-59

Age and residence	Percentage with chronic conditions and/or impairments
45 years and over	
Rural	69.5
Nonfarm	68.1
Farm	72.0
45-54 years	
Rural	60.1
Nonfarm	58.7
Farm	62.9
55-64 years	
Rural	69.9
Nonfarm	68.5
Farm	72.3
65-74 years	
Rural	78.2
Nonfarm	77.0
Farm	80.2
75 years and over	
Rural	87.5
Nonfarm	86.8
Farm	88.8

Source: Adapted from health statistics from the U. S. National Health Survey: U. S. Department of Health, Education, and Welfare, *Older Persons Selected Health Characteristics*, Series C, No. 4 (Washington, D. C., 1960), Table 2, p. 11.

Table 7. Rate per 1,000 Population of Selected Chronic Conditions and Impairments for Rural Persons Aged 45 and Over by Age and Residence in the United States, 1957 and 1959

Age and residence	Chronic conditions						Impairments		
	Heart condition	High blood pressure	Diabetes	Arthritis and rheumatism	Hernia	Asthma, hay fever	Visual	Aural	Paralytic, involving major extremities
45 years and over									
Rural	92.1	91.5	27.0	208.4	39.9	65.3	55.1	96.4	13.8
Nonfarm	91.5	89.8	26.9	191.1	36.1	66.2	54.9	97.3	13.9
Farm	93.0	94.7	27.1	239.7	46.8	63.5	55.6	95.0	13.8
45-54 years									
Rural	38.2	51.5	12.9	130.4	22.9	61.8	22.6	39.0	—
Nonfarm	37.8	47.1	12.0	112.4	20.9	61.3	21.1	37.5	—
Farm	39.0	59.9	14.7	164.2	26.8	62.8	25.6	41.9	—
55-64 years									
Rural	85.2	95.2	31.1	221.5	39.0	72.7	38.0	72.7	—
Nonfarm	86.4	93.6	31.2	203.6	31.8	77.2	36.9	76.3	14.8
Farm	83.4	98.0	30.9	252.3	51.4	65.0	40.1	66.6	—
65-74 years									
Rural	143.4	138.7	45.1	291.6	59.1	66.1	76.7	150.2	18.4
Nonfarm	142.0	142.5	47.8	273.8	55.2	65.9	81.2	149.9	18.6
Farm	146.0	132.0	40.4	323.4	66.0	66.8	68.5	151.0	18.2
75 years and over									
Rural	217.7	144.4	34.7	313.8	71.1	57.0	184.0	277.4	42.9
Nonfarm	217.1	145.9	34.4	306.8	70.4	57.0	182.7	284.2	38.6
Farm	218.8	141.8	35.6	326.7	72.4	57.0	186.4	265.0	50.8

Source: Adapted from health statistics from the U. S. National Health Survey: U. S. Department of Health, Education, and Welfare, *Older Persons Selected Health Characteristics*, Series C, No. 4 (Washington, D. C., 1960), Table 22, p. 36.

lient of these ailments among the rural elderly were arthritis and rheumatism, heart conditions, and high blood pressure; hearing problems constituted the most important impairment.

One of the possible consequences of chronic conditions and impairments is the limitation imposed on the activity of the afflicted individuals. Not only are chronic conditions and impairments more prevalent with increasing age but they are more likely to bring a reduction in activity. More than two-thirds of the rural individuals 65 years and over with a chronic condition or impairment reported that their activity was restricted to some extent, and one-quarter of rural persons 75 years and over reported major limitation on their activity. The aged residing on farms reported slightly more restrictions than did those living in nonfarm areas (Table 8).

Physical health conditions appear to be more favorable for the aged residing in an urban than in a rural environment. This is evident in the incidence of acute conditions; the rate for the

Table 8. Percentage of Rural Persons Aged 45 and Over with Chronic Limitation of Activity by Age and Residence in the United States, 1957-59

Age and Residence	Persons with no chronic conditions	Persons with 1+ chronic conditions		
		Limitation of activity		
		None	Partial	Major
45 years and over				
Rural	30.5	41.5	21.5	6.5
Nonfarm	31.9	41.4	20.0	6.7
Farm	28.0	41.7	24.1	6.2
45-54 years				
Rural	39.9	45.3	13.1	1.7
Nonfarm	41.4	44.8	11.9	1.9
Farm	37.1	46.2	15.4	1.3
55-64 years				
Rural	30.1	44.5	21.1	4.3
Nonfarm	31.5	43.9	20.1	4.5
Farm	27.7	45.4	22.8	4.1
65-74 years				
Rural	21.8	37.3	31.1	9.8
Nonfarm	23.0	37.5	29.1	10.4
Farm	19.7	36.9	34.7	8.7
75 years and over				
Rural	12.5	26.5	36.3	24.7
Nonfarm	13.2	28.3	34.2	24.3
Farm	11.2	23.1	40.3	25.4

Source: Adapted from health statistics from the U. S. National Health Survey, U. S. Department of Health, Education, and Welfare, *Older Persons Selected Health Characteristics*, Series C, No. 4 (Washington, D. C., 1960), Table 2, p. 11.

rural aged (117.4 per 1,000 persons per year) is somewhat higher than for those residing in standard metropolitan areas (113.0). Likewise, the incidence of injuries for the aged from the metropolitan area (180.7 per 1,000 persons per year) is lower than that for rural individuals 65 years and over (206.2). Urbanites 65 years and over not only report a lower percentage with chronic conditions, but those afflicted are less likely to be disabled than are the elderly residing in rural areas (Table 9). Prevalence rates on eight out of the nine selected chronic conditions and impairments favor older persons from urban areas over the rural (Table 10). It is only with respect to mortality rates that those from more urban settings fail to portray a more favorable physical status. Since nonmetropolitan areas cannot be defined as

Table 9. Percentage of Persons Aged 65 and Over with Chronic Conditions and/or Impairments by Age and Residence in the United States 1957-59

Age and residence	Chronic conditions and/or impairments	Chronic conditions and/or impairments with limited activity
65-74 years		
Urban	72.1	32.8
Rural	78.2	40.9
75 years and older		
Urban	80.9	51.8
Rural	87.5	61.0

Source: Adapted from health statistics from the U. S. National Health Survey: U. S Department of Health, Education, and Welfare, *Older Persons Selected Health Characteristics*, Series C, No. 4 (Washington, D. C., 1960), Table 2, p. 11.

completely rural, there is no way of ascertaining whether real differences in mortality rates exist between rural and urban aged populations. Data on life expectancy for rural and urban dwellers in the nation have been nonexistent since 1939. The findings up to that time showed greater longevity for those in rural areas, although the gap between the two residential areas appeared to be closing with the passing of time.

MENTAL HEALTH

Information about mental illness and emotional disturbance among the aged is extremely limited. Part of the data void may arise from a lack of consensus on basic concepts relative to men-

Table 10. Rate per 1,000 Population of Selected Chronic Conditions and Impairments for Persons Aged 65 and Over by Age and Residence in the United States, 1957 and 1959

Age and Residence	Chronic Conditions						Impairments		
	Heart condition	High blood pressure	Diabetes	Arthritis and rheumatism	Hernia	Asthma-hay fever	Visual	Aural	Paralytic, involving major extremities
65-74 years									
Urban	120.9	123.1	41.7	236.4	44.4	51.7	67.6	114.6	15.8
Rural	143.4	138.7	45.1	291.6	59.1	66.1	76.7	150.2	18.4
75 years and over									
Urban	170.5	122.2	35.8	269.6	60.8	41.9	156.4	248.8	28.1
Rural	217.7	144.4	34.7	313.8	71.1	57.0	186.0	277.4	42.9

Source: Adapted from health statistics from the U. S. National Health Survey: U. S. Department of Health, Education, and Welfare, Older Persons Selected Health Characteristics, Series C, No. 4 (Washington, D. C., 1960), Table 22, p. 36.

tal health.[6] There are indications, however, that the proportion of aged admitted to mental hospitals has been increasing. Goldhammer and Marshall point out that for those 50 years and older there has been a marked increase in the age-specific admission rates to mental hospitals between 1840 and 1940.[7] Several interpretations may be given to this trend. It may actually reflect a greater incidence of mental illness among the aged; it may indicate the increased availability of mental hospital facilities; and it may imply a decline in the support pattern of the family and a reluctance to maintain mentally ill aged members in the household. The question of whether or not rural and urban environments have differential effects on the mental condition of their respective populations remains undecided, and its problematic nature remains.

Self-evaluation of emotional stress is a common means of assessing mental health. A national survey conducted at the University of Michigan in 1957 focused on self-perceptions of adjustment and methods of coping with emotional problems of a national sample of adults 21 years and over.[8] Data concerning symptoms of psychological and physical anxiety were collected. Psychological anxiety referred to a conscious distress state indicated by affirmative responses to items such as loss of appetite, difficulties in sleeping, and dizziness. The findings indicated that among three age groups (young adults—21 to 44 years, middle-aged—45 to 54 years, and the old—55 years and over) residing in the rural areas of the nation, anxiety scores tended to rise with increased age. This is likewise true with respect to physical anxiety. The oldest adults reported a greater percentage of affirmative responses indicating physical anxiety symptoms (shortness of breath and "hard" heart beating) than the younger age groups (Table 11).

A number of other studies dealing with aspects of the mental health of the aged have been undertaken in various parts of the nation. Each of these studies relied on the self-rating of the respondent, although in each case different items were solicited. A study in a small community in Pennsylvania on a sample of adults 65 years and over reported that about one-third of the respondents evaluated their mental health as "poor." When the sample was categorized into three age groupings (65 to 74, 75 to 84, and 85 years and older), no significant difference was revealed between self-rating of mental health and chronological

Table 11. Percentage Distribution of Anxiety Scores for Rural Adults 21
Years and Over in the United States, 1960

Age and anxiety categories	Scores		
	High	Medium	Low
Psychological anxiety			
Young	3.8	59.1	37.1
Middle-aged	6.9	61.6	31.5
Old	17.3	50.4	32.3
Physical anxiety			
Young	2.6	32.2	65.2
Middle-aged	7.9	29.9	62.2
Old	15.3	41.3	43.4

Source: Unpublished data from University of Michigan survey and Gerald Gurin, *Americans View Their Mental Health* (New York: Basic Books, 1960).

age. A positive relationship was evident, however, between mental health and self-rating of physical health.[9]

A study in South Dakota reported that about one-third of the respondents (35 percent) had low personal adjustment (viz., morale), but no significant difference was reported between personal adjustment and chronological age. However, adjustment was significantly related to the respondents' self-concept of age and to his self-evaluation of his physical health.[10]

Several other studies on the rural aged have queried respondents on "despair" and on items related to personal adjustment.[11] Although the self-evaluation measures in these studies were found to be related to the self-rating of physical health, the relationship with chronological age for those beyond 65 years was inconsistent.

As part of the Hunterdon County Study on Chronic Illness, a clinical evaluation was made by medical personnel of 846 rural persons. The findings portray a somewhat different pattern for the mental condition of the aged than the previous studies reported. Whereas those 65 years and over had a slightly higher percentage of psychoses than either the age group 45 to 64 or 25 to 44 years, the converse is true with respect to psychoneuroses and personality disorders. In contrast with 9.9 percent for the middle-aged and 13.6 percent for the younger aged adults, 2 percent of the aged had these mental conditions. Percentages in this study were weighted in order to compensate for the differential sampling ratios that were employed.[12]

First-admission rates to public mental hospitals provide another source of data about the mental health of the rural aged. In nonmetropolitan areas of 12 states in 1960, individuals 65 years and over were more likely to be admitted to a mental hospital than younger adults. Those 65 to 75 years had a first-admission rate more than twice that of younger adult age groups; those 75 and over had a rate that exceeded that of the younger adults by more than seven times (Table 12).

Table 12. Rate of First Admissions to Public Mental Hospitals in 12 Reporting States for Nonmetropolitan Areas, 1960

Age	Rate per 1000 Population
25-44	44.8
45-64	40.4
65-74	100.9
75 and over	303.6
Total	40.6

Source: Unpublished data provided by the Office of Biometry, National Institute of Mental Health, Aug. 1966.

In 1960, a comparison of first admissions to public mental hospitals by place of residence indicated that rates per 100,000 aged persons were higher in nonmetropolitan than in metropolitan areas and, among persons 75 years and over, the lowest rates maintained for localities under 10,000 in population (Table 13). Data on first admissions of persons aged 65 and over to mental hospitals in the state of Wisconsin from 1960 to 1962 showed that counties with the highest urbanization scores have an admission rate (455 per 100,000 population) three times higher than coun-

Table 13. Rate of First Admissions per 100,000 Aged Persons to New York State Civil State Hospitals, 1960

Area from which admitted	Aged 65-74	Aged 75 and over
State	219	645
Total metropolitan areas	208	639
New York City	212	641
Other localities 10,000 and over	269	703
Localities under 10,000	144	558
Total nonmetropolitan areas	270	664
Localities 10,000 and over	370	969
Localities under 10,000	230	545

Source: Annual Report, State of New York Department of Mental Hygiene, 1960, with population data on age groups provided by New York State Department of Health.

ties with the lowest level of urbanization (182 per 100,000 population).[13]

The data presented here permit few generalizations about the mental health condition of the rural aged. Those 65 years and over tend to have self-perceptions of higher anxiety and lower morale than younger rural adults, but these self-perceptions are related to self-ratings of physical health and not chronological age. Rural older persons experience more psychoses but fewer psychoneurotic reactions and personality disorders than younger adults. However, as Trussell points out, "The presence of diagnosable conditions in the general classification of 'mental, psychoneurotic and personality disorders' understates somewhat the importance of emotional factors in disease."[14]

Few conclusions can be drawn about mental health conditions of the rural aged in comparison with those in urban areas. Rural older persons score slightly higher on self-perceptions of psychological and physical anxiety than the aged in small towns and cities, in suburbs of large cities, or in metropolitan centers.[15]

HEALTH SERVICES

An important consideration in maintaining the health of the population at a high level is the availability and use of health services. The distribution of medical and health care services has favored urban centers, evident in the concentration of research centers, hospitals, clinics, medical specialists, dentists, and ancillary medical personnel in the more populated areas. As shown in Table 14, health service ratios tend to increase as the population size of the county categories increases. Not only do rural counties have the lowest ratio of physicians but rural doctors are older and less likely to be trained in one of the specialties. In isolated rural counties of the nation in 1960, 84 percent of the practicing physicians were general practitioners, and 40 percent were aged 55 years or over.[16] In many sections of the nation there has been an exodus of doctors from rural to urban areas and there has been extreme difficulty in finding replacements for rural doctors. Shortages in other health services and personnel, including dentists, dental hygienists, and nursing homes, are found in many rural areas of the nation.[17]

Table 14. Ratio of Health Facilities to Population by County Group, in the United States, 1962

| County group | Number per 100,000 population | | | | | Number per 1,000 population |
	Den-tists	Nurses, active	Pharma-cists	Physicians, total	Sanitary engineers	Hospital beds
Greater metropolitan	71.0	327.5	81.2	205.3	4.1	4.0
Lesser metropolitan	52.0	339.6	65.2	153.0	3.5	3.9
Adjacent to metropolitan	38.7	254.2	51.3	91.5	1.5	3.2
Isolated semi-rural	40.6	242.8	56.0	100.4	1.5	4.1
Isolated rural	27.4	125.9	45.3	59.1	0.3	2.0

Source: Maryland Y. Pernell and Kathryn I. Baker, *Health Manpower Source Book, Section 19: Location of Manpower in 8 Occupations, 1962,* U. S. Department of Health, Education, and Welfare (Washington, D. C., 1965), p. 13.

The use pattern of medical doctors by the rural aged is shown in Table 15. Rural nonfarm residents made greater use of physicians than did those who lived on farms. However, very slight differences existed between rural farm and nonfarm aged in the time interval between visits to a physician (Table 16) or to a dentist (Table 17).

The use of hospitals by the rural aged is shown in Table 18. The discharge rates indicate that the greatest use of these facilities was made by the youngest adult group (25 to 34), followed by those 65 years and over. The aged had the longest hospital stay of any of the age groups. The average duration of hospital stay for individuals 65 and over (14.4 days) was almost three

Table 15. Average Number of Physician Visits per Person per Year for Rural Persons Aged 45 and Over in the United States, 1957-59

Residence	Aged 45-54	Aged 55-64	Aged 65-74	Aged 75 years and over
Rural	4.6	5.5	6.1	7.1
Nonfarm	5.2	5.9	6.2	7.6
Farm	3.6	5.0	5.9	6.2

Source: Adapted from health statistics from U. S. National Health Survey: U. S. Department of Health, Education, and Welfare, *Older Persons Selected Health Characteristics,* Series C, No. 4 (Washington, D. C., 1960), Tables 31, 32, and 33, pp. 49-51.

Table 16. Percentage of Rural Individuals Aged 45 and Over Reporting Visit to Physician Within a Year by Residence and Age in the United States 1963-64

Residence and age	Percentage
Outside of Standard Metropolitan Areas	
45-54 years	62.6
55-64 years	61.7
65-74 years	67.9
75 years and over	71.9
Nonfarm	
45-54 years	63.6
55-64 years	62.4
65-74 years	69.0
75 years and over	71.8
Farm	
45-54 years	58.4
55-64 years	58.8
65-74 years	62.5
75 years and over	72.6

Source: Adapted from health statistics from the U. S. National Health Survey, U. S. Department of Health, Education, and Welfare, *Physician Visits: Interval of Visits and Children's Routine Checkup,* Series 10, No. 19 (Washington, D. C., 1965), Table 5, p. 19.

times longer than that for persons 25 to 34 years (5.6 days). Use of hospitals and duration of stay varied with place of residence. The aged from the rural nonfarm areas made greater use of hospitals than did those who lived on farms.

Table 17. Percentage Distribution of Dental Visits for Rural Persons Aged 25 and Over by Age and Residence in the United States, 1957-59

| Residence and age | Time interval since last visit to dentist | | | |
	Within 1 year	More than 1 year	Never	Don't know
Rural				
25-44 years	60.7	33.9	3.0	2.4
45-64 years	40.6	53.5	2.5	3.4
65 years and over	19.3	70.9	3.1	6.7
Rural nonfarm				
25-44 years	62.9	32.8	2.0	2.3
45-64 years	43.9	50.8	1.9	3.4
65 years and over	19.3	71.1	2.7	6.9
Rural farm				
25-44 years	55.0	36.6	5.6	2.8
45-64 years	34.9	58.1	3.6	3.4
65 years and over	19.3	70.7	3.7	6.3

Source: Adapted from health statistics from the U. S. National Health Survey: U. S. Department of Health, Education, and Welfare, *Dental Care: Interval and Frequency of Visits,* Series B, No. 14 (Washington, D. C., 1960), Table 3, p. 14.

One of the means used to meet hospital and health care costs is health insurance. The National Health Survey collected information on three types of insurance coverage for 1959: hospital, surgical, and doctor's visit for rural adults 45 years of age and over. Of the three plans, hospital insurance was the most commonly held, surgical coverage was next, and policies covering doctor's visitations was least subscribed. Subscription to health insurance decreased markedly with age for rural dwellers. Individuals 45 to 54 years subscribed to hospital or surgical insurance

Table 18. Use of Short-Stay Hospitals by Rural Patients Aged 25 and Over by Age and Residence in the United States, 1958-60

Residence and age	Number of discharges per 1,000 population per year	Average length of stay in days
Rural		
25-34 years	179.0	5.6
35-44 years	122.8	7.3
45-64 years	121.5	9.5
65 years and over	155.7	14.4
Nonfarm		
25-34 years	184.1	5.7
35-44 years	124.9	7.1
45-64 years	131.4	9.7
65 years and over	161.7	15.2
Farm		
25-34 years	160.7	5.1
35-44 years	117.1	8.0
45-64 years	103.7	9.1
65 years and over	144.9	12.9

Source: Adapted from health statistics from the U. S. National Health Survey: U. S. Department of Health, Education, and Welfare, *Hospital Discharge and Length of Stay: Short-Stay Hospitals*, Series B, No. 32 (Washington, D. C., 1961), Tables 7 and 8, pp. 20 and 21.

plans about three times more often than did the aged. Middle-aged rural adults were covered by a doctor's insurance plans twice as often as were those 65 years and over. Regardless of the type of health insurance, the aged living on farms had less coverage than did those in nonfarm areas (Table 19).

Even when the rural aged subscribed to health insurance, they frequently had a smaller proportion of their medical costs met by an insurance plan than did middle-aged adults. This is evident from the proportion of the hospital bills covered by insurance for individuals discharged from short-stay hospitals. The elderly had a smaller proportion receiving three-quarters or more of their hospital bill from insurance than those 45 to 64 years. The health insurance plan held by those from nonfarm areas was more likely to cover more of the hospital bills than that possessed by older persons on farms (Table 20).

One of the pertinent questions related to the use of health services by the rural aged is whether or not changes occur with the passing of time. Data from the Cornell Health Survey con-

Table 19. Percentage of Rural Persons Aged 45 and Over With Health Insurance by Age and Residence in the United States, 1959

Residence and age	Type of coverage		
	Hospital	Surgical	Doctor's visit
Rural			
45-54 years	65.6	60.2	20.2
55-64 years	56.2	49.8	15.3
65 years and over	36.6	30.6	9.1
65-74 years	43.5	37.2	—
75 years and over	23.3	17.5	—
Nonfarm			
45-54 years	73.2	67.7	22.6
55-64 years	64.3	57.9	17.4
65 years and over	41.3	34.0	10.0
65-74 years	49.3	42.1	—
75 years and over	27.1	19.8	—
Farm			
45-54 years	50.8	45.5	15.6
55-64 years	44.1	37.6	12.1
65 years and over	28.3	24.3	7.6
65-74 years	34.1	29.4	—
75 years and over	15.7	13.0	—

Source: Adapted from health statistics from the U. S. National Health Survey: U. S. Department of Health, Education, and Welfare, *Health Insurance Coverage: United States*, Series B, No. 26 (Washington, D. C., 1960), Tables 1, 2, and 3, pp. 18-20.

ducted in six upstate New York nonmetropolitan counties permit a comparison of the same rural individuals at two points in time. The analysis focuses on seven health services used by rural males aged 55 and over in 1949-50 and the use of the same services in 1957-59. The health services included physical examination, chest X-ray, use of general practitioner, use of specialist, use of dentist, and health insurance.

Since knowledge and information about health care increased markedly between 1949 and 1959, it was expected that the rural

Table 20. Percentage Distribution by Fraction of Hospital Bill Paid for by Insurance for Rural Individuals Aged 45 and Over in the United States, 1958-60

Residence and age	Percentage of total discharges from short-stay hospitals			
	Any part paid by insurance	Under ½ paid by insurance	½ to ¾ paid by insurance	¾ and over paid by insurance
Rural				
45-64 years	70.5	6.1	11.0	53.2
65-74 years	49.0	9.8	10.4	28.8
75 years and over	27.9	6.5	6.1	15.3
Nonfarm				
45-64 years	74.9	6.0	10.5	58.3
65-74 years	54.2	10.5	9.7	34.0
75 years and over	29.4	8.1	6.6	14.7
Farm				
45-64 years	60.6	6.6	12.4	41.6
65-74 years	38.7	8.2	11.8	18.7
75 years and over	24.9	3.1	5.5	16.3

Source: Adapted from health statistics from the U. S. National Health Survey: U. S. Department of Health, Education, and Welfare, *Proportion of Hospital Bill Paid by Insurance*, Series B, No. 30 (Washington, D. C., 1961), Table 7, p. 20.

men would report increases in the use of the seven selected health practices. The findings, however, failed to confirm this expectation. With the exception of the use of the dentist for preventive purposes and the subscription to a health insurance plan, no significant increases are apparent, and the use of the dentist

Table 21. Percentage of Rural Males Aged 55 and Over Using Selected Health Services in Upstate New York in Two Surveys

Service	First survey (N = 347)	Second survey (N = 324)	X²
Physical examination	10	10	—
Chest X-ray	13	14	.21
Treatment by general practitioner	55	58	.55
Treatment by medical specialist	15	15	—
Preventative treatment by dentist**	3	10	5.38*
Curative treatment by dentist	14	9	3.99*
Health insurance	30	46	18.86*

* Significant at the .05 level of confidence.
** The definition applied to this item resulted in the exclusion of respondents who reported an endentalous condition or who were 75 years and over. The N for this item was reduced to 173 for the first survey and to 165 for the second survey.
Source: Unpublished data from research project: "Availability and Use of Health Resources in Upstate New York," Bert L. Ellenbogen, Department of Rural Sociology, Cornell University, 1966.

for curative purposes declined over the 8-year period (Table 21). Research has generally found a relationship between income and the use of health practices. Therefore, one might expect that those with high income would reveal greater acceptance of the selected health practices over the two points in time than those with low income. The data, do not support this hypothesis. Those rural men with higher incomes made greater use of the health practices at both points in time, but level of income was not a significant factor in increases in the practices (Table 22).

Comparisons of the overall use pattern of health services for the aged in rural and urban areas of the nation reveal some dif-

Table 22. Percentage of Rural Males Aged 55 and Over Using Selected Health Services in Upstate New York by Income Group in Two Surveys

	Low income		High income	
Service	First survey (N = 187)	Second survey (N = 160)	First survey (N = 221)	Second survey (N = 103)
Physical examination	8	8	13	13
Chest X-ray	11	13	15	17
Treatment by general practitioner	53	55	58	64
Treatment by medical specialist	8	12	23	23
Preventative treatment by dentist**	4	6	3	17*
Curative treatment by dentist	10	6	18	15
Health insurance	20	39*	42	61*

* Significant at the .05 level of confidence.
** The definition applied to this item resulted in the exclusion of respondents who reported an endentalous condition or who were 75 years and over. The N for this item was reduced to 97 for low-income group and to 76 for the high-income group for the first survey; and for the second survey the N's were reduced to 113 and 52 respectively for the two income groups.
Source: Unpublished data from research project: "Availability and Use of Health Practices in Upstate New York," Bert L. Ellenbogen, Department of Rural Sociology, Cornell University, 1966.

ferences. In 1960, the rural aged exceeded the urban in the use of a physician (both in the frequency of annual visits as well as in seeing a doctor within a one-year interval) and in the extent to which a short-stay hospital was utilized. The urban aged, compared to the rural, made greater use of dentists, remained a longer time in the hospital, subscribed more often to all three types of health insurance, and possessed insurance which provided more adequate coverage of hospital costs. The most disadvantaged category of aged in the use of health services was the farm segment (Table 23).

Table 23. Use of Health Services by Persons Aged 65 and Over by
Residence in the United States 1960-61

	Rural	Rural nonfarm	Rural farm	Urban
Average annual number of visits per person to physician[1]	6.4	6.7	6.0	6.9
Visit doctor within one-year interval[2]	69.3%	70.3%	66.4%	66.1%
Average number of dental visits per person per year[3]	0.5	0.5	0.5	0.9
Number of discharges per 1000 population from short-stay hospital[4]	155.7	161.7	144.9	140.3
Average number of days in short-stay hospital[4]	14.4	15.2	12.9	15.2
Health insurance coverage[5]				
Hospital plan	36.6%	41.3%	28.3%	51.3%
Surgical plan	30.5	34.0	24.3	40.8
Doctor's visit plan	9.1	10.0	7.6	10.8
Proportion of hospital bill covered by insurance[6]				
Any part	37.9%	40.3%	33.0%	55.7%
Three-quarters	22.1	24.5	17.7	34.1

[1] *Older Persons Selected Health Characteristics,* Series C, No. 4 (Washington, D. C.,
1960), Table 31, p. 49.

[2] *Physician Visits: Interval of Visits and Children's Routine Checkup,* Series 10, No.
19 (Washington, D. C., 1965), Table 5, p. 19.

[3] *Dental Care: Volume of Visits, 1957-1959,* Series B, No. 15 (Washington, D. C.,
1960), Table 2, p. 13.

[4] *Hospital Discharge and Length of Stay: Short-Stay Hospitals,* Series B, No. 32
(Washington, D. C., 1961,) Tables 7 and 8, pp. 20 and 21.

[5] *Hospital Insurance Coverage: United States,* Series B, No. 26 (Washington, D. C.,
1960), Tables 1, 2, and 3, pp. 18-20.

[6] *Proportion of Hospital Bill Paid by Insurance: Patients Discharged from Short-Stay
Hospitals, United States,* Series B, No. 30 (Washington, D. C., 1961), Table 7, p. 20.

Sources: The sources are adapted from health statistics from the U. S. National
Health Survey, U. S. Department of Health, Education, and Welfare, Washington,
D. C. They are as follows:

IMPROVING HEALTH CARE FOR THE RURAL AGED

Three conditions are important in improving the health care of
a population: availability of health services, a favorable orientation toward accepting such services, and the ability to pay for
them. These conditions are related to the health level of the
aged, especially the rural aged, among whom needs for health
care are substantially greater than among younger persons.

Two recent developments in American society have had a profound influence upon the conditions contributing to improved
health levels for the aged. One of these is legislation in the field

of health and the other is the growth of community health programs for older people. Since both of these topics are discussed elsewhere in this volume, only brief mention will be made here with special reference to health.

Prior to 1960, the ability of the aged to pay for health care costs depended upon personal economic resources or upon some financial assistance from the provisions of the Social Security Act of 1935. Legislative efforts during the 1940's and 1950's resulted in many proposals for a federally supported health program. The Kerr-Mills Act of 1960 and the Medicare program of 1965 firmly established the concept of medical assistance for the aged. Other legislation in recent years focused on physical and mental health services at the community level. The Community Health Services and Facilities Act of 1961 provides matching funds from the federal government to states for the construction of community health services for the chronically ill. The act also encourages local communities to explore, develop, and implement new and improved methods for out-patient community services, especially for the chronically ill. Efforts also have been made to overcome the critical shortage of physicians and to increase the supply of other types of health personnel. The Health Professions Educational Act of 1963, which was amended in 1965, makes federal funds available to develop new facilities and enlarge existing university centers for training persons in the health professions.[18]

These legislative acts make available financial resources for changes to be brought about with respect to: (a) aspects of the health organizational structure, (b) the distribution of medical technology (as well as stimulating further medical discovery), and (c) the financial arrangement by which the aged may obtain health care. To what extent the health care of the rural aged will be influenced by recent legislation remains to be seen. It appears that certain aspects of the Medicare program will cover almost the entire rural population 65 years and over. Whether the rural aged will be satisfied with the minimal coverage included cannot yet be determined. Indications are that the seclusion and physical isolation of many rural older persons may result in a considerable time-lapse before they become enrolled in the programs.

Community programs for health care of the aged have gained considerable impetus in recent years. As Rosen notes: "Organized community effort directed toward improving the health of the aging and dealing with these problems is only in the initial stages. Until very recently, custodial care and institutionalization were the means by which communities attacked the problem of the aging persons who suffered from severe forms of disease. Almshouses, charity cases in hospitals, and the like were used to discharge community responsibilities."[19]

One might say after examining the literature that community programs for the aged are becoming fashionable. There are innumerable accounts of the sponsorship of various community programs for the health care of the aged by one or another of public and private health agencies, service clubs, or a combination of these organizations. A few examples may be mentioned. There is the description of the process by which a community nursing home was established in Phoenix, Arizona,[20] and of the procedure followed in Santa Cruz, California, for establishing a geriatric program within the county department of health.[21] In Chicago, collaborative interagency efforts produced an organized visiting program for the hospitalized aged.[22] There is an account of the community program to provide meals to homebound elderly in Rochester, New York, in Greenwich, Connecticut, and in the metropolis of Philadelphia.[23]

Many other programs and projects for the health care of the aged have been carried out by health associations, the Visiting Nurses Association, the American Cancer Society, the Extension Service, the Heart Association, and other agencies and service clubs. One finds reports of a nursing care program provided to a rural county in Minnesota[24] and the rehabilitation services offered to the aged in a city of 10,000 in Ohio.[25] A demonstration project has been undertaken in a rural county by the State Department of Health in California in order to furnish nursing care for the chronically ill.[26] In Iowa, a town of 800 inhabitants has established a multipurpose program for the aged, including home-care services to the chronically ill.[27] Pilot programs have been initiated in several rural sections to devise organizations for health care for the aged in sparsely populated areas,[28] and extensive research is underway to raise the level of community health programs in smaller communities.

Despite these efforts, one gains the impression that there are substantially fewer and less comprehensive community health programs for the aged in rural areas than in urban centers. The structural characteristics in rural areas (population size and density, economic resources, and accessibility to medical services) serve as a deterrent in establishing community health programs for the aged. Sparse populations limit efficient administration and prohibit the raising of sufficient economic support necessary to develop and maintain health programs for the aged in most rural areas of the nation.

CONCLUSION

The foregoing data and observations in this chapter suggest the following conclusions.

(a) The physical health status of older rural people appears to be lower than that of persons of comparable age living in urban environments. This is shown in the incidence of acute conditions, of injuries, of disabilities, and of selected chronic conditions and impairments. Among the rural aged, those on farms appear to be more disadvantaged in physical health than those in nonfarm areas.

(b) The rural aged reveal more anxiety and lower morale than do younger rural persons, but these conditions appear to be related to physical health conditions rather than to age. The rural aged experience more psychoses but fewer psychoneurotic reactions and fewer personality disorders than younger rural adults.

(c) The availability of health personnel and health resources is less adequate in rural than in urban areas of the nation. Major shortages in rural areas exist in specialized medical personnel, as well as in adequate nursing homes and trained personnel for these homes.

(d) Recent health legislation and the growth of community health programs are contributing to the improvement of health levels of older rural people. However, data suggest that the acceptance and use of health programs by aged rural persons are impeded by the characteristics of rural areas in the United States.

NOTES

[1] Monroe Lerner and Odin W. Anderson, *Health Progress in the United States, 1900-1960* (Chicago: The University of Chicago Press, 1963).

[2] U. S. Senate, A Report of the Special Committee on Aging, *Development in Aging, 1959 to 1963* (Washington, D. C., 1963); Odin W. Anderson, et al., *Family Expenditure Patterns of Personal Health Services* ("Health Information Foundation Research Series," No. 14; New York, 1960); Agnes W. Brewster and Dorothy McCamman, *Health Costs of the Aged*, U. S. Department of Health, Education, and Welfare, Division of Research and Statistics, Report No. 20 (Washington, D. C., 1956); James D. Cowhig and Emily O. Stewart, *The Older Farm Family and Medical Costs*, U. S. Department of Agriculture, Agricultural Marketing Service, Information Bulletin No. 235 (Washington, D.C., 1960); U. S. Department of Health, Education, and Welfare, The Health Economics Branch, Division of Community Health Services *Medical Care Financing and Utilization* (Washington, D. C., 1962); P. O. Steiner and R. Dorfman, *The Economic Status of the Aged* (Berkeley: University of California Press, 1957).

[3] For example, see, Tom T. Sasasaki, *Fruitland, New Mexico: A Navaho Community in Transition* (Ithaca, N. Y.: Cornell University Press, 1960); Lyle Saunders, *Cultural Differences and Medical Care* (New York: Russell Sage Foundation, 1954); Sam Schulman, "Rural Healthways in New Mexico," *Annals of the New York Academy of Sciences*, 84 (1960); Harvey L. Smith, *Society and Health in a Mountain Community* (Chapel Hill: University of North Carolina Institute for Research in Social Science, 1961).

[4] Surveys have been conducted in selected rural areas of the nation which have been concerned with aspects of the health condition of the rural aged. For example, Courtney B. Cleland and Ernest Lovon, *The Senior Years: A Report on the South Dakota Survey of Aging*, The Governor's Committee on Aging (Bismarck, N. D., 1960); Bert L. Ellenbogen, et al., *Age, Status and the Diffusion of Preventive Health Practices* (New York State College of Agriculture at Cornell, Department of Rural Sociology Bulletin No. 64; Ithaca, N. Y., 1964); Gary Hansen, *Chronic Illness Disability and Aging in Morrison County, Minnesota* (Morrison County Research Reports No. 1; St. Paul: The University of Minnesota, 1962); Arnold M. Rose (ed.), *Aging in Minnesota* (Minneapolis: The University of Minnesota Press, 1963); Ray E. Trussell and Jack Elinson, *Chronic Illness in a Rural Area: The Hunterdon Study*, Vol. III (Cambridge, Mass.: Harvard University Press, 1959); E. Grant Youmans, *Health Problems in Selected Rural and Urban Areas of Kentucky* (Kentucky Agriculture Experiment Station Progress Report No. 104; Lexington, Ky., 1961).

[5] Youmans, *Health Problems;* Charles P. Loomis and J. Allan Beegle, *Rural Social Systems* (Englewood Cliffs, N. J.: Prentice-Hall, 1951).

[6] Marie Jahoda, *Current Concepts of Positive Mental Health* (New York: Basic Books, 1958).

[7] Herbert Goldhammer and Andrew Marshall, *Psychosis and Civilization* (Glencoe, Ill.: The Free Press, 1949).

[8] Gerald Gurin, et al., *Americans View Their Mental Health* (New York: Basic Books, 1960).

[9] James Montgomery, *Social Characteristics of the Aged in a Small Community* (Pennsylvania State College, College of Home Economics Publication No. 233; State College, 1965).

[10] Denton E. Morrison and G. Albert Kristjanson, *Personal Adjustment*

Among Older People (South Dakota State Agricultural Experiment Station, Technical Bulletin 21; Brookings, S. D., June 1958).

[11] For example, Cleland and Lovon, *The Senior Years;* E. Grant Youmans, "Pessimism Among Rural and Urban Persons," *Journal of Health and Human Behavior,* 2 (1961), 2.

[12] Trussell and Elinson, *Chronic Illness in a Rural Area.*

[13] *Wisconsin Mental Health Indicators,* State of Wisconsin, State Department of Public Welfare, Bureau of Research, Release No. 1, 2, and 3 (Madison, Wis., 1964).

[14] Trussell and Elinson, *Chronic Illness in a Rural Area.*

[15] Unpublished data provided by Dr. Joseph Veroff, University of Michigan, 1965.

[16] William H. Stewart and Maryland Pennell, *Health Manpower Source Book: Physicians' Age, Type of Practice and Location,* U. S. Department of Health, Education, and Welfare (Washington, D. C., 1960), Tables 3 and 5, pp. 13, 29.

[17] For example, Anton H. Anderson, *Health Resources in the Northern Great Plains* (University of Nebraska Agricultural Experiment Station Publication No. 4; Lincoln, Neb., 1954); C. Horace Hamilton, *Health and Health Services in the Southern Appalachians* (North Carolina Agricultural Experiment Station Progress Report RS-35; Raleigh, N. C., 1959); Donald G. Hay and Walter C. McKain, Jr., *Availability of Selected Health Care Resources in Rural Areas of Connecticut* (Storrs Agricultural Experiment Station Bulletin No. 367; Storrs, Conn. 1961); Byron S. Hollingshead, *The Survey of Dentistry* (Washington, D. C.: American Council on Education, 1961); C. Horace Hamilton, *Hospitals and Hospital Service in Wisconsin* (Madison; University of Wisconsin Press, 1960); Vernon W. Lippard, "Supply of Health Care Personnel," published in *Health Care Needs of the 1960's* (New York: Group Health Insurance, Inc., 1963); Reginald Robinson, "A Report on the Project on Community Resources in Mental Health," *American Journal of Public Health,* 53 (1963), 4; William H. Stewart, "Manpower for Better Health Services," *Public Health Reports,* 81 (1966), 5.

[18] U. S. Senate, *Development in Aging, 1959 to 1963.*

[19] George Rosen, "Health Programs for an Aging Population," in Clark Tibbitts (ed.), *Handbook of Social Gerontology* (Chicago: The University of Chicago Press, 1960), p. 543.

[20] Hersch Kaplan, "A Community Nursing Home," *Patterns for Progress in Aging,* U. S. Department of Health Education, and Welfare, Case Study No. 1 (Washington, D. C., 1961).

[21] Evelyn S. Byron, "A Friendly Visiting Program," *Patterns for Progress in Aging,* U. S. Department of Health, Education, and Welfare, Case Study No. 13 (Washington, D. C., 1961).

[22] Opal S. Harris, "A County Health Department Geriatric Program," *Patterns for Progress in Aging,* U. S. Department of Health, Education, and Welfare, Case Study No. 14 (Washington, D. C., 1961).

[23] National Council on Aging, "Home-Delivered Meals for the Ill, Handicapped and Elderly," *American Journal of Public Health,* Supplement to 55 (1965), 5.

[24] Alberta Wilson, "Long-Term Nursing Care in Rural Minnesota," *Nursing Outlook*, 12 (1964), 10.

[25] A. Clair Sidall, "The Oberlin Plan for Community Health Services," *American Journal of Public Health*, 54 (1964), 8.

[26] "California's Older People: Their Health Problems," *California's Health*, 17 (1950), 18.

[27] "A Small Town Organizes Basic Services for its Aging," *Aging*, 109 (1963).

[28] Edna J. Brandt, *et al.*, "A Home Nursing Service in a Rural County," *American Journal of Public Health*, 51 (1961), 9; William J. Meyer, "Rural Glaucoma Screening," *American Journal of Public Health*, 52 (1962), 1; John C. Dement and George F. O'Brien, "Contract Public Health Services for Rural Counties—A New Approach to an Old Problem," *American Journal of Public Health*, 47 (1957), 10.

JERROLD E. LEVY

The Older American Indian

Any discussion of contemporary North American Indians must first cope with the problems of definition and uniqueness. Indians make up only 0.25 percent of the population of this country, but their importance is not so much in their numbers as in their unique relationship with the federal government. In this sense they are difficult to compare with other ethnic groups, most of whom migrated to this country with the intention of making an adjustment to American society. In contrast, the various Indian tribes have been cultural islands engulfed by and resistant to the flood of white American settlement. It is thus important to outline briefly the pertinent sources of Indian diversity and uniqueness at the present time, as well as to define the population called Indian, the older members of which are the subject of this chapter.

The aboriginal or precontact period of Indian life allows for easier generalizing than the more recent periods. Despite the existence of over three hundred tribes on the North American continent and their division into some fourteen major culture areas, certain continentwide regularities exist with variations determined by a tribe's geographical location and level of economic development. Despite the diversity of cultures and languages or the differences between sedentary agriculturalists, seed-gatherers, and caribou nomads, there are generalizations that can be drawn.

The history of Indian tribes after conquest reveals divergent tendencies as often as parallel developments. Large, undesirable, and unsettled areas of the Southwest have allowed a degree of isolation to some tribes whereas the intensive settlement of the eastern half of the United States has led to the relatively rapid disintegration of many others. A history of changing policies toward American Indian groups has resulted in a situation in which many tribes continue to exist as federally recognized ethnic groups upon land that is held in special trust status by the government and that is apart from the economic and legal frameworks of the surrounding states. At the same time, other groups such as the Lumbee of North Carolina are not even recognized as ethnic Indians. Traditionally, the Bureau of Indian Affairs of the Department of the Interior has considered as being Indian *only* those enrolled members of the tribes for which the bureau is responsible. Moreover, eligibility for enrollment is determined by each tribe, according to its own rules. For this reason there has been no uniform definition even within the bureau itself, and agreement concerning the number of Indians in the United States is difficult to attain.

Description of the contemporary American Indian is complicated further by the lack of statistics for certain tribes and by the incomparability of existing data on other tribes. Data pertaining to the status of the aged would logically come from health and welfare agencies. However, these services are not provided uniformly by the same agencies for all tribes. In many instances it is not recorded whether the beneficiary of services is an American Indian or, if so, of which tribe he is a member.

The Bureau of Indian Affairs has maintained an estimated count of the Indian population that includes enrolled members of Indian tribes for which the government accepts responsibility and the estimated number of descendants of such members.[1] In 1955 this estimate was about 472,000, of whom 400,000 were included on tribal rolls. About 280,000 Indians lived on reservations, and about 55,000 lived near reservations. The remaining 137,000 resided more or less permanently in non-Indian areas. An increasing number of Indian families are taking up residence in the larger urban centers where jobs are more plentiful. The bureau estimates are consistently higher than those of the United States census.[2] Current (1965) estimates are in the neighborhood of 600,000, and the American Indian is considered one of the fastest growing minority groups in the United States.

The state with the greatest number of Indians and the largest proportion of Indians in its total population is Arizona, where Indians constituted 9 percent of the population in 1959. The states next in order by number of Indians are Oklahoma, New Mexico, North Carolina, South Dakota, California, Montana, Washington, New York, and Minnesota.[3]

The Indian population, in general, has high birth rates and high death rates, with the result that it is a young population. Half of the Indians in this country are less than 20 years old. The percentage distribution by age among Indians resembles that of the total United States population in 1880.[4] The population trends are for continued natural increase, although at rates as yet unpredictable, and for an increasing number of older people as medical care improves. A proportional increase of the older age groups will occur only if the birth rate tapers off in the years to come.

The federal government has been largely responsible for Indian education. Adult Indians today compare favorably with nonwhites in the general population although, along with other racial minorities, they have less schooling than is average for the white population. There are, of course, enormous extremes not expressed by the nationwide averages. On six Indian reservations, for example, more than one-third of the residents over 5 years of age are not able to speak English.[5]

The American Indians are an economically depressed group. Their income, housing, and employment possibilities are far below the national average. Efforts of the federal government since 1928 have consistently aimed at bringing the population up to a competitive level with the general population. The Indian frequently lives on an isolated rural land base unfit for agriculture and far from sources of wagework. Since World War II many young Indians have moved from rural areas to large cities, and attempts have been made to bring economic opportunity and development to the reservation areas themselves. In broad perspective, the problem of the rural Indian parallels that of other rural populations in the nation.

In this chapter, contemporary conditions of the aging Indian are represented by the case of the Navajo of Arizona, New Mexico, Utah, and Colorado. As the largest single Indian tribe in possession of the largest reservation, they are important in their own right. To some extent their history and present situation are typical of those of other tribes. This limiting of the discussion to one tribe will permit adequate description at the expense of representativeness. Wherever pertinent, contrasting material from other tribes will be presented.

THE AGED IN ABORIGINAL AMERICA[6]

Age is both an idea and a physiological actuality. When dealing with populations of a vanished era, it is dangerous to confuse the social definition of age with our own chronological expression of our idea of age. Equally dangerous is the tendency to confuse or equate the social ideal of the roles of the aged with the social reality or the actual conditions under which they lived. In many respects the aboriginal populations of the New World were different from their descendants of today; in more respects they were different from the white Americans who succeeded them. In this section a discussion of social ideals and roles will precede a consideration of physiological and ecological factors that both defined and placed limitations upon those ideals and roles.

One of the prime problems of aging individuals is to guarantee their physical survival. American Indian tribes had a variety of ways to provide food for their older members. These techniques varied from communal sharing among the hunting and gathering tribes such as the Eskimo, Shoshone, and Plains Indians who found the storing of a food surplus difficult, to the concept of family responsibility for the care of its own elders, as was found among the Pueblo Indian of the Southwest. The distribution of food to the aged out of public stores appears to have occurred only among the Aztec and Inca peoples, who were already civilized and were the possessors of centralized government and urban centers.

Supporting the various means of sharing or guaranteeing food for elderly persons were food tabus. Certain foods were thought to be good only for old people and dangerous for young people. Among the Omaha, for instance, the tender parts of the buffalo were reserved for the aged. Among the Crow the bone marrow was set aside.

American Indians provided economic security for the aged by reserving many roles for older people. Commonly, knowledge was considered to be a form of property. An old man frequently had more ceremonial knowledge than younger men and this he was paid for as he imparted it to his disciples. Payment was made for the treatment of illness, for dispelling witchcraft, and for divining the whereabouts of lost articles. Among some tribes very specific tasks were reserved for old people, for example, the care of men's boots by the aged Eskimo women.

In almost every instance, however, an individual looked to his own family for support in his declining years. The old people performed many of the household chores, freeing their own children for such tasks as herding or hunting, seed and root gathering, or the tanning of hides. It was the grandparents who told the children stories during the long winter nights and so began their education as members of the tribe, for these stories contained the rudiments of tribal history, cosmology, and world view. American Indian societies were kin-based, behavior between individuals being determined by the kinship relation existing between them. Thus a considerable number of relatives felt responsible for the well-being of the older people. Bonds between kinsmen are still strong. Navajos often make special trips over a period of several days to bring food to aging relatives. Among the Hopi, a healer will be called "father" by his patients, and because of this relationship they will continue to bring him gifts of food and clothing for many years.

It is not surprising, then, to find a considerable amount of prestige accruing to old age, although it might be more correct to say that the prestige was attached to the role rather than to old age itself. Thus, if a man had ceremonial knowledge he was known as a wise old man. But if during his active years he had done little to qualify himself for the roles to come, his later prestige would automatically be less. In general, the aboriginal Indian held the aged in respect. There was no retirement but instead a continued utilization of the individual for constructive purposes. In some ways, old age brought rewards. Many social and ceremonial restrictions did not apply to old people. In many tribes women were allowed greater sexual freedom after menopause. It was common for women to become healers and to participate in rituals after menopause.

Unfortunately, almost nothing is known about the personality structure of older Indians. Did the existence of productive roles and prestige for the aged provide for a happier, more secure, and satisfying aging process? David Gutman[7] has found that older traditional Navajos of today appear to have almost no themes of alienation or anxiety revealed in their responses to Thematic Apperception Tests. This type of evidence suggests that Indian aging was a pleasant and satisfying experience. But the individuals tested, although traditional, are not aboriginal for they do not live in the preconquest world of warfare, food shortages, and exposure to climatic extremes. Many of the statements concerning age recorded by anthropologists indicate the existence of a less happy state.

> It is bad to be old.
> Better to die young
> Fighting bravely in battle.
>
> *Song of the Blackfoot*
> *"Crazy Dog" warrior society.*[8]

This sentiment was common among the Plains Indians for whom the primary productive and prestigious roles were those of buffalo hunter and warrior and for whom the exigencies of a harsh nomadic life made the sedentary roles of the aged less important. Nevertheless, similar sentiments are recorded for both pastoralists and agriculturalists. The pastoral Navajo have made such statements as "old age is a bad time" and "after sixty it all slips away."[9] Moreover, for all the respect and ceremonial power accorded the aged, they were also feared because it was generally felt by the Navajo that an old person was very often a witch.[10] Even among the sedentary agriculturalists such as the Hopi, who cared for old people in permanent villages, there were some limitations placed upon the respect accorded old age. Old people continued to work on more restricted tasks until completely decrepit. "Even a blind man can weave in the ceremonial kiva." But the Hopi accorded respect to the aged only as long as they fulfilled some function. After senility set in, old age was a burden, and, despite the bonds and obligations of kinship, neglect of the aged by their own families was frequently observed during the Depression years of the 1930's.[11]

These statements concerning the undesirability of old age become even more meaningful when we consider the practices that applied to the period of decrepitude and senility. These may be described as socially sanctioned forms of murder, suicide, and abandonment and forms of neglect and maltreatment. The ritual murder of the aged was relatively rare among the Indians. The Iroquois, however, did allow an older man to give a large feast during which a favorite son would administer the *coup de grâce* from behind. More common was abandonment of the feeble, especially among the more nomadic tribes. Ewers has observed that on occasion even the extremely poor were abandoned by tribes of the North Plains.[12] Often enough, however, the old person chose the time of his own demise to avoid forcing the painful job upon relatives. Eskimo material has many accounts of old people who stole away from their families in the night and were never seen again. In any event, it is clear that for most tribes such behavior occurred only as a response to economic necessity, those times when the weak could not be moved without endangering the well-being of the group or when the food supply was dangerously low. And, it must be added, the malformed, the seriously ill, and the crippled were often so treated along with the aged.

These customs had a survival value that was both understood and accepted by the old people themselves. In fact, the values of these tribes emphasized group well-being so strongly that the aged would have had it no other way. They did, it seems, even emphasize the value of not being a burden and of accepting death as a natural counterpart to life. It is my general impression that old age and death were well understood and accepted and that the aged's departure from the world was most often quiet and dignified. The Plains Indians represent an extreme in their custom of committing suicide in battle to avoid the loss of status and prestige which were so firmly attached to the warrior role in a highly specialized and aggressive society.

It is inferred that the aboriginal American Indian defined age differently than most Americans today. Old age among the Indians was that period in the individual's life which began after childbearing for women and after hunting and warring for men and which ended with senility or decrepitude. All positive elements associated with old age were inextricably bound to the performance of socially productive roles. That such useful roles were available to most aged people was indeed fortunate, for with senility we find evidence of abandonment, neglect, and even maltreatment. It is to senility and to loss of prestige and productivity that such negative statements as "after sixty it all slips away" would apply. In most cases the Indian's old age was a prime of life. Freed from domestic chores, the leader of the family group, a possessor of practical, religious, or medicinal knowledge, the older Indian was actively engaged in leading, educating, and advising, the very roles generally associated with middle age and prime of life in contemporary American society.

It has not been made clear how long an individual Indian spent in any one of his life periods. What is the relationship between physiological and chronological age? If senility set in only a few years after the physically active life ceased and was itself a prolonged period of illness and dependence, then the social roles and attitudes mentioned would have meant little to the individual who would spend but a short time enjoying them. At what age was an Indian old and, once old, how long could he expect to live as an old man? Many of my answers to these questions are relatively subjective and are based upon personal observations rather than upon large amounts of accurate statistics gathered from truly primitive populations.

It has been observed that American Indians do not show the signs of age in the same way as do Caucasians.[13] Women of non-white races appear to lose their youthfulness soon after they begin bearing children but men appear youthful well into middle age. In American Indians, the signs of old age do not set in immediately after the disappearance of signs of youth. Balding is very uncommon among Indians. The hair grays but not as early and not in the same manner as among whites; gray flecking may start around fifty and a salt-and-pepper effect may remain until after the seventies. The only white-haired Indians I have known have all been over seventy and many octogenarians are still only partially gray. Especially important is the fact that skin wrinkling frequently sets in very late. Weathering by sun and wind may be seen in the face during the forties, but the body skin of women between fifty and seventy years of age is often smooth and supple. The darker skin color also remains uniform to the eye—blotching and uneven coloring are found only in the very old. Barring blindness or arthritic crippling, an Indian will appear middle-aged (i.e., between 40 and 50) until he is over 60 years old. Physically undistinguishable from individuals ten to twenty years younger, the Indian has no marks which would set him apart from others "in the prime of life." Preferred Navajo forms of marriage allow middle-aged women to marry young men and older men to marry young women. For the Navajo, at least, an aging male and sometimes a female may remain active in family life by virtue of marriage to a younger spouse. Indian standards of beauty and attractiveness do not accentuate features characterized by adolescence. Regular, pleasant features and a strong active body are most often mentioned as the criteria for feminine beauty.

Before the coming of the white man, the Indians were exposed to many types of illness of little importance today. Some of the degenerative diseases from which the aged suffered include diseases of the eyes and arthritic ailments. Blindness and crippling certainly have made many candidates for senility. On the other hand, the Indian appears to have been relatively free of arteriosclerotic heart disease,[14] cancer,[15] and the forms of diabetes known among whites. Diabetes, relatively common among the present-day Navajo, appears late in life and is very mild in form.

An individual who survived the enteric and respiratory illnesses of childhood and the traumas of accidents and warfare in adulthood[16] was likely to enter old age as a very healthy specimen. It has even been conjectured that the primitive Indian had a greater life expectancy at 50 than does the contemporary American Caucasian. Once having reached old age, Indians represented the fittest of their generation. It must be remembered, however, that remarkably few individuals ever reached 50 or 60.[17] The life expectancy of an Indian at birth was probably around 30-35 years. This only recently has changed.

In contrast with present-day Americans, then, the aging Indian was healthy and relatively youthful in appearance. He probably remained a fairly active old man until 70 or 80, when senility overtook him and death followed soon after.

The small number of aged Indians living at any given time had social implications of some import. The few individuals occupying the old-aged status were easy to provide for in an economy of scarcity and they posed no threat to the younger generations. Avenues to success were not blocked by large numbers of aging, high-status people and so no resentment between youth and age developed. The Cherokee refer to the old men who acted as advisors in the village as "beloved" old men.

It is not unreasonable to conclude that old age for the Indian was a satisfying time of life. The aged were few in number and healthy in constitution, and the society could use them as well as revere them. However, the positive aspects of old age pertained only to the productively functioning individual. Senility and debility were disvalued by young and old alike. Nor is it wise to attribute to a society that which was the result of a combination of circumstances, such as the relative absence of degenerative diseases and the few racial peculiarities of the aging process in the population. Moreover, a certain amount of ecological balance was characteristic. Social values and attitudes were consistent with social usages which in turn were adaptive to a relatively slowly changing environment. What satisfactions the Indian may appear to have experienced during his latter years may be due primarily to the fact that they were the realization of his expectations. As a result, the aged accepted abandonment, voluntary death, and even the idea of death with equanimity. Aging and death were an integral part of the expectations of a style of life which was repeated generation after generation and endured until the years of conquest by the white man and the engulfing of the tribal societies by the urban world of today.

CURRENT DEVELOPMENTS: THE NAVAJO EXAMPLE

The coming of the white man initiated a series of changes in Indian tribal populations. Whole tribes were decimated, not only by warfare but also by the introduction of many infectious diseases. The restriction of the Indians to reservations and the destruction of wildlife brought to an end the aboriginal subsistence economies. Government subsidies and health care programs fostered overcrowding and further diminution of the inadequate reservation land base. Attempts to adjust to new economic activities have further disorganized the tribal social organizations and these have important implications for the position of the older person in contemporary Indian society. By using the Navajo as an example, it is possible to see in some detail how these various changes have operated.

With the Treaty of 1868 the Navajo began their lives as reservation Indians. Prior to this time they had lived approximately two centuries in the Southwest, expanding in size as they learned agriculture from the Pueblos and pastoralism from the Spaniards. Geographic expansion from a land base of perhaps 3,000 square miles in what is now northern New Mexico gradually interpenetrated the Pueblo country to the south and west. The original reservation of 3,314,330 acres was considered adequate for some 9,000 Navajos in existence at that time. With the exception of raiding, traditional economic pursuits were not curtailed and the tribe continued to expand. Today the Navajo number between 90,000 and 100,000 and occupy a reservation that has been added to by executive order on several occasions until it constitutes the largest Indian reservation in the United States. The area, about the size of the state of West Virginia (approximately 24,000 square miles), comprises an estimated 14,250,000 acres.[18]

The Navajo were fortunate in two respects. Being semi-nomadic and living in an isolated and arid part of the country, they escaped the full effects of the great cholera, measles, and smallpox epidemics. Their population has continued to expand as the figures above so amply illustrate. Unlike the hunters and gatherers who had their game supplies destroyed, the Navajo were able to continue their agriculture and pastoralism with considerable success until the 1930's, a period of almost seventy years. At this time overgrazing, erosion, and a sudden decline in the wool and lamb market necessitated a drastic curtailment of the traditional pursuits. The years since the Depression have been marked by an increased reliance upon wagework; an opening of the reservation to the outside world by the building of roads in an effort to increase the tourist trade, attract small industry, and permit the Navajo access to off-reservation jobs; and a prodigious expansion of health, education, and welfare activities aimed at preparing the Navajo for this new type of life.[19]

By reviewing traditional Navajo roles for the aged in the light of new developments, it is possible to highlight the position the older Navajo occupies today. Property holdings of the old people have been seriously affected by current developments. The stock reduction program has not only curtailed the amount of wealth controlled by the individual but has put considerable pressure upon the older stock owner to relinquish his grazing pursuits to his heirs so they can support their own growing families. Government agents have encouraged the practice, pointing out that an elderly person without livestock may qualify for old age benefits. Although total income for the kin group may be increased thereby, this practice strips the elderly of the managerial roles and the prestige that goes with them. The value of traditional knowledge in general and of ceremonial knowledge in particular is decreasing rapidly. The experienced stock-raiser has nothing to teach a younger person who cannot increase his flocks but who must learn wagework skills and modern stock-raising techniques that the older people do not know. Young people, unable to increase or inherit flocks, find it impossible to pay for the long years of apprenticeship to a ceremonial healer. The peyote religion is offering more easily obtained ceremonial roles to the younger men. Free medical services as well as the peyote ceremonies are competing with the very expensive and elaborate traditional healing rituals. Only the best medicine men are able to make a full-time living and few are finding young men to carry on after them.

The shift to wagework has encouraged the development of the nuclear family at the expense of the extended family. Old people are a burden to young couples operating in a cash economy with the low incomes of unskilled workers. The domestic skills of the traditional aged are less important in a small household. Now almost all the children are either in a government boarding school or a public school. Only the infants are at home to be cared for. Much of the domestic economy for the younger wage workers involves knowledge of English and arithmetic to cope with shopping in the new cash stores that are springing up all over the reservation. These new stores are supplanting the old trader who dealt in credit based on a family's annual production of wool and lamb.

The shifting economy has produced hardships for the young at the same time that it has almost completely destroyed the productive roles and economic holdings of the older traditionalists. More uncomfortable perhaps has been the resultant destruction of the education and advising functions of the experienced older person. Unwise in the ways of the white world, he can no longer advise adequately in the political councils of his community. With the children away at school during the winter months (the traditional time for recounting the myths and legends), the older person can no longer function as educator and imparter of tribal morality and world view. To compound the tragedy, it is becoming increasingly apparent that the younger, educated Navajos do not want much of what the old people have to offer. Young mothers complain that their parents do not care for the infant grandchildren properly. They are said to be unsanitary, careless, and do not "discipline" the children. The schools, missionaries, and government personnel have taught that the old ways are finished, that modern health practices must take the place of the traditional religion. The shifts in the economy have created new goals which are devaluating the older people as effectively as the destruction of their traditional roles. These changes are no easier for the young people than for their elders. It is difficult to respect a parent or grandparent who is not only an economic burden but who is often in disagreement with the way the family is being run. Equally difficult is the process of rejecting a loved one, a person whom one has been taught to respect.

Before proceeding further, some qualifications must be made. The changes described are not happening everywhere at the same rate on the reservation. Wagework communities reveal the tendencies more strikingly than do the more isolated areas of the reservation. Nor is change effected in a single generation. The young, acculturated Navajo may feel estranged from their grandparents but the parents stand midway between them and represent a buffer generation. There are still many areas of the reservation where pastoral pursuits continue, where the matrilineal extended family is the rule, and where cash income is obtained by young men who leave their wives and children with the larger kin group for several months each year to go on migratory labor circuits to Utah and California. These shifts in living pattern are diffused throughout the population, and the presence of older traditional Navajos who appear calm and full of wisdom all too often obscures the magnitude of the changes that are taking place.

That the position and life pattern of the aged Navajo are changing is revealed further by the changing population and health status of the tribe. The increase in the tribal population from ca. 9,000 in 1869 to almost 100,000 in 1965 has already been noted. By conservative estimates the rates of increase are as follows:

> 1870-1900: 1.50–2.00 percent per annum
> 1900-1930: 1.75–2.25 percent per annum
> 1930-1950: 2.40–2.18 percent per annum
> 1950-1960: 2.40–3.30 percent per annum

The number of Navajo people aged 60 and older has increased from approximately 1,225 in 1910 to 4,303 in 1961, with present estimates putting them at about 5,600 in 1965. Throughout the last fifty years and perhaps for the last century the percentage distribution of the population by age groups has remained essentially unchanged, the age group of 60 years and over constituting only about 5 percent of the population. In 1960, male and female persons aged 65 years and over constituted 2.0 and 1.8 percent, respectively, of the total population on the Navajo reservation.[20] The population profile is still close to that of primitive groups. It has not changed more radically because of the relatively late development of modern health services on the reservation. It was only in 1955 that the Public Health Service assumed responsibility for Indian health programs and reasonably adequate budgets and facilities became realities. The stages in population growth were initially small but have increased steadily with government subsidies for food in poor years and recently with improved medical care. These advances have primarily affected the younger age groups so that more and more young people are surviving to old age. Advances in medical care have been less rapid for the elderly and for the chronically ill. The survival of children with congenital heart defects and other crippling ailments may well swell the ranks of aging people with less healthy specimens than heretofore.

Today, obesity and gall bladder diseases are frequent among middle-aged Navajo. These do not appear to have been characteristic of the aboriginal Indian populations nor is it known to what extent these illnesses are the results of shifts from the aboriginal diet to the reservation diet of today. It is clear that treatment and care for people with these ailments is now possible and, as they age, they are increasingly the responsibility of the younger relatives. The pneumonias and accidents which in an earlier day ended in death are now cared for in modern hospitals, guaranteeing the survival of weakened or crippled persons. The growing number of old people will include more who need protracted care through a lingering period of debility and senile dependency. Examples of this sort are seen by social welfare personnel almost daily. The functioning of welfare programs and Navajo utilization of them are illustrative of the changes already being felt.

Before 1941 welfare for the Navajo consisted primarily of emergency assistance in the form of rations during time of extreme crisis. Since that time public assistance has expanded in all areas of Navajo life as the major means of shoring up the economy during the period of transition. Free schooling and medical care, a surplus commodities program, and such tribal programs as clothing for school children, when considered along with more conventional welfare programs as Aid to Dependent Children and Aid to the Disabled, compose approximately 30 per cent of the total income for the Navajo economy. Payments to Navajos on Old Age Assistance in New Mexico alone increased from $6,153 in 1950 to $40,099 in 1960. The number of cases doubled during that time, with 686 cases handled in 1960. In Arizona where the larger portion of Navajos reside, $669,440 was disbursed as Old Age Assistance in 1960 as opposed to $483,241 in 1952.[21] The administering of all these programs is the responsibility of a variety of federal, state, and tribal agencies.[22] The utilization of these benefits is being urged upon the Navajo who, with an average per capita income of $521, certainly needs all the help he can get.[23]

Urged to sign his grazing permit over to his heirs by an agricultural expert who wants to see the younger families become economically active, the older Navajo loses his source of authority in the family. The family income is then increased when the elderly person qualifies for old age benefits. But without prestige and authority the older person is all too often seen as nothing more than an added source of income. The development of this attitude is not conducive to good familial care of the elderly and frequently generates bitter disputes between relatives about who will care for the old people and so receive the welfare check. The growing number of families who find it a burden to care for the aged has recently led to discussions between the tribe and the Public Health Service concerning the feasibility of constructing a nursing home on the reservation. The expansion of welfare services certainly recognizes economic needs and strives to answer them. Inadvertantly, and perhaps inevitably, the encouragement of the use of welfare programs fosters the destruction of the image of the wise and active old man and substitutes one of dependency and debility.

The dilemma does not pertain to the aged alone. Changing roles and statuses and the breakdown of the traditional patterns and norms are the inevitable results of economic change. Change among the Navajo is not being achieved without social and personal maladjustment and pain. Alcoholism, a rising suicide rate, family instability, and anomie are all in evidence on the reservation. The shift from rural tribalism to urbanism is inevitable for the greater portion of Navajos, as well as for the American Indian in general. Health, education, and welfare services are the accepted forms of support for populations in transition. All this is clear, yet it is at this juncture that the American Indian stands apart from other recipients of welfare.

The Indian accepts and even demands support to help him survive. He recognizes that his children face a different future and need new schools and job opportunities. Yet he bases these demands and expectations not upon his rights as an American or upon his desire to succeed in American life but upon the terms of the treaties made between the various tribes (as sovereign powers) and the United States government. His view is ethnocentric and his goal pluralistic.

Cultural pluralism is not new on the American scene. Nor, it may be pointed out, is it the goal of all Indians. It is, however, the prevailing position taken by organized Indian groups, whether these be intertribal political organizations, tribal councils, or communities. Cultural pluralism presents a peculiar challenge to the planner of social change and, to the extent that some ethnocentricity is found in all minority groups, poses a problem of some magnitude.

As the old man applies for his welfare check in order to eat he often does so with the realization that he is being pushed into a mold that is alien to him. He believes his own values to be superior to those of the whites. He submits to change rather than working toward it. This is not simple conservatism. The Indian sees the problems of the white unemployed, of the old white man alone in a nursing home, and he does not want them. His frustration and resentment are then aimed at the very welfare agencies that are organized to help him. Expression of this resentment has been explicit recently as the war on poverty has gathered momentum in Indian country.[24] The welfare program itself has been attacked as the means by which the government will destroy the identity of the Indian. It is clear that such an attitude on the part of beneficiaries can only subvert the goals of such programs and eventually lead to the formation of a population that consumes welfare benefits as a means of expressing aggression.

To the social analyst, the changes operating upon the Indian populations are inevitable. Anomie and personal maladjustment may also be an integral part of the price. And, ironic as it may appear, it is probably inevitable that the Indian must be blessed with the evils of civilization before these evils can be eradicated or alleviated.

Many Indian leaders believe that solving their problems for them adds to their peoples' frustrations and thus is both undesirable and avoidable. They point out that Indians have never believed human dignity to be diminished by a lack of material goods. It was the white man who told them they were poor and that they should be ashamed of poverty. And it was the white man who measured the Indian by his income and his house. Now many Indian leaders are asking that aid be used to create opportunity and not to support the indigent and that it not be administered by the old local professionals.

It is too soon to say whether current aid will have more success than the more conventional ones. Possibly there is no desirable alternative to current trends. In this case the Indian will continue in his present direction toward white norms. Health programs will preserve a growing number of dependent and ailing old people for whom larger and cleaner nursing homes must be built. It is poor consolation to realize that in passivity the Indian will perform a new constructive role: his very dependency will create more jobs for young acculturated descendents who will care for him as nurses and social welfare workers.

NOTES

[1] U. S. Department of the Interior, Bureau of Indian Affairs, *Problems in Determining Population Data* (processed, 1952).

[2] U. S. Department of Health, Education, and Welfare, Public Health Service, Office of the Surgeon General, Division of Public Health Methods, *Health Services for American Indians,* Public Health Service Publication No. 531 (Washington, D. C., 1957), p. 8.

[3] *Ibid.,* p. 8

[4] *Ibid.,* p. 10

[5] *Ibid.,* p. 19

[6] Except where specifically noted, the data utilized in this section are from Leo W. Simmons, *The Role of the Aged in Primitive Society* (New Haven: Yale University Press, 1945).

[7] David Gutman, Dept. of Psychology, University of Michigan, *Personal Communication.*

[8] C. Wissler, *Societies and Dance Associations of the Blackfoot Indians* "American Museum of Natural History Anthropological Papers," Vol. XI, part 4; (New York, 1913), p. 387.

[9] D. Leighton and C. Kluckhohn, *Children of the People* (Cambridge, Mass: Harvard University Press, 1948), pp. 89-91.

[10] *Ibid.,* p. 90.

[11] E. A. Kennard, "Hopi Reactions to Death," *American Anthropologist,* 39 (1937), 494.

[12] John C. Ewers, *The Horse in Blackfoot Indian Culture,* Bureau of American Ethnology Bulletin 159 (Washington, D. C., 1955), pp. 243f.

[13] I am indebted to Dr. Marshall T. Newman, Chairman of the Anthropology Department, Portland State College, for putting many of these observations into a meaningful perspective.

[14] Cornell University, *Final Report of the Navajo, Cornell Many Farms Project* (processed, 1964).

[15] Recent research points out that although cancer is present among Indians, that of the lung, breast, and prostate gland are almost entirely lacking. The incidence of carcinoma is still unknown and its effects upon the aboriginal population may have to be reassessed. John Porvasnick, M.D., "Recent Experiences with Cancer on the Navajo-Hopi Reservation," *The Tuba City Indian Hospital Bulletin,* 3 (Sept. 1962).

[16] Diseases of an epidemic nature such as smallpox, plague, cholera, and measles were probably entirely absent. The prevalence of other infectious illnesses is impossible to determine but they appear to have been more prominent in Mexico and Peru where the higher population concentrations and warmer climates foster the survival and spread of the agent.

[17] Accurate population profiles for aboriginal Indian populations are non-existent. Observers were unable to gauge chronological age. It does appear certain that many tribes had a disproportionate number of females due to the toll taken by warfare. J. C. Ewers, *The Horse in Blackfoot Indian Culture,* p. 212.

[18] Robert Young, *The Navajo Yearbook,* Bureau of Indian Affairs, Gallup Area Office, Navajo Agency (Window Rock, Ariz., 1961), pp. v, 210ff.

[19] *Ibid.,* p. 211.

[20] George A. Hillery, Jr., and Frank J. Essene, "Navajo Population: An Analysis of the 1960 Census," *Southwestern Journal of Anthropology,* 19 (1963), 297-313.

[21] Robert Young, *The Navajo Yearbook,* p. 303.

[22] *Ibid.,* pp. 227ff., 287-309.

[23] *Ibid.,* p. 228.

[24] Cf. "Poverty Conference in Tucson", *Indian Voices,* Feb. 1965, p. 2.

OLEN E. LEONARD

The Older Rural Spanish-Speaking People of the Southwest

The Spanish-speaking people in the United States are second only to the American Indians in the length of time they have occupied American soil. Moving north from the high plateaus of Mexico around the first part of the seventeenth century, they occupied the central valley of what is now New Mexico almost two decades before the first permanent English colonists landed in New England. Until about 1850 few descendants of these pioneer settlers had left the area. Today they are concentrated in the five southwestern states of Arizona, California, Colorado, New Mexico, and Texas. Unlike descendants of many European groups, the Spanish-speaking people retain much of their original language, religion, values, and beliefs. Only within the past few decades have there been marked tendencies to break with the past. Improved schools and teaching, more regular attendance at school, and jobs involving contacts with outsiders have contributed to the breakdown of the traditional culture. At present, individuals who retain clear and salient traits of the old ways are mainly older persons often living in remote rural areas and those who have moved recently into the area from a Spanish-speaking country such as Mexico.

This chapter is concerned primarily with the older rural Spanish-speaking people of the Southwest. It assesses their social, economic, and health status, examines their family and community roles, and indicates some of their problems. It is recog-

239

nized that many Spanish-speaking persons live elsewhere in the United States, but information about them is extremely limited, and data on them are not included in this chapter.

CHARACTERISTICS OF THE POPULATION

In 1960 approximately three and a half million white persons with Spanish surnames lived in the five southwestern states. Although heavily concentrated pockets of these people were in New Mexico, southern Colorado, and Arizona, most of them lived in California and Texas.[1] Some 139,000 were 65 years of age or more. California had the largest number and Texas the second largest; Arizona and Colorado had the smallest number (Table 1).

Table 1. Number of White Persons Aged 65 and Over with Spanish Surname by State and Residence for Five Southwestern States, 1960

State	Urban (thousands)	Rural nonfarm (thousands)	Rural farm (thousands)	Total (thousands)
Arizona	6	1	.*.	7
California	50	6	2	58
Colorado	5	2	.*.	7
New Mexico	6	6	1	13
Texas	44	8	3	54
Total	111	23	6	139

* Less than 500.
Source: U. S. Bureau of the Census, *United States Census of Population: 1960, Subject Reports, Persons of Spanish Surname,* Final Report PC(2)-1B (Washington, D. C., 1963), Table 2.

An important characteristic of the older Spanish-speaking population of the Southwest is its predominantly urban residence. In 1960 about 80 percent of the group was living in towns or cities. This shift from rural to urban environments has been marked in the last two decades. Many immigrants from the other Americas, including the recent migrants from Cuba and the steady stream from Puerto Rico in past decades, have settled in the larger cities. However, as late as 1950 only 68 percent of the group lived in urban communities.

Older rural Spanish-speaking persons constitute a small proportion of the total population of their group. In 1960, about 3.4

percent of the Spanish-speaking rural farm population was 65 years of age or more, compared with 9.7 percent for the total white rural farm population (Tables 2 and 3). The percentage for the females was less (2.8 percent) than for the males (3.9 percent). Percentages for the rural nonfarm population were slightly greater, with about the same ratio between sexes. The small proportion the aged makes of the total population results from higher birth rates of the rural Spanish-speaking people and from a steady stream of relatively young migrants from Spanish-speaking countries.

Table 2. Percentage of the Rural White Population Aged 65 and Over with Spanish Surname by Sex and Residence for Five Southwestern States, 1960

Residence	Total	Male	Female
Rural farm	3.4	3.9	2.8
Rural nonfarm	4.2	4.5	3.9

Source: U. S. Bureau of the Census, *United States Census of Population: 1960, Subject Reports, Persons of Spanish Surname,* Final Report PC(2)-1B (Washington, D. C., 1963), Table 2.

Immigration into the Southwest is mostly from Mexico. Targets of the migration have been both rural and urban districts. Concentration becomes less as distance from the border increases. Since recent immigrants are willing to accept lower wages, the movement tends to push the native Spanish-speaking people farther into the interior of the country.

Paralleling a trend in the general population, relatively fewer foreign-born Spanish-speaking persons were in the rural population in 1960 than in 1950. There were more males than females

Table 3. Distribution of Total White Population with Spanish Surname by Sex and Residence for Five Southwestern States, 1960

Sex	Rural farm (thousands)	Rural nonfarm (thousands)	Urban (thousands)	Total (thousands)
Male	106	287	1,362	1,755
Female	77	255	1,379	1,711
Total	183	542	2,741	3,466

Source: U. S. Bureau of the Census, *United States Census of Population: 1960, Subject Reports, Persons of Spanish Surname,* Final Report PC(2)-1B (Washington, D. C., 1963), Table 2.

in the Spanish-speaking population of the Southwest, in part a reflection of the migration from Mexico. The difference was especially great in the rural farm areas where 106,000 males and only 77,000 females were estimated to be living in 1960 (Table 3). There was little difference between the numbers of males and females living in the cities.

The assimilation process for Spanish-speaking persons in the Southwest has proceeded to the point that many persons today question efforts to distinguish them from other groups. Certainly the task of doing so is becoming increasingly difficult. A number of studies during the last 20 years demonstrate clearly the accelerating rate at which the traditional culture is breaking down. Some of this is planned change, as in the schools. Other changes result from extended contacts with outsiders through job and training opportunities. There is, however, evidence that a hard core of traits has been retained, especially among the aged and among the more tradition-minded persons who have remained in the rural areas. These individuals may be identified by a common use of Spanish, the clinging to a few old customs, values, and beliefs, and a birth rate that is higher than in most parts of the nation.

SOCIOECONOMIC STATUS

A number of factors, both historical and physical, combined during the colonial period to produce in the southwestern United States a two-class system that is still in evidence in many areas. Colonists from Spain, and later from Mexico, were granted large holdings requiring major inputs of hired labor. The scarcity and location of the principal water supplies gave their possessors vast power over others. The system of agriculture that prevails in much of the area today—extensive in the dry uplands and intensive in the irrigated valleys—dictates a condition favoring large units dedicated to commercial agriculture or else a highly fragmented system of family-operated units employing small equipment and large inputs of hand labor that can shift during certain seasons to paid labor on the large commercial properties.

A major part of the paid farm labor of the Southwest is furnished by the Spanish-speaking population. The relatively low earnings and the seasonality of the work are reflected in the low levels of living in the area, a condition which is pronounced among the older rural people.

EDUCATION

The formal educational attainment of the older Spanish-speaking people of the Southwest clearly reflects the poor quality of schools in the area during the early part of the twentieth century. Not only were the schools of poor quality but the system of education was designed primarily for English rather than Spanish-speaking children. The consequences of these conditions are seen today: one of the highest illiteracy rates for older people in the nation.

In 1960 almost 42 percent of the Spanish-speaking male population of the Southwest living on farms and 65 years of age or over had no formal schooling, compared with 6 percent of the same age group for the United States rural farm population as a whole. These percentages were about the same for the older rural farm female population (Table 4). Equally impressive is the fact that 73 percent of the rural farm males 65 years or more in the area had completed no more than four grades of formal schooling, compared with 21 percent of the total older rural farm male population in the United States. If the completion of a minimum of five grades is considered the dividing line between functional and nonfunctional literacy, as is frequently the case, about three-fourths of the rural-farm Spanish-speaking males of the Southwest 65 years of age or over are illiterate. This figure is highly similar to literacy figures for many countries of the world generally considered by North Americans to be among the underdeveloped. As Table 4 shows, literacy figures for the farm and nonfarm Spanish-speaking people in the Southwest are almost identical.

Literacy levels between the different southwestern states are far from uniform. States with the largest numbers of Spanish-speaking people (California and Texas) have the highest rates of adult illiteracy. Texas has the highest ranking, with more than 56 percent of its Spanish-speaking rural farm males reporting no formal schooling in 1960. The state of Colorado, which includes fewer Spanish-speaking people, had the lowest rate of illiteracy among its rural farm aged, with only 14.5 percent of the group reporting no formal schooling.

Table 4. Rural White Persons Aged 65 and Over with Spanish Surname by Residence, Sex, and Grade of School Completed for Five Southwestern States, 1960

Grade completed	Rural farm				Rural nonfarm			
	Male		Female		Male		Female	
	Number	Percent	Number	Percent	Number	Percent	Number	Percent
0	1,702	42	996	46	5,468	43	4,581	46
1-4	1,289	31	499	23	3,864	30	2,680	27
5-6	428	10	195	9	1,390	11	854	9
7-8	372	9	265	12	1,309	11	1,085	11
9-11	150	4	59	3	370	3	329	3
12	61	2	54	3	193	1	150	2
Some college	87	2	54	3	193	1	150	2

Source: U. S. Bureau of the Census, *United States Census of Population: 1960, Subject Reports, Persons of Spanish Surname,* Final Report PC(2)-1B (Washington, D. C., 1963), Table 2.

INCOME

The older Spanish-speaking citizen of the Southwest occupies a deprived economic position in the community. He does enjoy certain advantages, however, largely denied to this Anglo-American counterpart, in that old age does not remove him from a position of prestige and some usefulness to his friends and relatives. As an urban study in California points out, Spanish-speaking families generally are devoted to the elderly and working relatives do not resent elderly persons' leaning on them for financial and other aid.[2]

United States census data for 1960 show that the huge majority of Spanish-speaking males of the Southwest 65 years of age or over had annual incomes of less than $3,000 per year, a functional poverty line set by the Office of Employment Opportunity in 1964. The percentages were 86 for the rural farm males and 91 for the rural nonfarm males. Of white males 65 years of age or older in the total population, 68 percent had incomes under $3,000.

These figures coincide with findings from a 1961 study of Spanish-speaking people in San Antonio and Atascosa counties, Texas. This study found that 56 percent of the local rural Spanish-speaking males 65 years of age and older generally had earnings of less than $3,000.[3] Data from the same study also show very sharp drops in annual income for these people when they reach 65 years of age.

Actually, combined data for the two counties show a steady and marked decline in income for each age grouping, beginning with age 35. Males 35 to 44 years of age, for example, had median incomes of approximately $2,600 in 1960-61. This dropped to $2,480 for the 45 to 54 year group and to $1,144 for those 65 years of age and older. The drop in the arithmetic mean earnings was even more marked, from $2,567 per year for the 35 to 44 year group to only $277 for the group 65 years of age and older. The pattern was almost identical for the two counties.

HOUSING AND LIVING CONDITIONS

Living conditions among rural Spanish-speaking people are relatively poor, especially for the aged. Incomes for most older per-

sons, even if they are employed, are scarcely large enough to provide the bare essentials for living. Aspirations for retirement
hinge on hopes for Old Age Assistance and help from children.
At present, many adults expect to move to the major towns or
cities when they retire. Such attitudes often result in reduced
interest in improving homes in the country, since these homes
will only be abandoned when retirement age is reached.

Few consumption studies exist for the Spanish-speaking population of the Southwest and none for the older members of this
group. Information available from other sources shows that a
large proportion of the rural people do not possess many of the
items usually considered to be part of the American way of life;
refrigerators and television sets are not found in many rural
homes of the Southwest. A study in north-central New Mexico
found that 27 percent of the rural farm families were without a
refrigerator in 1960, 67 percent had no television, 60 percent
were without running water, 70 percent were without a flush
toilet, and 74 percent did not take a daily newspaper.[4] Although
there are no statistics available that give the incidence of these
items among older Spanish-speaking households in the area, there
is reason to believe that such households are no better equipped
than those of younger members.

Substandard housing conditions obtain for much of the
Spanish-speaking population. Saunders, who has spent many
years studying health and living conditions in the Southwest,
advises that

> whether Spanish-speaking southwesterners live in the city
> or country, their housing is likely to be poor. Houses are
> generally small and old. Sanitary facilities are frequently
> substandard or are lacking entirely. Overcrowding is com-
> mon. At one extreme is the brush hut of the wetback in the
> border counties, providing little more than an overhead
> shelter. The housing of Mexican-American agricultural work-
> ers, whether migrant or not, is probably not so good as that
> of the villagers.[5]

There are few good sources of information on housing conditions among the rural Spanish-speaking population of the Southwest. Some idea of the situation can be had, however, from the
analysis of United States Census of Housing data on a few counties that are predominantly inhabited by Spanish-speaking people, such as: Moro and San Miguel of New Mexico, Conejos and

Costilla of Colorado, and Zapata and Starr counties of Texas. About 60 percent of the houses in these counties were rated as being in sound condition in 1960, and 10 percent were dilapidated. Only 38 percent, including those in the towns, had plumbing facilities and 36 percent had no water piped into the house; 5 percent of the Spanish-speaking people were living in one-room houses and 18 percent in two-room houses.

Although these figures include all family heads, it is assumed that housing conditions for the older persons are as bad or worse except for those residing with their children or other relatives. These conditions are the result of many factors, among which are: the reduced size of many holdings, poor quality of much of the land, inadequate water, poor educational background, lack of complete familiarity with Anglo-American ways, and, at times, job discrimination. A study of a Spanish-speaking village in northern New Mexico in 1940 shows that a group of farmers in the village owned, as an average, less than two acres of irrigated land, the only sort of land that could be counted on to produce each year.[6] The situation is similar in many other settlements in the New Mexico and Colorado area.

WELFARE AND DEPENDENCY

No adequate information is available that permits a measure of the relative importance played by welfare payments in the lives of the older rural Spanish-speaking population of the Southwest. That which does exist, however, indicates that participation of the older rural population in welfare programs is common. The study in two Texas counties shows that 82 of the 103 rural Spanish-speaking persons 65 years of age or over interviewed in 1961 were receiving old age pensions.[7]

A high rate of participation by this group in welfare, and especially in Old Age Assistance programs, reflects not only the relatively underprivileged economic position they occupy but also a set of attitudes that includes little inhibition to receiving assistance, whether of old age or some other type. To the extent that the Spanish-speaking population of the Southwest is still influenced by the social and cultural system of its antecedents, the people are not reluctant to accept help in old age. Spanish tradition and custom impose rigid class differences that include a set of rights and duties concerning the needy. Aging rural people expect their landlords and other employers to provide them with a minimum level of subsistence in old age. This is not considered charity but rather a type of deferred payment for services. Obviously, it is not a major transfer to shift this attitude to the state. This is, as Saunders points out, simply a matter of role playing in existing institutional relationships.

LABOR-FORCE PARTICIPATION

As pointed out earlier, the value orientation of Spanish-speaking people permits retirement from work as a natural and expected thing to do. There are no social rewards for employment to avoid idleness. However, retirement is more pronounced among the urban and rural nonfarm residents than among the rural farm population. Census data for 1960 show that only 26 percent of the rural nonfarm Spanish-speaking males of the Southwest 65 years of age or over considered themselves in the labor force, and 92 percent of these were employed. The percentage was only 4 for the corresponding group of females and 92 percent of this group was employed. The situation was quite different for those living on farms. Here 53 percent of the males 65 years of age or older were in the labor force and 97 percent of the group was employed. Corresponding percentages for the females were 6 and 95.

As one would expect, most of the older rural Spanish-speaking persons who are still employed are in farm work, either as operators or laborers. About one-third are employed as farm laborers or as foremen. The remainder are scattered among a wide variety of skilled and unskilled jobs.

The older females living on farms participate in various forms of work, including many farm tasks. A few own or manage small shops or other businesses. Most employed rural nonfarm women perform domestic work. About a fifth of this group reported that they were working but gave no specific occupation.[8]

These data clearly demonstrate a concentration of the Spanish-speaking population of all ages in the unskilled and poor-paying jobs. Discrimination may account partly for this situation, but the major factors are lack of education and training, little work experience, and a limited knowledge of English. The last, of course, is particularly true for jobs where the use of English is of fundamental importance.

The tendency for older Spanish-speaking people of the Southwest to remove themselves from the working force at a relatively early age has been noted by various students of the area.[9] Such behavior is in keeping with the traditional value orientation which encourages relatively early transfer of work responsibilities. Too, work, at least for the older Spanish-speaking citizen, is valued only as a means to get something done and makes no sense as an end in itself. This does not mean that work is thought unimportant. It may be an exclusive means for getting something one desires or has to have. It would not be understood, however, in the traditional American social context as a rational decision to avoid the ills of idleness.

HEALTH STATUS

Poor and inadequate health and medical care and antiquated and obsolete sanitary facilities and practices are inevitable consequences of low incomes. Despite notable improvements that have taken place during the last two decades, this condition still is widespread in much of the Spanish-speaking Southwest, particularly in the rural areas.

The problems of health among rural Spanish-speaking people of the Southwest have received little research attention. Accumulated research data show that the general level of health of these people is lower than that for the general population in the region. Water for household use is often a major problem. In many rural households it is taken directly from unprotected irrigation ditches or polluted streams. This, and related conditions, contribute to a high incidence of dysentery and even death among infants, especially in the more isolated rural villages where medical care is distant and expensive.[10]

Study and observation in sections of the rural Southwest indicate some improvement in the health status of Spanish-speaking people during the past two decades. This improvement has resulted from somewhat larger incomes, more regular work, greater participation in educational programs, and from the increased efforts of welfare agencies of state and federal governments.

There are no data, however, that demonstrate this clearly. Saunders thinks that "the health of the Spanish-Americans who have remained in their native villages is probably not greatly different now from what it has been in the past quarter century although a somewhat adequate diet, and the influence of such organizations and agencies as the New Mexico Health Council, the Catholic Maternity Institute, and the State and local health departments of Colorado and New Mexico have made medical personnel and facilities more available and have brought about improvements in water supply and sanitation in some areas."[11] These changes probably have benefited the older rural Spanish-speaking persons of the Southwest, but not as much as other age groups.

FAMILY AND KINSHIP SYSTEM

Many elements of the traditional Spanish-speaking family are still much in evidence among the older people of the rural Southwest, especially in New Mexico and Colorado.[12] Once essential for survival, the extended family is bowing to pressures to conform to the dominant national pattern. Among the elements that remain are those concerned with attention to older relatives, particularly parents and grandparents. Strict norms of the family system prescribe that older people will be cared for by a wide variety of relatives and that they will be visited, consulted, and made to feel that old age is not a barrier to remove them from roles considered useful by the society of which they are a part. Among Spanish-speaking people, the arrival at old age may be considered something of an accomplishment and achieving it an honor. It is a goal to which many look forward. Retirement is a time to rest and to dole out, little by little, the store of wisdom gleaned from many years of experience.

An important function of the older person in the more rural sections of the Spanish-speaking Southwest is to maintain a link, both horizontally and intergenerationally, between members of extended families. This function may involve a wide range of activities, including acting as spokesman for the larger group in a crisis or an event threatening the group welfare and judging the extent to which families are performing their responsibilities with regard to religion, child orientation, child training, and other matters affecting family members. Since these many duties require a substantial amount of time, the older person has relatively little reason to complain about idle time and uselessness.

The older Spanish-speaking female performs many roles considered important to the well-being of the group. Mothers and grandmothers are major sources of folklore concerning health and health practices. Their counsel is sought by girls contemplating matrimony and by young mothers facing new obligations as wives and mothers. Despite competition from public health technicians during the past two or three decades, the older married or widowed female retains important responsibilities in the health care of rural families, particularly for those living in the more isolated rural areas.

LIVING ARRANGEMENTS AND PATTERNS OF CARE

Clear definitions of individual and family obligations in the traditional Spanish-speaking family system avoid many of the in-law and intergenerational problems that often plague Anglo-American marriages. As indicated previously, there are definite expectations concerning the responsibilities of children for their parents, for older people, and for other members of the family. Married children often encourage older parents to live with them. If this cannot be arranged, then one or more offspring may be delegated to live with the elderly person or couple. Such responsibilities extend to the care of children of a widowed parent who would otherwise not have someone on whom to depend for support.

Although all children are expected to contribute to the support and maintenance of elder relatives, a major part of this responsibility is likely to fall on the sons. Employed daughters, however, and especially those who are unmarried, are expected to help.[13]

AUTHORITY ROLES IN THE HOME

Much has been written on the comparative roles of different members of the traditional Spanish-speaking family. Almost without exception the roles of husband and wife are characterized as dominant and submissive with unilateral decision expectations associated with the male. Unfortunately, characterizations such as these are often arbitrary, made by observers relatively unfamiliar with the traditional culture, a condition not conducive to accuracy. Careful and prolonged observations of situations within the Spanish-speaking family of the Southwest, and in other countries where the same original culture is present, suggest that females, especially homemakers, exert substantial influence in the making of decisions. This conclusion seems valid not only in the towns and cities but also in isolated villages or settlements. Although situations involving the public appearance and participation of both sexes will portray the male as an autocratic decision-maker for the family, this apparent authority seldom carries over into behavior less accessible to an outside audience. In the home, when outsiders are absent, the wife is extremely likely to take strong and decisive stands on matters involving the family budget, the discipline of the children, and the management of all home activities. Studies show that the wife, even in the most unassimilated Spanish-speaking family, has a voice in domestic decision-making equal in importance to that of the wife in an Anglo-American family of comparable economic level.

The opinions and judgments of the homemaker in decisions affecting family affairs become increasingly important with age. The advisory role of the mother continues to be important long after her daughters establish their own families. Serious consideration of maternal advice is based on two major premises: a deep reluctance to disturb the mother emotionally and a general feeling of confidence in the mother's advice and general counsel. The rural daughter is likely to have an especially high regard for the experience of her mother. The importance of mother's opinion about economic matters may be limited but great pains may be taken to assure that such opinions are never rejected outright.

Both the younger and the older people in the rural Spanish-speaking communities of the Southwest admit that adaptation to local Anglo-American culture has resulted in less appreciation for the counsel and guidance of older people. This, obviously, is part of a widely based change pattern that has done much to widen the ideological chasm separating the older and younger age groups. This change is highly traumatic for many older persons who see sons and daughters abandon traditional ways. A cultural complex is extremely sticky, however, and can hardly be discarded completely in a generation. Much of the cultural heritage of the area has disappeared in the recent past and in an unbalanced fashion, i.e., certain elements have been more quickly and easily abandoned than others. This imbalance also has characterized the acceptance of new traits. Values generally associated with the early Protestant ethic have been adopted by the younger group. Many of the traditional values associated with basic Spanish culture, such as the restricted interpretation of family roles, have been retained. There is little doubt that unless present trends are reversed most of the Spanish-speaking young people now entering the compulsory school attendance ages will be different from their Anglo-American neighbors in name only.

PARTICIPATION IN COMMUNITY ACTIVITIES

Formal organizational participation for the rural Spanish-speaking families of the Southwest is limited largely to the church and church-sponsored activities. Attendance at these is often minimal both as a result of distance and as a matter of choice. An older study in north-central New Mexico showed an average annual attendance of males at religious meetings of 144 and for females 146, or about three times per week. This was the only organizational activity of any importance reported for the year.[14]

Sunday Mass, when this service is available, is attended regularly by the older individuals, both male and female. Where a priest is not available an older male or female may conduct a substitute service. This responsibility frequently is assigned to a leading elder or to a younger male or female who has demonstrated qualities of leadership and whose loyalty to the church is not under question.

Homes of older people in the Spanish-speaking communities are the centers of much informal activity, especially in communities where the houses are grouped closely together, as is common in rural New Mexico, Colorado, Arizona, and certain parts of California. Children, grandchildren, and others call frequently, not only for counsel and advice but to offer assistance and to visit. Children and other relatives are expected to visit older people. It has been observed that these visits are decreasing, since better roads and improved means of transportation enable younger people to go more frequently to nearby towns.

Among Spanish-speaking people, older persons have an important role in certain activities of the young. When physical conditions permit, older people are expected to be present at all social affairs such as weddings, christenings, and dances. They serve as chaperons at all social affairs in which young people participate. The presence of older people lends a respectability to such affairs that otherwise would not obtain.

USE OF LEISURE TIME

Retirement for the rural Spanish-speaking person is often little more than a change of status and position in the local community situation. Retirement does not mean complete withdrawal from useful roles. In farming, for example, when a son takes over the chief work roles, the male parent may become a technical supervisor whose counsel is much more than perfunctory. Although the son may not feel obligated to accept the counsel of an elder, it would be considered extremely discourteous for him not to listen to it. This relationship is not limited to parents and children. It also may include grandchildren and others falling under the rather broad umbrella of the extended family.

Older males and older females hold the places of honor in the households. Special chairs and special places may be set aside for them in the homes of children. Active participation from such favored positions give the older people a strong sense of importance to the group.

Thus, in a cultural setting in which leisure is not considered evil and in which being fully occupied has no special virtue, the older people perform active family roles. In such a situation, no apology is needed for being old.

PROBLEMS OF ADJUSTMENTS

Periodic migration of workers from Mexico and geographic isolation from the remainder of the United States have produced what George I. Sanchez has called a case of "cultural indigestion" in the Southwest.[15] It is only within the past 30 years that improved roads, a greater dissemination of information, better schools, and more regular attendance at school have combined to bring the Spanish-speaking people of the Southwest into fairly close contact with the dominant culture of the nation. The result is change that is proceeding at a rate not dreamed of two decades earlier. Even in the most isolated rural areas Spanish is giving way to English, younger people are moving out into wider political and social arenas, and general behavioral differences that characterized the Spanish-speaking peoples a few years ago are disappearing. In brief, assimilation is well along the way in the entire Southwest.

The more obvious traits of Spanish culture, such as language, special types of music, and art today are salient only among recent immigrants from Mexico and the older rural residents who occupy the more isolated small valleys, mountain plateaus, and mining towns scattered over much of the Southwest. Some of the younger people still understand and can speak a form of antiquated Spanish, but it is now the preferred language only of the older people. Today, even in isolated rural areas, it is the older people who converse in Spanish while the younger ones use English. Only the older people can recite key events of Spanish and Mexican occupation of the area. It is the older persons who know the songs, music, sayings, folklore, and superstitions peculiar to the early Spanish Southwest. Among the younger people these are being replaced by comics and tales of space and astronauts as related through radio and television. Many of these changes are considered by the older people to be good. Both children and grandchildren are encouraged to remain in school, to learn a trade, to study for a profession, and to leave the land that has offered their fathers relatively little. These attitudes accelerate change in the rural Spanish-speaking Southwest. They have been important factors in producing a mass migration of Spanish-speaking people from the rural Southwest during the past two decades.

MODES OF ADJUSTMENT

As indicated earlier, the traditional norms of the Spanish-speaking family accept the care of relatives in old age as a family responsibility. Recently these norms have undergone some change, especially among the younger age groups. As with values and attitudes, change in norms and rules has come more slowly for the older population. They have not been able to accept completely the idea of shifting all responsibility for their care and attention to the state. However, many older Spanish-speaking people have moved from rural areas to towns and small cities in the Southwest in order to receive greater assistance from the state. In contrast with earlier retirement practices of moving in with the children, increasing numbers of older parents and grandparents are now moving into town where they live with older children or else purchase or rent inexpensive living quarters.

SOURCES OF CONFLICT AND ANXIETY

The highly integrated nature of the family among the Spanish-speaking people of the Southwest is an important factor in diminishing the intensity of many of the sources of anxiety of older people. Worries about children living in distant places and the resultant inability to visit with them are mitigated by the efforts of nearby relatives to make up for this loss by increasing the number of their own visits. This pattern of responsibility also compensates for the isolation of older Spanish-speaking people from their Anglo-American neighbors, who are unable to communicate for lack of a common language.

The high degree of integration characterizing the Spanish-speaking family seems to maintain even among rural migratory families who move about not only in the Southwest but in other areas as well. Horacio Ulibarri, professor of education at the University of New Mexico, found in his recent studies of the Southwest that "the migrant and ex-migrant families tend to be closely knit units where all members seem to enjoy great status and esteem."[16] He found, also, that "an attitude of complete contentment seemed to prevail within the family unit" and that concern was expressed over the welfare of a wide range of poor relatives, even though economic conditions limited their ability to help. One of the few major worries of the older people was that they had not been able to do more for their children. The predominance of this attitude may well reflect the adoption of certain aspects of Anglo-American culture. Although unassimilated Spanish-speaking parents are concerned with what they are unable to do for their children, self-recrimination in the traditional Spanish culture is less common than among the Anglo-Americans.

PSYCHOLOGICAL AND SOCIAL DEPENDENCY

The conditions of psychological dependency that have been pictured for older people in the general population do not appear appropriate for the older Spanish-speaking population of the Southwest, especially for those who live on farms or in the smaller towns and villages. As indicated earlier, the older citizen of the rural Southwest, whether gainfully employed or retired, occupies a position of status and prestige in the community. Far from feeling useless and dependent in old age, older Spanish-speaking persons consider themselves needed persons performing important roles in advising sons, daughters, and others. Some of the older persons consider themselves important links to the past, charged with the task of acquainting younger people with Spanish history and tradition. Having such key responsibilities, they do not feel useless nor burdensome, even though they depend on charity or on what sons and daughters can provide. Few would argue that key advice in the area of morals and history is not worth the price of food and shelter.

A few students of the area have called attention to the influence of both geography and the Spanish and Mexican Land Grant Policies in the development and stability of a system of agriculture involving large land holdings and corresponding political power. Under both the colonial and early republican systems, the owner or "patron" furnished tenants everything needed for crop operations except labor, such as tools, credit, church facilities (often building the church and paying the expenses of visiting priests), health, and education. Families and individuals were tied closely not only to the land but to specific persons (the patrons) who rewarded their services with nominal wages or limited use of land during their working lives and with a semblance of maintenance in old age.[17] This system began to break down during the latter part of the nineteenth century, when public lands were widely distributed throughout the area, and continued through World War II. At that time a large percentage of all able bodied workers moved to more remunerative jobs elsewhere. However, much of the earlier feelings of dependence remain for the older members. Unfortunately, little research has been done on this highly complex problem but such evidence as is available shows that present rates of economic dependency, measured by pensions and old age benefits, follow about the same pattern as for the nation as a whole.

ECONOMIC AND SOCIAL TRENDS

The volume and the rate of economic and social change in the Southwest since the beginning of World War II in both rural and urban areas have been among the greatest in the nation. These changes continue today, but at a slower rate. Census information indicates that migration from the rural areas, so marked in the 1960's, is much reduced. A study of economic conditions in northern New Mexico, completed in 1957, shows that the size of the rural population of that area of the state is about the same as it was 10 years ago even though the 234 rural households visited for purposes of the study reported a total of 332 children, or about 1.5 persons per household, permanently away from home. About half of these were still in the sample area and approximately 35 percent lived outside the state. Most of the out-of-state migrants were male.[18]

Insofar as income depicts well-being, the situation for the Spanish-speaking people of the Southwest has improved markedly during recent years.[19] This improvement largely is the result of the rapid industrial growth of the West since World War II, particularly along the coast of California. This growth has drawn in large numbers of workers, as well as older relatives, from farms and small towns of New Mexico, Texas, Colorado, and Arizona. Farm wage rates and prices for farm products have risen. For the older population, a major factor in their improved well-being has been their participation in state Old Age Assistance plans. In many cases this assistance has enabled older persons to leave farms and to live in towns and cities. However, despite these recent improvements, the incomes of the Spanish-speaking people of the Southwest are still among the lowest in the nation, a condition which obtains not only for persons of working age but also for the older population, both those who are employed and those who are retired.

The changing structure of the rural economy of the Southwest, greater contact of the rural people with members of the dominant society, widening participation in life outside village and community limits, and increased mobility have produced a cumulative effect contributing to the breakdown of the traditional life of the area. The once highly integrated and extended family system characteristic of the area has been, and continues to be, giving away to the smaller and more mobile nuclear family responsible only to its own members. Roles within the family have changed, and a more democratic structure has developed, permitting greater freedom of action and participtaion in all decisions affecting the group. More females, especially single females, are working. Relatively more children, rural as well as urban, are attending schools that have become better equipped to meet the educational problems of the area.

An important continuing change characteristic of the Southwest is its rapid shift toward a native population. Despite a constant stream of immigration from Latin America, Puerto Rico, and, especially, Mexico, relatively more of the population each year is of native stock. In 1960 the U. S. Bureau of the Census estimated that only 15 percent of the Spanish-speaking population of the Southwest was foreign born as compared with 17 percent in 1950 and 21 percent in 1940.

Another of the more important changes taking place among the Spanish-speaking people of the Southwest is their rapid shift in residence from rural to urban. Whereas they constituted a predominantly rural population before 1940, by 1960 they were largely urban. By 1950, approximately 66 percent of the population was living in centers of 2,500 or more and by 1960 the percentage had increased to 79. Almost 61 percent of the latter group was living in urban places of 10,000 or more, indicating that much of the recent growth in the urban population has been in the larger towns and cities.[20]

The rate of urbanization for the population 65 years of age or over seems to be keeping pace with the urbanization of the total Spanish-speaking group. In 1950, about 68 percent of this older age group lived in places of 2,500 or more, and by 1960 this percentage had increased to 80. As would be expected from the shifting industrial picture of the Southwest, this urbanization was far from uniform in pattern among the five southwestern states. The U. S. census of population returns show that 85 percent of older Spanish-speaking people of California lived in places of 2,500 or more in 1960, compared with only 58 percent in New Mexico, where a substantial portion of the rural Spanish-speaking population lives on owner-operated farms.

The major trend among the Spanish-speaking people of the Southwest, both rural and urban, is toward a rapid assimilation into the dominant culture of the nation. For older persons living in the more isolated rural areas of the Southwest, who tend to cling to their Spanish traditions, this cultural transition presents problems of adjustment and concern. They recognize they are approaching the end of their lives and with their passing the cultural traditions which mean so much to them will also pass. When this occurs, the phrase "Persons of Spanish Surname" may have little meaning in the United States.

NOTES

[1] Numbers used here are based largely on estimates from a 25 percent sample, U. S. Bureau of the Census in 1960. Data published in a special report of the census, *Spanish Surname Population, 1960,* PC(2)-1B (Washington, D. C., 1963).

[2] Margaret Clark, *Health in the Mexican-American Culture* (Berkeley: University of California Press, 1959), p. 145.

[3] A study made in Michigan during the same year finds that earnings for older Spanish-speaking migrant workers in the state are more. Most of these migrants were originally from Texas. Unpublished data gathered by Michigan State University under a study sponsored by the Farm Population Branch, Economic Research Service, U. S. Department of Agriculture, 1960-61.

[4] Marlowe M. Taylor, *Rural People and Their Resources* (North-Central New Mexico, New Mexico State University, Bulletin 448; Las Cruces, 1960), p. 14.

[5] Lyle Saunders, *Cultural Difference and Medical Care* (New York: Russell Sage Foundation, 1954), p. 73.

[6] Olen E. Leonard, *The Role of the Land Grant* . . . (Ann Arbor, Mich.: Edwards Brothers, Inc., 1940).

[7] Robert L. Skrabanek, "Study of Spanish-Speaking Population of Two Texas Counties," 1961 (unpublished).

[8] See U. S. Bureau of the Census, *United States Census of Population: 1960, Subject Reports, Persons of Spanish Surname,* Final Report PC(2)-1B (Washington, D. C., 1963), Table 8.

[9] This awareness is breaking down as the Spanish-speaking group becomes assimilated into the dominant culture. This assimilation has been moving at an accelerated rate since World War II, when large numbers of persons from the areas in which these people were concentrated were pulled into the industrial West and North. More and better schools, better prepared teachers, and more regular attendance have also been important contributing factors. It is somewhat doubtful today that many of the younger Spanish-speaking children could be classified as culturally distinct from Anglo-Americans.

[10] Leonard, *The Role of the Land Grant*, pp. 53-54.

[11] *Cultural Difference and Medical Care*, p. 76.

[12] Paul A. Walter, Jr., "The Spanish-Speaking Community of New Mexico," *Sociology and Social Research*, 24 (Nov.-Dec. 1939); Olen E. Leonard and Charles P. Loomis, *Culture of a Contemporary Community*, U. S. Department of Agriculture, Rural Life Studies 1 (Washington, D. C., 1941); Horacio Ulibarri, "Social and Attitudinal Characteristics of Migrant and Ex-Migrant Workers in New Mexico, Colorado, Arizona, and Texas" (The College of Education, University of New Mexico, unpublished, 1964).

[13] This seems especially to be the case when the old people choose to remain in their local villages or rural communities. They may remain in their own homes or move in with a local son or daughter. Such support as would not come from Old Age Assistance plans would be supplied by working sons and daughters. See Saunders, *Cultural Differences and Medical Care*, p. 48; and also Leonard, *The Role of the Land Grant*, pp. 62-65.

[14] Leonard, *The Role of the Land Grant*, p. 60.

[15] "Spanish-speaking People in the Southwest" (University of Texas, unpublished, 1950).

[16] "Social and Attitudinal Characteristics of Migrant and Ex-Migrant Workers in New Mexico, Colorado, Arizona, and Texas" (University of New Mexico, 1964, unpublished), p. 21.

[17] Saunders, *Cultural Difference and Medical Care*, pp. 133-35; Leonard, *The Role of the Land Grant*, pp. 72-104.

[18] Ulibarri, "Social and Attitudinal Characteristics," p. 18.

[19] Saunders, *Cultural Difference and Medical Care*, pp. 174-225. No effort has been made to establish the relationship between local increases in income and real improvement in living. This is a point about which there is much discussion but little valid information. One could probably show that the shifting of responsibility for the support of older rural couples to the state from the child has resulted in the use of more consumption goods by the latter.

[20] U. S. Bureau of the Census, *United States Census of Population: 1960, Subject Reports, Persons of Spanish Surname*, Final Report PC(2)-1B (Washington, D. C., 1963), and *United States Census of Population: 1950, Subject Reports, Persons of Spanish Surname*, Final Report P-E, No. 3C (Washington, D. C., 1953).

STANLEY H. SMITH

The Older Rural Negro

Very little information is available about aged Negroes in American society, and even less is known about the social category which is the focus of this chapter—older rural Negroes. The National Urban League recently published a report called *Double Jeopardy: A Profile of the Older Negro in America Today*,[1] which suggests that the status of the aged Negro is different from the aged white primarily because he is Negro. Another report entitled *Health Care and the Negro Population*[2] examines the health status of the aged Negro, analyzing this phenomenon within the framework of subcultural differences. Of relevance also is "The Aging Negro: Some Implications for Social Welfare Services" by Walter M. Beattie, Jr.,[3] which contains implications for planning welfare, health, and leisure-time activities for older Negroes. By means of surveys, agencies of the federal government are making important contributions to the body of knowledge about the older rural Negro. Prominent among these is *The Aging Nonwhite and His Housing* by the Housing and Home Finance Agency,[4] which examines housing conditions of aged nonwhites in terms of adequacy and comfort.

In recent years attention has been focused on the "other America"—areas in the United States inhabited by persons classified as poor in an affluent society.[5] Available evidence indicates that substantial portions of the aged in American society may be placed in the poverty group and that many pockets of poverty exist in rural areas of the nation. It is well known, also, that minority groups in the United States have a lower standard of living than the white population. However, diligent search has revealed extremely few studies of persons who share three characteristics commonly associated with poverty: old age, rural residence, and minority-group status. Thus, a systematic body of knowledge is lacking about substantial portions of the population in American society.

SOURCES OF INFORMATION

The paucity of published information about the aged rural Negro in the United States poses a critical problem. Rather extensive literature exists about Negroes living in urban areas of the United States, and one approach might have been to sift this literature and draw inferences about older rural Negroes, but since such inferences might have dubious validity, this approach was rejected. It was decided to attempt a chapter, incomplete as it might be, based upon existing data about older rural Negroes. One source of such information is the U. S. Census Bureau materials.[6] Although these materials have limitations, they provide the opportunity of making meaningful comparisons between older rural farm and rural nonfarm Negroes, and between these two categories and older urban Negroes. These materials also provide a national standard for many comparisons, but these national standards, by definition, include all aged persons—rural as well as urban. Consequently, comparisons between older rural Negroes and national standards for all aged persons do not reveal the sharp differences that may exist. In addition, it is difficult to draw inferences about the full significance of existing differences. Minority groups, especially many Negroes, do not necessarily compare themselves or their conditions of life with some national standard. More probably they contrast their lot in life with that of white, urban, middle-class persons as portrayed in various mass media. Thus, it is very doubtful that inferences drawn from national census materials can reveal how the older rural Negro feels about his conditions of life.

Another source of data relating to older rural Negroes is found in a southern regional study in rural sociology.[7] These data also have limitations. The project was not designed to study the aged and the information about older persons was thus incidental to the main purposes of the project. The title of the study was "Factors in the Adjustment of Families and Individuals to Changing Conditions in Low-Income Rural Areas of the South." The regional sample drawn for this study was not representative of all areas of the rural South. It was a selected sample of rural families living in lower economic areas of seven states in the southeastern United States. This sample included 396 heads of households aged 65 and over, of whom three-quarters were male and one-quarter female, and of whom 74 percent were white and 26 percent Negro. The responses obtained from these 396 heads of households to very limited categories of questions are used in this chapter. One important advantage of these data is that they permit comparisons between aged Negroes and whites who share a common condition of life: both groups live in low-income rural areas of the South.

In cases where the census data and the regional data overlap, it is expected that some differences will exist, differences probably accounted for by the nature of the sampling. However, the intent in presenting the regional data is not to make comparisons with the national data but to compare the aged Negroes and whites in the southern region.

Materials in this chapter include some selected demographic characteristics of aged rural Negroes; data on educational level, employment, and income; some data on the involvement of aged rural Negroes in American life; and a small amount of data which are designed to allow an assessment of some of the subjective reactions of aged rural Negroes to their social and economic conditions. It is hoped that the materials presented contribute to an understanding of an important category of persons in the United States who possess three poverty-linked characteristics: old age, rural residence, and minority-group status.

SELECTED DEMOGRAPHIC CHARACTERISTICS

In 1960, there were 367,091 Negroes aged 65 and over living in rural areas of the United States, 275,100 in rural nonfarm areas and 91,991 in rural farm areas. Slightly more aged Negro females than males lived in rural nonfarm areas, but in the rural farm areas the males outnumbered the females. Rural aged Negroes constituted almost one-third (32 percent) of all Negroes aged 65 and over in the nation. In 1960, only 7 percent of aged rural Negroes lived in regions outside of the South. In the southern region there were 253,047 aged Negroes living in rural nonfarm areas and 89,466 living in rural farm areas (Table 1).

Table 1. Regional Distribution of Negroes Aged 65 and Over in the United States by Residence and Sex, 1960

Sex and Rural distribution	Region				
	United States	North-east	North Central	South	West
United States					
Total	1,167,880	156,178	190,493	776,800	44,409
Male	540,523	70,491	90,419	359,517	20,096
Female	627,357	85,687	100,074	417,283	24,313
Rural					
Total	367,091	8,380	13,457	342,513	2,741
Male	181,784	4,455	7,331	168,468	1,530
Female	185,307	3,925	6,126	174,045	1,211
Rural nonfarm					
Total	275,100	8,044	11,583	253,047	2,426
Male	132,637	4,264	6,258	120,774	1,341
Female	142,463	3,780	5,325	132,273	1,085
Rural farm					
Total	91,991	336	1,874	89,466	315
Male	49,147	191	1,073	47,694	189
Female	42,844	145	801	41,772	126

Source: U. S. Bureau of the Census, *United States Census of Population: 1960, Nonwhite Population by Race,* PC(2)-1C (Washington, D. C., 1963), Table 1.

Data on residential mobility give some index of the spatial movements of older rural Negroes. Residential mobility is assessed from the numbers of aged persons in the United States who moved to a different house between 1955 and 1960. According to this index, the rural aged Negroes changed household addresses less often than the urban aged Negro and slightly less often than all aged persons in the United States. As shown in Table 2, this generalization obtained for aged rural Negroes of both sexes. These data suggest less spatial mobility for the rural aged Negro, but they also suggest the existence of more limited opportunities for changing homes in rural areas. Undoubtedly more opportunities of this kind exist in urban than rural areas of the United States, for both white and Negro aged populations.

Available data on marital status in 1960 suggest that aged Negroes in rural areas have greater family stability than those in urban areas. As shown in Table 3, larger proportions of older rural male and female Negroes were married and living with their spouses. Also, smaller proportions of rural than of urban aged Negroes were separated, divorced, or widowed. Substan-

Table 2. Residential Mobility Within the United States of Persons Aged 65 and Over for the Total Population and for the Negro Population by Sex and Residence, 1955-60

Residential mobility and sex	Total population	Negro population		
		Urban	Rural nonfarm	Rural farm
Males				
Same house	70.7%	67.0%	72.7%	78.2%
Different house	27.5	30.2	25.8	21.5
Not reported	1.8	2.8	1.5	0.3
(Number)	(7,308,985)	(358,739)	(132,637)	(49,147)
Females				
Same house	69.6	67.4	74.5	76.0
Different house	28.7	30.4	24.4	23.7
Not reported	1.7	2.2	1.1	0.3
(Number)	(8,898,252)	(442,050)	(142,463)	(42,844)

Source: U. S. Bureau of the Census, United States Census of Population: 1960, Characteristics of the Population, PC(1)-1D (Washington, D. C., 1963), Vol. I, Table 164; and United States Census of Population: 1960, Nonwhite Population by Race, PC (2)-1C (Washington, D. C., 1963), Table 19.

tially larger proportions of aged Negro women than of men in rural areas were widowed: slightly more than one-fifth of the men, compared to more than half the women. The data in 1960 indicate that the marital structure of the aged Negroes in rural areas is slightly less stable than that of the total aged population in the United States, which is predominantly white. A larger proportion of aged rural Negroes than of the total aged in the United States were married more than once, and a larger proportion of aged rural Negroes than of the total aged population were separated or widowed.

Table 3. Percentage Distribution of the Total Population and the Negro Population in the United States by Marital Status and Sex, 1960

Marital status	Total population	Negro population		
		Urban	Rural nonfarm	Rural farm
Males				
Single	7.7%	6.6%	4.8%	3.3%
Ever married	92.3	93.4	95.2	96.7
Married, spouse present	66.9	56.4	63.2	71.1
Married, spouse absent	2.4	3.2	3.1	1.4
Separated	1.5	5.3	4.0	2.6
Widowed	19.1	25.6	23.2	20.6
Divorced	2.4	2.9	1.7	1.0
Married more than once	19.8	37.8	39.2	38.9
(Number)	(7,308,935)	(358,739)	(132,637)	(49,147)
Females				
Single	8.5	4.8	3.7	3.5
Ever married	91.5	95.2	96.3	96.5
Married, spouse present	34.7	23.2	32.0	42.1
Married, spouse absent	1.7	2.0	2.0	1.0
Separated	1.0	3.8	2.4	1.7
Widowed	52.1	63.7	58.9	51.0
Divorced	2.0	2.5	1.0	0.7
Married more than once	15.0	31.0	30.3	27.1
(Number)	(8,898,252)	(442,050)	(142,463)	(42,844)

Source: U. S. Bureau of the Census, *United States Census of Population: 1960, Characteristics of the Population,* PC(1)-1D (Washington, D. C. (1963), Vol. I, Table 164; and *United States Census of Population: 1960, Non-white Population by Race,* PC(2)-1C (Washington, D. C., 1963), Table 19.

EDUCATIONAL LEVEL

In recent years, Negro people in the United States have pressed for improved educational opportunities in an effort to raise their social and economic status. Although such efforts will undoubtedly benefit many younger Negroes, the aged Negro population will probably be affected very little. Older Negroes in the United States, particularly those in rural areas, have received relatively little formal education, and the prospects for altering this disadvantage appear rather remote.

The low formal educational levels of rural aged Negroes in the United States are revealed in the census data. In 1960, the educational levels of rural Negroes aged 65 and over were substantially lower than those of urban Negroes of comparable age and substantially lower than national levels for aged persons. At a time in American society when considerable education is mandatory for all citizens, it is significant that 90 percent of male and 84 percent of female aged rural Negroes had received less than eight years of formal education (Table 4). Aged Negroes in urban areas were only slightly less disadvantaged in formal educational levels. The proportions of aged urban Negro males and females who had received less than eight years schooling in 1960

Table 4. Percentage Distribution of Persons Aged 65 and Over for Total Population and Negro Population in the United States by Sex and Years of School Completed, 1960

Years of school completed and sex	Total population	Negro population		
		Urban	Rural nonfarm	Rural farm
Males				
None	7.9	16.2	27.1	23.0
Elementary: 1-4 years	15.7	34.8	44.9	46.3
5-7 years	23.0	23.8	18.0	20.2
8 years	26.0	11.1	5.0	5.6
Secondary: 1-3 years	10.4	6.2	2.5	2.6
4 years	7.8	3.8	1.2	1.1
College: 1-3 years	4.9	2.2	0.7	0.8
4 years or more	4.3	1.9	0.6	0.4
(Number)	(7,315,525)	(358,739)	(132,637)	(49,147)
Females				
None	6.6	12.7	19.5	17.4
Elementary: 1-4 years	11.5	31.1	40.5	40.7
5-7 years	20.8	26.5	25.1	26.2
8 years	27.5	12.9	7.3	7.6
Secondary: 1-3 years	12.8	7.8	4.0	4.4
4 years	11.6	4.9	1.7	1.8
College: 1-3 years	6.0	2.4	1.2	1.1
4 years or more	3.2	1.7	0.7	0.8
(Number)	(8,882,309)	(442,050)	(142,463)	(42,844)

Source: U. S. Bureau of the Census, *United States Census of Population: 1960, Educational Attainment,* PC(2)-5B (Washington, D. C., 1963), Table 1; and *United States Census of Population: 1960, Nonwhite Population by Race,* PC(2)-1C (Washington, D. C., 1963), Table 19.

were 75 and 70 percent, respectively. The corresponding percentages for older people in the nation were 47 and 39, respectively.

Additional evidence of the low educational level of the rural aged Negro is strikingly apparent when comparisons are made of aged persons in the United States who had received no more than four years of formal education. Approximately 70 percent of rural aged Negroes were in this educational category in 1960, more than one-third greater than the proportion for the urban aged Negro and almost three times the proportion for all older persons in the United States (Table 4).

Data from low-income families in the southern region also reveal the low educational level of aged rural Negroes. These data permit comparisons between white and nonwhite heads of household in which income level is held relatively constant. As shown in Table 5, the educational disparity between white and nonwhite heads of households is clearly shown in the proportions who reported they had received no formal education whatsoever. About one-fourth of aged rural Negroes in the sample had received no formal schooling, but only about 7 percent of the aged whites gave such a report. These findings add evidence of the inadequacy of the educational provisions existing in rural areas of the South.

Table 5. Educational Level by Percentage of Heads of Households Aged 65 and Over in Low-income Families of the Rural South by Race, 1959

Years of school completed	White		Negro	
	Rural farm (N = 111)	Rural nonfarm (N = 182)	Rural farm (N = 33)	Rural nonfarm (N = 70)
0	6.3	8.7	27.3	22.9
1-4	24.3	29.7	36.3	34.3
5-7	25.2	28.6	9.1	25.7
8	27.9	15.8	9.1	4.3
9-11	7.2	9.9	9.1	4.3
12	4.5	5.5	3.0	1.4
13-15	3.6	0.6	6.1	1.4
16	—	0.6	—	1.4
No response	1.0	0.6	—	4.3

EMPLOYMENT

It is generally recognized in the United States that most men withdraw or retire from the major occupational role at about age 65. One exception to this generalization are the farmers, who tend to remain in the labor force on a part-time basis. Older rural Negroes in the United States tend to conform to these patterns. According to the census data in 1960, about three-quarters of the aged Negro males who lived in rural nonfarm areas were not in the labor force. This proportion was slightly higher than that for aged urban Negro males and slightly higher than that for all males aged 65 and over in the United States (Table 6). However, almost half the aged rural Negro males who lived on farms considered themselves in the labor force in 1960 and practically all of these were employed. Nine-tenths of the aged rural Negro females were not in the labor force in 1960, and this proportion was about the same as that for aged urban Negro females and for all aged females in the United States. However, a smaller proportion of aged Negro females in rural areas than in urban centers of the nation reported they were employed in 1960 (Table 6).

Table 6. Employment Status by Percentage of Persons Aged 65 and Over for the Total Population and for the Negro Population by Sex, 1960

Employment status	Total population	Negro population		
		Urban	Rural nonfarm	Rural farm
Males				
Civilian labor force	30.5	28.7	24.1	47.6
Employed	28.8	26.1	22.2	46.5
Unemployed	1.7	2.6	1.9	1.1
Not in labor force	69.5	71.3	75.9	52.4
(Number)	(7,308,985)	(358,739)	(132,637)	(49,147)
Females				
Labor force	9.9	14.7	8.9	8.7
Employed	9.5	13.9	8.4	8.2
Unemployed	0.4	0.8	0.5	0.5
Not in labor force	90.1	85.3	91.1	91.3
(Number)	(8,898,252)	(442,050)	(142,463)	(42,844)

Source: U. S. Bureau of the Census, *United States Census of Population: 1960, Characteristics of the Population,* PC(1)-1D (Washington, D. C., 1963), Vol. I, Pt. I, Table 194; and *United States Census of Population: 1960, Nonwhite Population by Race,* PC (2)-1C (Washington, D. C., 1963), Table 37.

The kinds of work performed by aged rural Negroes in the United States in 1960 are shown in Table 7. As might be expected, male Negroes in rural areas of the country were heavily concentrated in farm and farm-related occupations. Small proportions of aged Negro males in rural areas were engaged in professional, other white-collar occupations, or in skilled work. About 10 percent of the aged nonfarm Negro males were engaged in service and household work, compared to about 30 percent for the aged urban Negro males. The kinds of work done by aged rural Negro females followed a pattern similar to that of the men, with one important exception: a large proportion of aged Negro females, both urban and rural nonfarm, performed private household work. The low-paying jobs performed by most rural Negroes in the South suggest that very modest social security benefits would be forthcoming.

Table 7. Occupations by Percentage of Employed Persons Aged 65 and Over for the Total Population and for the Negro Population by Sex, 1960

Occupation	Total population	Negro population		
		Urban	Rural nonfarm	Rural farm
Males				
Professional, technical, and kindred workers	8.3	5.2	2.6	0.5
Farmers and farm managers	15.7	1.3	22.3	70.1
Managers, officials, and proprietors, except farm	13.9	4.7	2.4	0.5
Clerical and kindred workers	6.1	3.2	0.5	0.1
Sales workers	8.2	2.1	1.1	0.3
Craftsmen, foremen, kindred workers	14.3	9.8	5.3	1.1
Operatives and kindred workers	9.6	13.2	8.0	1.9
Private household workers	0.4	2.7	1.8	0.5
Service workers, except private household	10.6	26.8	8.7	1.0
Farm laborers and foremen	3.1	2.2	25.5	20.2
Laborers, except farm and mine	5.8	20.8	19.2	2.8
Occupation not reported	4.0	8.0	2.6	1.0
(Number)	(2,112,521)	(93,646)	(29,507)	(22,830)
Females				
Professional, technical, and kindred workers	13.1	4.2	3.2	2.8
Farmers and farm managers	2.2	0.1	3.3	24.2
Managers, officials, and proprietors, except farm	6.5	1.7	1.5	1.0
Clerical and kindred workers	13.8	2.0	0.4	0.1
Sales workers	8.9	1.4	1.2	1.3
Craftsmen, foremen, kindred workers	1.1	0.4	0.1	—
Operatives and kindred workers	10.5	6.1	4.0	1.0
Private household workers	19.3	58.7	62.8	32.2
Service workers, except private household	15.6	15.5	9.7	5.6
Farm laborers and foremen	1.1	0.6	8.9	25.2
Laborers, except farm and mine	0.4	0.6	0.7	0.5
Occupations not reported	7.5	8.7	4.2	6.1
(Number)	(879,998)	(61,493)	(11,908)	(3,521)

Source: U. S. Bureau of the Census, *United States Census of Population: 1960, Characteristics of the Population,* PC(1)-1D (Washington, D. C., 1963), Vol. I, Table 201; and *United States Census of Population: 1960, Nonwhite Population by Race,* PC (2)-1C (Washington, D. C., 1963), Table 37.

INCOME

Employment status and income are closely related. Since aged persons tend to withdraw from employment, their incomes are typically low. The incomes for aged rural Negroes in 1959 are shown in Table 8. Whereas the median income for all aged males in the United States was $1,766, the medians for aged male Negroes, urban and rural, were substantially less—$1,226 and under $1,000, respectively. The low incomes of the aged rural Negro males are strikingly evident when incomes of less than $1,000 are compared. Whereas seven-tenths of the aged rural Negro males had incomes of less than $1,000 in 1959, only about four-tenths of the aged urban Negro males and about three-tenths of all males in the United States received this amount.

Additional data on the annual incomes of aged rural Negroes are presented in Table 9, which shows comparisons between

Table 8. Income Level by Percentage of Persons Aged 65 and Over for the Total Population and for the Negro Population by Sex, 1959

Income	Total population	Negro population		
		Urban	Rural nonfarm	Rural farm
Male				
(Number)	(6,875,832)	(334,332)	(121,940)	(46,720)
$1-$999	27.6	43.3	72.2	72.5
$1,000-$1,999	29.2	29.7	19.4	22.4
$2,000-$2,999	15.4	12.2	0.5	3.8
$3,000-$3,999	8.2	6.5	0.1	1.1
$4,000-$4,999	5.7	4.2	0.1	0.5
$5,000-$5,999	4.2	2.3	—	0.2
$6,000-$6,999	2.6	0.8	—	0.1
$7,000 and over	3.7	0.5	—	0.1
(Median Income)	($1,766)	($1,226)	$\left(\begin{array}{c}\text{Under}\\ \$1,000\end{array}\right)$	$\left(\begin{array}{c}\text{Under}\\ \$1,000\end{array}\right)$
Female				
(Number)	(6,672,682)	(343,885)	(114,970)	(33,120)
(Median Income)	$\left(\begin{array}{c}\text{Under}\\ \$1,000\end{array}\right)$	$\left(\begin{array}{c}\text{Under}\\ \$1,000\end{array}\right)$	$\left(\begin{array}{c}\text{Under}\\ \$1,000\end{array}\right)$	$\left(\begin{array}{c}\text{Under}\\ \$1,000\end{array}\right)$

Source: U. S. Bureau of the Census, *United States Census of Population: 1960, Characteristics of the Population*, PC(1)-1D (Washington, D. C., 1963), Vol. I, Pt. I, Table 219; and *United States Census of Population: 1960, Nonwhite Population by Race*, PC (2)-1C (Washington, D. C., 1963), Table 37.

aged white and Negro heads of households selected from the lower economic areas in the southern part of the United States. Thus, economic status of these two racial categories is held relatively constant. Despite this control, it is evident that the aged Negro heads of households in the rural South received smaller annual incomes than did the white aged heads of households. For example, seven-tenths of the aged rural nonfarm Negroes in the sample had incomes of less than $1,000, compared with five-tenths for the aged nonfarm whites. Whereas more than half the aged farm Negroes had incomes of less than $1,000, about one-third of the aged whites had this amount.

Table 9. Family Income Level by Percentage Reported by Heads of Households Aged 65 and Over in Low-income Families in the Rural South by Race, 1959

Family income	White		Negro	
	Rural farm (N = 111)	Rural nonfarm (N = 182)	Rural farm (N = 33)	Rural nonfarm (N = 70)
$1–$249	4.5	2.1	6.1	3.0
$250–$499	3.6	8.8	3.0	12.8
$500–$749	11.7	17.0	21.2	30.0
$750–$999	14.4	17.5	18.2	18.5
$1,000–$1,499	18.0	21.8	30.3	14.3
$1,500–$1,999	15.3	12.5	12.2	8.6
$2,000–$3,999	24.3	13.6	3.0	4.3
$4,000 or more	7.2	2.8	—	1.4
No information	1.0	3.9	6.0	7.1

INCOME SATISFACTION

Satisfactions with one's lot in life probably varies from generation to generation. Many Negroes in the United States, especially younger urban Negroes, are forcefully expressing their dissatisfactions. One important source of dissatisfaction to the Negro, as well as to many other groups of people, is inadequate income. Two important questions thus are: To what extent are aged Negroes living in rural areas dissatisfied with their incomes? What reasons do they give for this dissatisfaction?

Data relevant to these questions are reported for a sample of aged household heads in low economic areas of the South. It has been pointed out (Table 9) that both white and Negro heads of households had very low incomes, but the incomes of the aged rural Negroes were lower than those of the whites. This relatively low income position of the aged rural Negro is reflected in his reported satisfactions. As shown in Table 10, the aged Negroes in the rural South revealed more dissatisfaction than the aged rural whites. About one-quarter of the aged whites in the sample said they were dissatisfied, but almost one-half of the aged Negroes expressed dissatisfaction. The reasons for dissatisfaction are also indicated in Table 10. The dissatisfaction of the aged farm Negro in the rural South centered on high farm costs, poor crops, inadequate pensions, and lack of employment. The dissatisfactions of the aged nonfarm Negro in the rural South related to two main items: inadequate pensions and disabilities from age or poor health. It is to be noted that none of the aged heads of homes in the rural South, either white or Negro, mentioned lack of education as a reason for dissatisfaction. It is inferred that these aged heads of households in the rural South see little relation between their condition of life and their educational levels.

Table 10. Attitude Toward Family Income by Percentage Among Heads of Households Aged 65 and Over in Low-income Families in the Rural South by Race, 1959

	White		Negro	
Satisfaction	Rural farm (N = 111)	Rural nonfarm (N = 182)	Rural farm (N = 33)	Rural nonfarm (N = 70)
Degree of satisfaction				
Very satisfactory	3.6	0.6	3.0	5.7
Satisfactory	53.1	44.5	45.5	28.6
Unsatisfactory	25.3	27.4	51.5	45.7
No information	18.0	27.5	—	20.0
Reasons given for unsatisfactory income				
Lack of employment	—	4.0	11.8	3.1
Disability, age, or health	21.4	54.0	—	34.4
Inadequate pension or retirement	17.8	24.0	23.5	50.0
High farm cost	7.1	—	35.3	—
Lack of education	—	—	—	—
Poor crop	7.1	2.0	23.5	3.1
Other	28.8	10.0	5.9	6.3
No information	17.8	6.0	—	3.1

COMMUNICATION FACILITIES

America has been designated an affluent society. One index of this affluence is the prevalence of various instruments and media of communications—automobiles, radio and television sets, telephones, and many kinds of printed materials. Urban families, especially white, middle-class urban families, have access to many of these facilities. In contrast, many rural families are not so fortunate. The lack of communication facilities is particularly evident among many older rural residents, who have grown up when many of the present communication facilities were rather uncommon and who now lack the financial resources (and sometimes the desire) to acquire them.

It is pertinent to inquire into the communication facilities available to older rural Negroes in the Unted States. Data on this topic give additional evidence of the economic status of aged Negroes in rural areas and, to some extent, indicate the aged rural Negroes' involvement in the mainstream of American life. Unfortunately, relevant data are severely limited. Use is made of information obtained from a selected sample of white and Negro household heads aged 65 and over who live in lower economic areas of the rural South.

As shown in Table 11, aged Negroes in the rural South possessed fewer automobiles than did aged rural whites. Whereas slightly more than one-third of farm and nonfarm aged rural whites and slightly more than one-third of aged farm Negroes possessed a car, only about one-fifth of the aged Negroes in rural nonfarm areas owned an automobile. Paved roads for the use of such vehicles appear to be rather scarce in the rural South, and the aged rural Negro has less access to them than does the aged rural white. The data in Table 11 suggest that many of the homes of the rural aged Negroes are located in areas inaccessible by paved or hard-surface roads.

Slight differences were reported between aged white and Negro heads of homes in the rural South in the possession of radios. As is characteristic of most rural areas in the United States, the possession of some kind of radio was common to both white and Negro rural aged in the sample. However, substantial differences were found between white and Negro heads of homes in the

Table 11. Communication Facilities by Percentage Available to Homes
with Household Heads Aged 65 and Over in Low-income Families
in the Rural South by Race, 1959

Facility	White		Negro	
	Rural farm (N = 111)	Rural nonfarm (N = 182)	Rural farm (N = 33)	Rural nonfarm (N = 70)
Type of road				
Paved, hard surface	39.6	50.0	15.2	34.3
Other	60.4	48.9	84.8	64.3
No information	—	1.1	—	1.4
Automobile				
Yes	37.8	35.7	39.4	18.6
No	62.2	63.8	60.6	75.7
No information	—	0.5	—	5.7
Radio				
Yes	82.8	83.0	84.8	77.2
No	17.2	16.5	15.2	18.5
No information	—	0.5	—	4.3
Television				
Yes	54.1	51.6	33.3	34.3
No	45.9	47.8	66.7	61.5
No information	—	0.6	—	4.2
Telephone				
Yes	29.7	31.7	9.1	4.3
No	70.3	67.7	90.9	91.4
No information	—	0.6	—	4.3

proportions who reported they had access to television sets or to
telephones. About one-third of the aged Negroes in the rural
South sample said they had access to a television set, compared
to about one-half of the aged whites. Negro-white differences in
access to a telephone were even more pronounced. Only 7 percent of the rural Negro homes in the sample had the use of a
telephone. This contrasted rather sharply with the percentage
reported by the white heads of homes aged 65 and over: slightly
less than one-third (Table 11).

Available data on access to printed materials in homes with
heads aged 65 and over in the rural South revealed marked differences between whites and Negroes. Slightly more than one-
third of the aged rural whites reported that they subscribed to a
daily newspaper, but only about one-seventh of the aged Negroes
made such a report. Substantial white-Negro disparities were
also found in subscriptions to weekly newspapers, to farm or

trade magazines, and to other journals. In each instance, substantially smaller proportions of aged Negroes than of whites in the rural South reported they had access to these publications (Table 12).

The impact of mass media on social and psychological changes which the Negro is experiencing has not been adequately explored. Impressionistic judgments suggest that these media, particularly television, in urban areas have played important roles in bringing about changes in the Negro's concept of himself, his

Table 12. Availability of Printed Materials by Percentage to Homes with Household Head Aged 65 and Over in Low-income Families in the Rural South by Race, 1959

Printed materials	White		Negro	
	Rural farm (N = 111)	Rural nonfarm (N = 182)	Rural farm (N = 33)	Rural nonfarm (N = 70)
Daily newspaper				
Yes	39.6	37.9	9.1	17.2
No	60.4	61.5	90.9	78.6
No information	—	0.6	—	4.2
Weekly newspaper				
Yes	56.7	32.5	12.1	11.4
No	43.3	67.0	87.9	84.3
No information	—	0.5	—	4.3
Farm or trade magazine				
Yes	57.6	39.0	36.4	21.4
No	42.4	60.5	63.6	74.3
No information	—	0.5	—	4.3
Other weekly and monthly magazines				
Yes	24.3	22.0	15.1	10.0
No	75.7	77.5	84.9	84.3
No information	—	0.5	—	5.7

role in society, and his relationships with other persons. The lack of availability of these media to the aged rural Negro is thus noteworthy. The lack of good roads, the scarcity of automobiles, and the absence of telephones contribute to his social isolation. Although his meager financial resources may deter him from purchasing television sets or telephones, there is also the strong possibility that the aged rural Negro has not attached significance to these media and is probably reluctant to exert unusual effort to obtain them. The low level and lack of interest in education and the consequent high rate of functional illiteracy among the aged rural Negro may partly account for the paucity of subscriptions to newspapers and journals.

SOURCES OF SATISFACTION

It is commonly observed in the United States that advancing age often brings a constriction in interests and activities and a narrowing of sources of satisfaction. Restrictions in investments in persons and objects in the environment are important negative components of old age.

The household heads aged 65 and over in the rural sample of the South were asked what their major sources of satisfaction were. As shown in Table 13, the major source of satisfaction to aged white and Negro heads of households comes from family relationships. About a third of both groups mentioned this source. The second source of satisfaction named by the aged men in the sample was religion, but substantially more of the aged Negroes than whites named this source. Few whites and Negroes indicated they obtained satisfaction from their work, and even fewer said they found satisfaction in civic, recreational, or educational activities.

The sources of satisfaction outside the home available to this sample of aged persons in the rural South coincided with their participation in community organizations. Church-related organizations were the predominant community activity. All the

Table 13. Sources of Satisfaction by Percentage to Household Heads Aged 65 and Over in Low-income Families in the Rural South by Race, 1959

Source of satisfaction	White		Negro	
	Rural farm (N = 111)	Rural nonfarm (N = 182)	Rural farm (N = 33)	Rural nonfarm (N = 70)
Family	34.3	34.6	39.5	25.7
Religion	23.4	15.4	42.4	38.6
Work	13.5	10.4	9.1	2.9
Civic	0.9	2.2	6.0	—
Recreation	1.8	2.2	—	1.4
Education	1.8	—	—	—
No information	24.3	35.2	3.0	31.4

Negroes aged 65 and over said they took part in some form of religious organization, and no other organizations were mentioned by the Negroes. About nine-tenths of the aged whites took part in church related activities, and the remainder mentioned school organizations, farm and extension groups, labor unions, and civic, patriotic, or fraternal organizations (Table 14). The fact that the aged Negro heads of homes in the South mentioned only church-related activities is noteworthy. In the rural South few community organizations are open to Negroes which give them a sense of belonging. The church traditionally has been the center of social life for the rural Negro and has

Table 14. Community Organizations by Percentage Participated in by Household Heads Aged 65 and Over in Low-income Families in the Rural South by Race, 1959

Community organization	White		Negro	
	Rural farm (N = 111)	Rural nonfarm (N = 182)	Rural farm (N = 33)	Rural nonfarm (N = 70)
Church related	92.8	90.1	100.0	100.0
School related	3.6	4.9	—	—
Farm and extension	3.6	—	—	—
Labor unions	—	1.2	—	—
Civic, patriotic, fraternal	—	3.8	—	—

served as an important cohesive force in the Negro community. As Heyman and Jeffers reported in their study of aged Negroes and whites, low-income rural Negroes placed more importance on religious activities than did middle-class Negroes.[8]

A GLANCE AT THE FUTURE

Three important indicators of a group's position in the social structure—education, employment, and income—point to the extremely low socioeconomic status of the aged rural Negro. In the United States, this group is severely limited in its involvement in the mainstream of American life. Moreover, as pointed out in a report by the United States Commission on Civil Rights, the poverty gap between Negro and white rural residents in the South has increased in recent years. A preconception appears to exist that Negro farmers have limited needs, capabilities, and aspirations. Thus, many rural farm Negroes have not been encouraged to diversify their crops, to acquire larger holdings, or to make their small acreages more productive. Relegated to a separate, inferior, and outdated agricultural economy, many farm Negroes are sinking to even lower levels of subsistence.[9]

NOTES

[1] New York: National Urban League, Inc., 1964.

[2] National Urban League, *Health Care and the Negro Population* (New York: National Urban League, Inc., 1965).

[3] *Phylon*, 21 (Summer, 1960), 131-35. See also Joseph Himes and Margaret Hamlett, "The Assessment of Adjustment of Aged Negro Women in a Southern City," *Phylon*, 23 (Summer, 1962), 139-48.

[4] Washington: Housing and Home Finance Agency, 1963.

[5] Michael Harrington, *The Other American* (New York: Macmillan, 1962), and Herman Miller, *Rich Man, Poor Man* (New York: Thomas Y. Crowell, 1964).

[6] U. S. Bureau of the Census, *The U. S. Census of Population: 1960, Subject Reports, Nonwhite Population by Race*, PC (2)-1C.

[7] Permission to use these data was obtained from J. E. Dunkelberger of Auburn University on behalf of the Technical Committee of the S-44 project.

[8] Dorothy K. Heyman and Francis C. Jeffers, "Study of the Relative Influences of Race and Socio-economic Status Upon the Activities and Attitudes of a Southern Aged Population," *Journal of Gerontology*, 19 (April 1964), 225-99.

[9] U. S. Commission on Civil Rights, *Equal Opportunity in Farm Programs*, Special Publication No. 3 (Washington, D. C., March, 1965).

MARVIN J. TAVES

GARY D. HANSEN

Programs for
the Rural Elderly

Most programs designed to help older persons—whether federal, state, or local—have either assumed the absence of significant rural-urban differences or have chosen to ignore such differences. Among federal programs some exceptions to this generalization are the exclusion of farmers and farm workers from social security benefits for almost 20 years after the enactment of the Social Security Act in 1935, long after most other nonprofessional groups had been included. Another was the home-improvement grant program designed specifically to improve rural housing. Although there has been no attempt to exclude the rural elderly from federal or state programs, a number of conditions have prevented these persons from full participation in such programs. Among these are the difficulties of administering programs for this group, the greater distance from service centers, the nature of rural occupations, the sparseness of rural population, the lower level of rural schooling, predominating attitudes of self-sufficiency, and a more limited access to means of mass communication.

Programs presently available to rural older people in the United States have received little attention. In almost every rural area there are problems of the aged that will require the development of imaginative programs that can best be accomplished by cooperative action; federal and stage agencies, private institutions, business and voluntary organizations, and various civic groups have important parts to play in such action programs. The older person may receive service in a variety of different ways and in many different settings. For example, he or she may be: a social security beneficiary; a patient in a hospital or clinic; a resident of public housing; a citizen protected by laws and the courts; a student in an educational program; an older worker seeking retraining or employment; a participant in a social center; or a family member in need of marital, social, or psychological counseling, guidance or therapy.

This chapter examines the foundations of local, state, and federal programs for the aged, describes some of the more salient federal legislation that affects older rural people, examines some aspects of federal-state-community coordination, and gives examples of action programs for older persons now in progress in various rural communities throughout the nation.

FOUNDATIONS FOR PROGRAMS FOR THE AGED

The foundations of programs for older persons carried out by counties, states, and the federal government might begin as recently as the passage of the Social Security Act in 1935 or as early as the codification of the Elizabethan Poor Laws in 1601.[1] American patterns and traditions in this regard borrow heavily from the British from the time of Elizabeth I through the inauguration of the present so-called Beveridge Plan. The Elizabethan Poor Laws became the model for relief policies of the American colonies and consequently for many aspects of state and local public assistance throughout American history. This carryover included several ideas still apparent in American society, such as relatives' and local responsibility for their "own" poor and the notion that indolence and dissipation make the able-bodied poor dependent on others. These principles dominated British welfare policy until the passage of the National Assistance Act in 1948 replaced them with the philosophy of the so-called Beveridge Plan. Under the Beveridge Plan it was held that the total society had certain responsibilities for the health and well-being of each citizen regardless of financial status of the family or of the local residence of the individual.

The American experience parallels that of England at many points. Before the Depression of the 1930's, the well-being of an older person who could no longer care for himself financially or otherwise was held to be the responsibility of his family, his immediate community, or at most the county in which he lived. At the turn of the century most local public bodies in the United States had in one way or another accepted a certain basic responsibility for the aged and infirm. In some cases this was reflected in the form of public employment which in reality was more pension than work, of a county home or other home for the aged and infirm. In other cases, fraternal orders were subsidized from the public treasury to carry on programs of aid to the aged. By the time of the great Depression a form of "outdoor aid" was also being paid in meager amounts by counties to the indigent poor.

One observation made concerning the availability, adequacy, and use of such programs was their tremendous variability from one locale to another. To many students of the early twentieth century, that variability was related less to the needs of the elderly than to the efforts of relatives and others to salve their consciences about their responsibilities for older persons and others less fortunate than themselves. Generally, the amount of assistance given was a pittance, and frequently even this pittance went only to those who complained too loudly to be ignored. There is no reason to believe that this practice was less prevalent in rural than in urban areas of America.

The marked increase in numbers of older persons in the United States and the economic stresses of the 1930's were important factors in shifting certain responsibilities for the well-being of older people to the federal government. This shift was by no means an abdication of local and state responsibility but rather a recognition that economic security was no longer either wholly the consequence of individual effort or a simple matter to achieve.

If the 1930's focused on the identification of dependency as a social problem, the 1940's and 1950's served to identify the aged as a group prone to dependency. This identification was associated with, and probably a forerunner of, a change in the concept of social welfare itself. This change involved enlarging the sense of social responsibility from assistance in economic crisis to maintenance of economic viability of the members of the dependent group. By mid-century there was evidence of a growing public consensus that favored the institutionalization of a broader ongoing framework of services designed to help older persons attain more satisfying levels of physical and mental health and social acceptance. During the 1960's there has emerged a new image of normal wholesome, healthy aging. No longer does the term "old man" necessarily connote disability, isolation, and dependency. The role of the "older person" today permits vigorous retirement.

THE SOCIAL SECURITY ACT

The impetus behind the passage of the Social Security Act was not so much concern for the well-being of the elderly as concern for others, especially the working-age children who needed relief from the financial burdens of caring for elderly parents. In addition, the heads of growing families saw their opportunities in the job market enhanced by the encouragement of retirement of the older worker through the Old Age and Survivors Insurance Act. Some employers also saw in the legislation assistance in replacing inadequately trained or physically and mentally declining older workers with more efficient younger employees at lower wages. As already noted, the social legislation of the 1930's had only limited direct implications for the rural farm population, as farming was an occupation not covered initially under the insurance portion of the legislation. The rural farm and nonfarm elderly, however, were eligible for federal grants in aid to states for Old Age Assistance. Of course, any one employed in "covered employment" participated in all aspects of social security regardless of rural or urban residence.

The federal government made loans and, later, grants to the states to pay for direct relief and work relief as early as 1932. There also followed federal emergency relief and public works programs. At the same time the specially created Committee on Economic Security presented its recommendations, which President Franklin D. Roosevelt incorporated in his proposal to Congress for economic security legislation. The resulting Social Security Act was signed into law in August 1935.

The social security program has undergone several significant changes since its initiation. Rather than being merely a program for retired workers, it has become an old age insurance system for the total family. It now includes benefits to certain dependent members of the wage-earner's family after his retirement and survivor benefits after his death. The basis for computing benefits has been changed from total lifetime earnings to average monthly earnings in covered work over a more advantageous portion of time. In 1950, coverage was broadened to cover many jobs that had virtually been excluded because it was thought necessary first to develop ways to report earnings and collect contributions. Among the groups first covered in 1950 were regularly employed farm and household employees and most persons who worked for themselves, other than farmers and certain professional workers. Further extensions of coverage brought farm operators and participating landlords into the program in 1954, and most self-employed professional people in 1956. A recent report points out that as of 1964, "all gainfully employed workers are now covered, with the exception of some Government employees who have separate retirement protection, self-employed doctors of medicine, farm and domestic workers who are not regularly employed, and very-low-income self-employed people."[2] A significant addition to the national social insurance system occurred with provision for severely disabled workers, age 50-64, in 1956, and to dependents of such disabled workers in 1958. These benefits have been extended to all such workers before age 65 without a minimum age requirement.

Some other specific provisions are: benefits can now be paid for widows at age 60 if they decide to accept a reduced monthly amount. The amount of work required under the new law is less for certain people 72 and over than it has ever been before. The amount of earnings that can be received without loss of benefits has been increased. Eligibility for disability benefits has been relaxed. At present, an insured worker whose disability is expected to last for at least a year may qualify for benefits beginning with the seventh month of his disability. A provision helpful to divorced women was enacted and widows who remarry are now eligible for the larger of either of two benefits: either one-half the retirement benefit of the former husband or one-half the benefit of the earnings of the present husband.

There is a change in coverage for farmers. A self-employed farmer whose gross earnings from farming in any year after 1965 are $2,400 or less may report two-thirds of gross earnings instead of net earnings for social security purposes. If gross income from farming is more than $2,400 and net earnings are less than $1,600, he may report $1,600 for social security purposes. For some years now there have been some special provisions for farm operators and farm employees under social security. A farm operator receives social security credit if his net earnings from self-employment are $400 or more in a year. Although rental income is not ordinarily covered under social security, farm rental income does count if the farm landlord "materially participates" in the actual production of the farm commodities or in the management of such production. The term "landlord" in this case means anyone who rents or leases land to another person regardless of whether he owns the land or rents or leases it from someone else. A farm employee is entitled to social security credits if the employer pays him $150 or more in cash during the year for farm work or if he does farm work for his employer on 20 or more days during the year for cash wages figured on a time basis.

MEDICAL ASSISTANCE FOR THE AGED

Medical dependency among those who had enough income to meet their needs is dealt with by a program of federal grants entitled "Medical Assistance for the Aged." Most of the states now participate in this program, which was designed to prevent impoverishment because of medical costs to the elderly. Again, the states are free to set their levels of financial eligibility, but they are required to submit state plans which guarantee that the state will provide some noninstitutional and institutional care and services, that all residents of the state are eligible, and that no property lien can be imposed prior to the death of the recipient, and no recovery of benefit payments can be made before the death of both the recipient and his spouse.

Financial eligibility for MAA as established by the states is generally less restrictive than the needs test for OAA. Most state programs disregard reasonable amounts of life insurance and liquid assets in determining eligibility. Maximum allowable income tends to be about $1,500, while the highest for any state is $2,-

100 for a single aged person. The variation in eligibility and benefits from one state to the next is reflected in the variations in average monthly amounts paid per recipient.

Beginning July 1, 1966, nearly all persons in the United States aged 65 and over became eligible for health protection under the Medicare provisions of the Social Security Act, which at the present time pay the cost of services for:

1. Up to 60 days in a hospital (except for the first $40) and all but $10 per day for an additional 30 days for each spell of illness.

2. Up to 20 days in an extended-care facility, e.g., a skilled nursing home, and all but $5 per day for an additional 80 days for each spell of illness. (The extended-care benefits began on January 1, 1967.)

3. Up to 100 home health visits for 80 percent of the cost of outpatient diagnostic tests in a hospital with a deductible of $20. In addition, there is voluntary medical insurance for those over 65 years old. Eligible persons are covered if they enroll for this coverage and pay a premium of $3 monthly. This voluntary, supplementary medical insurance generally pays 80 percent of the charges with a deductible of $50 in a calendar year for: (a) Physicians' and surgeons' services, (b) home health services without the need for prior hospitalization, (c) other medical and health services.

As in most other programs, these benefits may be modified gradually to assist individuals to cope with changing social and economic conditions. Therefore, these guidelines, percentages, and dollar amounts are dated but have been included here because of their historical significance.

OLD-AGE ASSISTANCE

The Social Security Act requires the states to include under old-age assistance needy persons who are age 65 or over. However, the OAA payments vary considerably from state to state, ranging from $39 in Mississippi to $102 in California for the month of October, 1966, and the national average for all recipients was $67. Variations reflect differences in items included in the budget, differences in income, in ceilings in the money payments, and in use of the option to disregard specific amounts of earned income in determining need and amount of payment. Many of the states apply maximums or other devices to reduce payments so that the recipient receives less than his needs even as determined under the state's assistance standards.

OTHER RECENT LEGISLATION

Growing interest in the problems of older people is reflected in recent federal and state legislation. Over the last decade the U. S. Employment Service of the Department of Labor and its affiliated state employment services have endeavored to strengthen placement, job development, and counseling services to older workers, particularly those aged 45 to 60. A few states have formed "self-help" organizations in which older workers cooperate in developing job opportunities and in finding work for each other. Several states have participated in establishing training courses for older workers in cooperation with state vocational education departments. These efforts to date have been limited to demonstration programs, which in most cases have not served the rural population.

The Economic Opportunity Act of 1964 provides opportunities for older people in each of its action titles. Directed particularly at poverty in rural areas is Title III, which authorizes grants up to $1,500 for low-income rural families to acquire and improve real estate, improve the operations of farms, or for other purposes. Also authorized are loans to such families of up to $2,500 for financing enterprises that supplement their incomes from farming. Another section provides for the organization and financing of family-farm development corporations to enable farm families to become owners and operators of family-sized farming units.

The act also authorizes loans to assist qualified persons in establishing retailing and service enterprises employing three or fewer persons. The program envisages support of such businesses as luncheonettes, filling stations, barber shops, shoe repair establishments, dry cleaners, tailors, and many others. The program is administered by the Small Business Administration.

Many older persons, including some from the rural areas, have availed themselves of the Vista Program (Volunteers in Service to America). Volunteers participate in job crops and work-training programs, and in community action programs as teachers, aides, counselors, and advisors. They also can be assigned to work in various programs which are the responsibility of the federal government for the purpose of combating problems of poverty. A stipend not to exceed $50 a month above and beyond living allowance, housing, supplies, equipment, and counseling may be furnished such volunteers.

In recent years there has been a marked increase in number of states that set up officially designated committees or commissions on aging to provide a central clearinghouse for activities for the aged. By the mid-sixties, 43 states listed a state government agency specifically designated to provide for the orderly development of the state's program on aging. Although the roles of these agencies vary from state to state, they tend to focus on the following: coordinate plans and policies, activities and services of the varied state agencies that serve older persons; set priorities in meeting needs and assuring proper emphasis in various agencies; gather and disseminate information about action programs and create public awareness and understanding of the needs and potentials of older persons; stimulate the development of local organizations on aging; and organize demonstration or pilot programs; identify research areas; provide consultation and evaluation of training projects; and encourage the setting of standards for programs for older persons.

INTEGRATION OF PROGRAMS FOR THE AGED

One of the more salient developments in the aging field has been recent attempts to integrate various programs and services into a coordinated whole at all levels—federal, state, and local. Evidence of this shown in Table 1, which summarizes some of the federal programs. For example, the Department of Agriculture's research program sheds new light on nutritional needs and problems of older people, the Department of Commerce provides valuable data on the growing number of older persons and their characteristics, the Department of Defense provides hospital and medical care for many older military personnel and their dependents, the Small Business Administration makes loans which generate health facilities for the elderly, and the Veterans Ad-

Table 1. Federal Agencies Also Serve the Older American Indirectly

Agency	Income	Health, medical care, and rehabilitation	Housing	Employment	Education and training	Social services
Agriculture	Benefits: surplus commodity donations, food stamps. Research.	Research on nutrition.	Direct loans. Loan guarantees. Grants. Research.	Research on farm labor working force.	Programs conducted by Extension Service.	Consultation and technical assistance.
Civil Service Commission	Benefits: civil service retirements, survivors annuities, payments to life insurance beneficiaries, health benefits payments.	Administers Federal Employees Health Benefits Act.		Administers Federal Competitive Civil Service system (no age restrictions). Serves as central personnel agency.	Inservice training of federal employees. Promotion of preretirement planning programs.	
Commerce	Census and other surveys and statistical services.		Census and other surveys and statistical services.	Census and other surveys and statistical services.		
Department of Defense	Benefits: military retirement, military disability retirement.	Hospital and medical care for retired military personnel and dependents.				
Health, Education, and Welfare	Benefits: old-age insurance, survivors insurance, disability insurance, old-age assistance, aid to the blind, aid to the permanently and totally disabled, medical assistance to the aged. Research.	Research. Construction of health facilities. Grants. Training. Direct services. Technical assistance and consultation. Food and drug protection. Vocational rehabilitation.	Consultation and technical assistance. Standards. Research.	Consultation and technical assistance. Grants for vocational education. Vocational rehabilitation.	Consultation and technical assistance. Grants for vocational education. Adult education and library services. Grants for training and research. Preretirement preparation education.	Consultation and technical assistance. Grants. Direct services. Research. Demonstrations. Referral services.
Housing and Home Finance Agency	Mortgage insurance for proprietary nursing homes.		Mortgage insurance.* Rental contributions.* Construction subsidies.* Direct loans. Research in housing for the elderly.		Consultation and technical assistance. Inservice training.	Consultation and technical assistance.

		Experimental housing mortgage insurance. Demonstration grants. Consultation and technical assistance.		
Labor	Benefits: unemployment compensation. Training allowances. Research.		Employment counseling. Testing. Placement. Occupational and labor market information. Training. Research. Technical assistance. Labor standards.	Manpower development and training.
Railroad Retirement Board	Benefits: railroad retirement, railroad disability retirement, survivor annuities, railroad unemployment and sickness insurance.			
Small Business Administration		Loans to privately owned health facilities (hospitals, convalescent and nursing homes; medical and dental laboratories).	Consultation and technical assistance to small businesses.	
Treasury	(Tax benefits: age 65 double exemption, retirement income credit, medical expense deduction)			
Veterans Administration	Benefits: disability and survivor benefits to veterans and certain dependents; life insurance proceeds to beneficiaries.	Direct services: in- and outpatient care, medical and vocational rehabilitation for service-connected disability; hospitalization for certain war veterans. Medical research.	Employment counseling (limited eligibility).	Direct services (limited eligibility).

* Public Housing Administration.

ministration provides many direct services and indirectly contributes significantly to knowledge about aging in general through its medical and vocational rehabilitation programs. The rural population benefits directly from a few of these, such as the rural home-improvement grant already mentioned.

The growing recognition that federal, state, and local efforts need to be more closely integrated is reflected in federal legislation specifically creating organizations to help older persons. The Committee on Aging and Geriatrics (1951) became the Special Staff on Aging (1963), which was replaced by the Administration on Aging (1965). The Administration on Aging has been established to provide a strong central focus and responsibility within the federal government on all matters of concern to older people and to those who work with older persons.

The Administration on Aging is one of the major operating units of the U. S. Department of Health, Education, and Welfare and is headed by a Commissioner on Aging, appointed by the President. It is the channel for exchange of information and help between state organizations in aging and the federal government. It works closely with all operating units of the Department of Health, Education, and Welfare, wherever aging is involved. It has the functions of a clearing house for information and for certain federal programs relating to the aging. It cooperates also with other federal agencies, with national and local voluntary organizations, and with colleges, universities, and other educational institutions in efforts to develop new knowledge and stimulate new programs. It has special competency of its own in the areas of state and community organization, leisure-time activity, preretirement preparation, and development of education in gerontology. It provides general information about older people and specifics on services and opportunities available to them. It concerns itself with the role and status of older people as well as with their care. It also develops, plans, and conducts and arranges for research, development, and demonstration programs in the field of aging.

COMMUNITY PROGRAMS FOR THE RURAL AGED

Some selected examples of community programs for older persons are presented below. These examples illustrate cooperative efforts of federal, state, and local organizations in meeting the needs of rural older people.

AITKIN, MINNESOTA[3]

Aitkin County, Minnesota, covers an area of almost 2,000 square miles of rural, relatively unfertile land dotted with lakes and swampy bogs. Many of its 1,800 older people live in isolation and loneliness. Most live on low incomes and experience considerable hardship. The proportion of older people is more than half again as high as that for the state or the nation. Aitkin is the county's largest community with a total population of less than 2,000 persons. To do something to make life richer and days less desolate for the elderly has been a challenge to the county for a number of years.

The Aitkin County Citizens' Committee on Aging, appointed by the Board of County Commissioners, is solving some of these problems. A Senior Center was established and staffed by a paid hostess and volunteers in charge of music, dances, education, crafts, hobbies, games, picnics, trips, and other activities. The efforts and accomplishments of the county committee were not confined to Aitkin but extended to the whole county through the varied activities of several Golden Age clubs in outlying hamlets. Local estimates indicate that half of the older people in the county participated in various aspects of the program each year.

The program has various meanings for different people. Doctors have recommended participation to their patients; one daughter believes the center may have saved her mother from a mental institution; a disabled arthritic gained incentive for physical exercise and social life; older citizen leaders in the community have dedicated themselves to making the program work, expanding it and serving others. The multipurpose Committee on Aging is firmly rooted in the county government structure, with a constitution, by-laws, and operating budget.

The Committee on Aging in Aitkin County experienced a relatively slow beginning but gained the respect and support of the community. Current activities and the glories of success did not blind them to the future. They view long-range planning as important in solving the remaining problems and unmet needs of older persons in this rural low-income county. Low-cost public housing, sales outlets for crafts, new centers and clubs, and the services of professional staff are part of a long-range plan.

EARLHAM, IOWA

Earlham is a small town of approximately 800 people in Madison County, which has a total population of about 12,500. Precisely 17 percent or 136 of Earlham's residents are 65 and over. A comprehensive program to extend a helping hand to the aged and chronically ill of the Earlham area was undertaken and supported by the community, the Iowa State Department of Health, the Iowa State Heart Association, and the United States Department of Health, Education, and Welfare. The variety and utilization of services offered under the Earlham Care Program, designated as "An Experiment in Community Living," are indicated in Table 2.

These services were coordinated by the office of the director of the project. An activity center for recreation, entertainment, and education was established. Other experimental programs included a clearinghouse for information on housing, private insurance coverage for home-care services, and a special committee for the sick at home.

The project staff, volunteers, and community leaders were especially concerned about continuation of the program. A survey was made to assess public opinion about the project. Questionnaires were completed by recipients of services, by their families, and by selected community leaders. Of all respondents, 93 per-

Table 2. Services Available and Utilized from September 1963 to June 1964

Service	Number of Clients	Services rendered
Homemaker	24	1,437 hours
Visiting nurse	8 families	341 visits
Meals on wheels	6 families	115 meals
Handyman	—	135 services
Counseling	—	no information
Transportation	—	132 trips
Friendly visitation	—	858 visits
Telephone contacts	20+	—
Employment service	18	all age groups

Source: Compiled from the "First Annual Report on the Earlham Care Program to the Iowa State Department of Health, July 1, 1964," prepared by John R. Carson.

cent indicated a favorable opinion of the project; 89 percent expressed no dissatisfaction with any phase of the program; and 79 percent wanted the program to continue when federal and state government grant money was no longer available. About 6 in 10 favored the use of local tax money to help finance the continued program.

Some who expressed dissatisfaction with the program reasoned that the church should care for the chronically ill and aged or that a charge should be levied for services. Paradoxically, some felt that the staff had no right to be active in certain areas, and some said the community was not aware of the national recognition attained by the project. Criticisms of new programs are to be expected. Some of this stems from a lack of information and understanding and can be remedied by personal contact and public educational efforts.

YORK COUNTY, MAINE

In 1961, the governor of Maine appointed a committee to study the problems of older people throughout the state. The appointees in York County organized the York County Advisory Committee on Aging in cooperation with the County Extension Association. At the request of this committee, the Department of Agricultural Business and Economics and the Experiment Station at the University of Maine conducted a countywide survey of the needs of aged people. Over 200 volunteer workers in York County provided the manpower needed to carry out this task. Using these studies as bases, the York County Advisory Committee and Nasson College offered a seven-week training session on community leadership. Participants met one night each week. By the fall of 1965, these leaders had started the following programs in their particular communities:

(*a*) A Golden Opportunity Center was located in a vacant store, which was given, heat and rent free, by the Sanford Trust Company. In 1964, the daily attendance was about 30 elderly persons, and this number increased during 1965. Classes in knitting, stenciling on glass, square dancing, and charcoal drawing were started in 1965.

(*b*) Two 50-Plus clubs were started, one in Sanford, Maine, sponsored by the YMCA, and one in the town of York, referred to as the "Yorksters." These clubs held monthly meetings and their programs were limited to business meetings and community sings.

(c) Friendly Visitor Services were established in seven towns and cities of Maine. Training for these friendly visitors was given by the Cooperative Extension Service of the University of Maine and by the U. S. Department of Agriculture, under the sponsorship of the Community Health Association.

(d) The Sanford YWCA invited the York County Council on Aging to develop a preretirement program, to be carried out by the Cooperative Extension Service.

LITTLE FALLS, MINNESOTA

Another example of community effort to help the aged was found in Morrison County, Minnesota. It involved public and private, local, state, and federal cooperation, a pattern which is common in community programs for older people. The Little Falls community program enlisted the help of the Governor's Consultant on Aging, who served as a catalyst for the project. One of the first steps was to organize a Commission on Aging, which made a countywide self-survey of the needs of the chronically ill, the disabled, and the aged. Various organizations helped with the survey, such as the Rural Sociology Department of the University of Minnesota, the Minnesota Department of Public Welfare, the State Department of Health, the County Welfare Department, the Nursing and Medical staff of the County Health Department, and the administrator and staff of the Catholic Hospital School of Nursing. Over 500 volunteers donated some 15,000 hours of travel time, as well as other expenses. Personal interviews were completed by 6,226 persons on health needs and resources, and by 2,786 persons on various aspects of aging. In the process, the people of the county and professional staffs became better acquainted, better informed, and more concerned about each other and they became more familiar with problems and possible solutions.

The survey established a detailed, factual basis for the development of programs, services, and facilities. It identified 1,356 chronically ill persons and 363 disabled amputees or accident victims. It located 127 registered nurses, 27 licensed practical nurses, 162 who had nurse's-aide training, and 102 with home-aide training. In addition, 521 untrained persons reported being willing to serve as home aides.

The community project was organized into three main parts: (a) public health home nursing-care services, (b) home-aide services, and (c) social and recreational services. Each program was assigned to a project staff member who had training for his particular area. A project supervisor helped direct the activities of each unit and provided team leadership. Consultants from occupational and physical therapy, vocational rehabilitation, nutrition, and public health nursing also participated. The entire project and staff were under the direction of the Minnesota Department of Health. However, final responsibility and control were in the hands of the county nursing board and the Morrison County commissioners. An advisory committee representing citizens and agencies on a countywide basis gave guidance and support to the project.

The goals of the project's three sections were similar. Each attempted to extend health and social services to the chronically ill and aged commensurate with their need.

The home-aide program provided services to 94 individuals from July 1962 to July 1964. Most individuals served were chronically ill and a high proportion of these had heart disease. Most patients were women. The average age was 68. The average number of hours per case was 522 at a cost of $266 per case. About one-third of the patients were welfare recipients. Reports for the period indicate a saving of $28,000 through the aide services to the patients and the public welfare agency in Morrison County.

A total of 79 home aides were on the roster and available for service at different times during the 2-year period. Of these, 61 had completed 9 to 16 hours of training given by the home-aide coordinator. As with many new services, the sponsoring organization changed. In this case it started in the Demonstration Project, moved to the County Nursing Service, and then became a part of a more comprehensive Home Care program at the local hospital. The frustrations, conflicts, and disappointments that accompanied these transitions are documented in the project reports.

Efforts to extend the home nursing-care program were handicapped by several factors which may affect other rural counties: (a) inadequate communication between new project staff and the existing staff of the county nursing service, (b) rural family pride in self-care and rejection of public health nursing because they believe it is part of the county welfare program, (c) lack of knowledge about skills, services, and benefits of public health nursing, (d) professional definitions of need for services without the accompanying consumer public demand, (e) reluctance of nurses and county officials to accept innovation that would expand the organization and demand for public funds somewhat more rapidly than constituents would endorse and provide.

The services and facilities that were developed included a day center, an annual hobby show, a friendly visiting program (to 92 homes in 1964), and a preretirement education program entitled "Fitness for the Future." The senior citizens club doubled in membership in two years and expanded social, informational, and educational offerings for members. The project staff engaged regularly in various efforts to inform the public about the needs of and resources for older people.

ST. JOHNS, MICHIGAN

"In the lush farmlands of Clinton County, Michigan, (St. Johns, population 5,636), an exciting community program is under way for and by older people. The senior citizens of Clinton County are relying on their own resources to improve their income, health, housing, and recreation. The St. Johns group is perfecting a well-rounded program which could serve as a model for other communities." This quotation, taken from a metropolitan Detroit newspaper, is indicative of the enthusiasm and inspiration of the Clinton County programs.

Clinton County is about 20 miles north of Michigan State University and the same distance from the state capital. Personnel from the state government and from the university have been helpful but probably not indispensable to the Clinton County program.

Few statistical records are available on the activities and accomplishments of the senior citizens in Clinton County. The formal beginnings of this program were marked by the incorportation of the "Senior Citizens of Clinton County" and the "Clinton County Commission on Aging." The same leaders directed both organizations, although the membership and purposes are different.

One of the first major steps was to establish a Drop-In Center. Negotiations with the Grand Trunk Railroad resulted in obtaining the use of an unused freight office at a rental of one dollar a year. Volunteers responded to a call for help and with donated labor, materials, and furnishings, the gloomy, dingy interior was transformed into an inviting lounge. The Drop-In Center is open several days a week and is manned and maintained by volunteers. It is the hub of social, recreational, educational, and creative activities. Volunteers staff a limited information, referral, and employment service.

The senior citizens are identified as one of the more progressive and active groups in the community. This reputation stems from a number of services rendered by members and recreational activities planned by members for the whole community. Ice cream socials, birthday celebrations, pot luck lunches, bake sales, card parties, dances, a band, a bowling league, parades, scenic trips, and guided tours of Michigan institutions and corporations add up to a diversified community program. The Drop-In Center also is rented to the city Recreation Department for various youth and community activities.

An important activity of the older people was to give furniture, clothing, food, and a Christmas to a family of twelve who lost their home and possessions in a fire. This family reported "that Christmas was the happiest day we've ever had." A friendly visiting program provides companionship for patients in the county infirmary and older citizens generally. Shut-ins receive their special attention during the holiday season. Materials for quilts and embroidery work were given to the county infirmary, corsages were presented to patients in the local hospital, and bandages were rolled for a leper colony in Africa. Senior citizens volunteered for the Cancer Drive. Some became engrossed in political activities and participated energetically and knowledgeably in debates on the issues, campaigns, and elections.

The Senior Citizen Employment Service activities have been of outstanding importance in St. Johns and in Clinton County, because the services of a public employment agency were not available. A local manufacturing plant provided work opportunities for senior citizens to supplement their incomes. Many older women did part-time sewing for working women. The senior citizens gave considerable attention to housing. Zoning laws and building codes were studied and modifications to meet special needs of the aged were obtained. Plans were made to build an apartment house for senior citizens near the downtown area.

MT. ANGEL, OREGON

Special interest and concern about the aged was first expressed in Mt. Angel by a zealous Catholic priest who organized a group of parishioners and citizens to plan a home for the aged. Mt. Angel is a small town in Marion County in the Willamette Valley of Oregon. About one-fifth of the 1,700 residents are 65 years of age or older. The original concept of the "home for the aged" called for a "village" of small houses near the parish church. Plans changed and progressed until a large brick home was purchased and remodeled to accommodate 20 patients.

The Benedictine Sisters, who had been primarily engaged in elementary, secondary, and college education, were asked to administer and staff the nursing home. After two years, the fruits of experience and its reputation of excellence and quality of care created a demand for service that far exceeded the capacity of the small facility. A modern, 63-bed, nursing-care home was built in 1957 on land adjacent to the Mt. Angel College campus and Convent of the Benedictine Sisters. In 1963, 25 beds were added, bringing the capacity to 88.

The administrator and staff of the Benedictine Nursing Home were concerned about the "total needs" of each resident-patient: physical, social, psychological, and intellectual. Efforts were directed at developing balanced programs of activities and services necessary to maintain the highest functional levels.

Care of the aged was not confined to the nursing home but was extended to others in the community. Some who lived in a nearby apartment complex received home-care services and benefited from central dining facilities and recreational and creative activities and participated in worship services held in the nursing home. Since the town had no hospital, the staff viewed the nursing home as a community health facility which offered a variety of services to residents of the larger community. Under physician's orders, allergy shots and vitamin shots were given to outpatients, equipment was sterilized for home use, and families were taught how to care for an ill member. Some vocational rehabilitation programs were started for young and middle-aged patients. Mt. Angel Towers, a 210-unit high-rise and garden apartment retirement home with an infirmary opened in 1965 to accommodate about 250 people.

In 1965 the Oregon Gerontology Study and Training Center was established at Mt. Angel. It is concerned with education, research, consultation, and services for older people. Cooperative projects are being developed with nursing and retirement homes, hospitals, housing developments, and senior citizens centers, and with federal, state, and local health and welfare and related agencies. These projects will provide opportunities to students majoring in the field of gerontology. The Gerontology Study and Training Center is especially interested in developing guidelines for cooperative community action to help older people.

POTENTIAL PROGRAMS AND SERVICES

As in most rapidly developing programs for human betterment in aging, a variety of solutions have developed at different rates in various regions of the nation. A review of services and programs shows that no community is without some, nor does any community have all of them. Most of the more broadly accepted programs and services are listed below. Such a list can be used by leaders in a community to assess the adequacy of opportunity for healthy aging and the resources available for care of chronic illness and disability. The list could also be used by those who are conducting an evaluative search for a home and community during retirement.

INCOME MAINTENANCE AND ECONOMIC SECURITY

Part-time employment
Savings, investment, and insurance counsel
Public and old age assistance
Aid to the blind, disabled, and handicapped
Social security coverage and benefits
Surplus food
Loans for private housing
Public housing subsidies
Rent supplements

Reduced fares on public transportation
Discounts on drugs and other products
Income tax dependent allowance and other reductions
Homestead tax exemptions and property tax relief

PHYSICAL AND MENTAL HEALTH

Periodic comprehensive physical examinations
Individual testing for specific diseases
Immunization clinics
Home visitation nursing
Physical, occupational, and speech therapy
Social work and family counseling
Homemaker and housekeeping aid
Health education series on nutrition, safety, and sanitation
Loan closets of wheelchairs, hospital beds, and other equipment and appliances
Meals on wheels

SOCIAL, EDUCATIONAL, AND RECREATIONAL PROGRAMS

Senior citizen clubs
Senior citizen centers
Information and referral services
Public parks and recreational areas
Retirement education classes
Adult or continuing education
Hobby and craft facilities
Volunteer service and leadership opportunities
Entertainment, drama, concerts
Travel opportunities
Transportation for those without cars

HOUSING AND HEALTH CARE FACILITIES

Individual, small modern homes
Low-rent housing, public or private
Age-integrated apartments
Homes for the aged
Retirement homes or manors
Adult or retirement communities
Nursing homes
Convalescent and rehabilitation centers

GOVERNMENTAL AGENCIES AND ORGANIZATIONS

Offices, councils, commissions, and committees on aging
Health and mental health departments

Educational institutions
Welfare and social service agencies
Employment and vocational rehabilitation departments
Housing authorities and urban planning and renewal agencies
Veterans' administration and veterans' affairs agencies
Social security offices
Governor, legislature, mayor, city council, and county
    commissions

CONCLUSION

The development of federal, state, and local programs for older
people has been characterized by two general principles. One is
increasing societal responsibility for the well-being of older persons and consequent attempts to help older persons attain more
satisfying levels of living. Social, economic, and health programs
have been directed to these ends. A second functional principle
is that to achieve optimal effectiveness, agencies must find expression at the local level, that is, in the communities where older
people live. Special conditions of rural life have prevented many
older rural persons from full participation in such programs.

NOTES

[1] For an extended discussion see, "Government Functions and the Politics
of Age" by Fred Cottrell in *Handbook of Social Gerontology,* Clark Tibbitts
(Chicago: University of Chicago Press, 1960).

[2] U. S. Department of Health, Education, and Welfare, Social Security
Administration, *Social Security Programs in the United States* (Washington,
D. C., Dec. 1964).

[3] Information taken from: U. S. Department of Health, Education, and
Welfare, Welfare Administration, Office of Aging, *A Rural County Cares for
its Aging, Patterns for Progress in Aging,* Case Study No. 17 (Washington,
D. C., 1964).

Contributors

WARD W. BAUDER
Economic Research Service
U. S. Department of Agriculture
Department of Economics and
 Sociology
Iowa State University

JEAN O. BRITTON
Department of Psychology
Pennsylvania State University

JOSEPH H. BRITTON
Department of Child Development and Family Relationships
Pennsylvania State University

JON A. DOERFLINGER
Department of Economics and
 Sociology
Iowa State University

BERT L. ELLENBOGEN
Department of Rural Sociology
University of Minnesota

GARY D. HANSEN
Institute of Gerontology
Mt. Angel College

JUANITA M. KREPS
Department of Economics
Duke University

OLEN E. LEONARD
Economic Research Service
U. S. Department of Agriculture
Mississippi State University

JERROLD E. LEVY
Department of Anthropology
Portland State College

WALTER C. McKAIN, JR.
Department of Rural Sociology
University of Connecticut

JAMES E. MONTGOMERY
Department of Home and Fam-
 ily Life
Virginia Polytechnic Institute

ARNOLD M. ROSE
Department of Sociology
University of Minnesota

HENRY D. SHELDON
Population Division
U. S. Bureau of the Census

STANLEY H. SMITH
Division of Social Science
Tuskegee Institute

MARVIN J. TAVES
Administration on Aging
U. S. Department of Health,
 Education, and Welfare

E. GRANT YOUMANS
Economic Research Service
U. S. Department of Agriculture
Department of Sociology
University of Kentucky

Name Index

Adams, B. N., 52, 70
Adkins, W. G., 42, 43
Agan, T., 177, 194
Albrecht, R., 62, 73, 81, 89, 93, 94
Alleger, D. E., 37, 43, 190, 194
Anderson, A. H., 219
Anderson, E. M., 177, 194
Anderson, N., 92
Anderson, O. W., 217, 218
Axelson, L. J., 54, 71

Baill, I. M., 42, 43
Baker, K. I., 208
Baldwin, E. D., 42, 43, 56, 71, 93, 94, 95
Barker, L. S., 73
Barker, R. G., 73
Barron, M. L., 57, 71, 94, 95, 111, 116
Bauder, W. W., 2, 42, 43, 56, 71
Beal, G. M., 42
Beattie, W. M., Jr., 262
Beegle, J. A., 218
Bergler, E., 69
Berry, B. J. L., 41
Bertrand, A. L., 69
Beyer, G. H., 71, 177, 179, 180, 193, 194
Biggar, J. C., 42, 43
Birren, J. E., 93
Bloedow, G., 21
Bohlen, J. M., 42
Boyd, R. R., 62, 73
Brandt, E. J., 220
Brewster, A. W., 218
Britton, J. H., 2, 53, 63, 70, 73, 89
Britton, J. O., 2, 53, 70, 73
Brown, R. G., 60, 72
Bruce, I. C., 171, 193
Burchinal, L., 51, 69, 70
Burgess, E. W., 55, 89
Byron, E. S., 219

Carson, J. R., 294
Cavan, R. S., 61, 72, 89
Chapin, S., 82
Charlesworth, J. C., 96
Christensen, H. T., 68

Clark, M., 260
Clawson, M., 96
Cleland, C. B., 218, 219
Cottrell, F., 303
Cowhig, J. D., 150, 167, 218
Cowles, M. L., 178, 194
Crockett, J. A., 167
Cumming, E., 42, 97, 115

Davidson, J. D., 73
Dement, J. C., 220
Deutscher, I., 54, 70
Dinkel, R. M., 53, 70
Doerflinger, J. A., 2, 21
Donahue, W., 48, 69, 96
Dorfman, R., 218
Ducoff, L. J., 42, 43, 56, 71, 167, 168
Duncan, O. D., 42, 56, 71
Dunkelberger, J. E., 280
Durkheim, E., 23, 41

Eickhoff, E., 171, 193
Elinson, J., 218, 219
Ellenbogen, B. L., 4, 212, 213, 218
Epstein, L. A., 163, 167, 168
Essene, F. J., 238
Ewers, J. C., 227, 238

Fanshel, D., 72, 95
Feld, S., 45, 68
Folkman, W. S., 71
Form, W. H., 22, 41
Fuguitt, G. V., 68
Fuller, W. A., 58, 72, 80, 93, 94, 95

Galloway, R. E., 42, 43
Glasser, L. N., 63, 73
Glasser, P. H., 63, 73
Glick, P. C., 68, 69
Goldhammer, H., 204, 218
Goldstein, S., 167
Gravatt, A. E., 54, 70
Green, A. W., 95
Gross, I. H., 69
Gumpert, M., 96
Gurin, G., 45, 68, 205, 218
Gutman, D. L., 50, 69, 226, 238

Subject Index

Aboriginal: diet, 234; diseases, 234; Indians, 221, 225, 227; population, 224; subsistence, 230. *See also* Indian tribes; Navajo

Activities: and adjustments, 89; advisory, 91; attitudes about, 112-13; church related, 114-15; classification of, 83; clearinghouse for, 289; creative, 85; and disengagement, 107-13; and expectations, 86; explorative, 84-85; free time, 76; and income, 88; index of participation in, 90; informal, 83-88; intergenerational differences in, 10-11; and leisure, 112-13; and loneliness, 17; most popular, 108; needed by aged, 17; need for, 113; of older persons, 76, 299; opportunities for social, 16-17; participation in, 81; passive, 83; and physical health, 201; reading, 84; recreation, 79; and research, 79; in rural areas, 88, 293; sedentary, 79; service, 76; and social participation scores, 80; among Spanish Americans, 250, 253-54; and state programs, 289; unstructured, 77; and values, 3; variables in, 82-83; withdrawal from, 88; youth-centered, 76. *See also* Associations; Free time; Hobbies; Leisure time; Organizations; Participation; Politics; Religion; Visiting

Adjustment: and activities, 89; and change, 37; with children's families, 10; in climacteric years, 55-56; and community, 89; and despair, 205; to economic conditions, 114; and emotional health, 204; of ethnic groups, 221; in farming, 160-61; and health, 38; and housing, 178-79; intergenerational, 10; in later years, 89-90; marital, 54-55; and migration, 67; among Navajo, 235-36; and physical health, 205; problems of women, 36; and retirement, 27, 37-38; and social participation, 89; among Spanish Americans, 254-56, 260; and work roles, 34. *See also* Subjective

Administration on Aging, 292

Affluence: of America, 275; ethical problem of, 27; and leisure, 76; and Negro, 262. *See also* Income; Poverty

Age-grading: and occupation, 32; and retirement, 32; in rural areas, 32; and voluntary associations, 9, 16

Aging: in aboriginal America, 224-30; in America, 7; attitudes toward, 9-10; and chronic illness, 199; commissions, 289; and conservatism, 18; developmental theories of, 26; and disease, 216, 230; factors in, 2, 6; and family norms, 63-66; generational factor in, 6-7; and group consciousness, 20; and illness, 199; and income, 14; among Indians, 225-26, 228, 229; knowledge about, 292; among Navajo, 229; new image of, 284; and new social roles, 20; and political action, 20; and prestige, 9; process, 2, 66, 76; research in, 1, 66; and satisfactions, 278; and senility among Indians, 226-27; undesirable, 76; and voluntary associations, 9, 20

Agriculture: and age-grading, 32; commercialized, 40; decline in, 158, 161; employment for older men, 161; and farm products, 159; of Indians, 223; labor force, 33; among Navajo, 230-31; nonrational factors in, 24; and rural Negro, 280; and social security, 39-40; among Spanish Americans, 242, 257; and style of life, 24; success in, 40; and work, 77. *See also* Farming; Occupation

American Negroes: dissatisfactions of, 273-74; involvement in American life, 275, 279; limited data on, 263-64; and regional research, 264

Anxiety: and age, 217; among aged, 207; and declining income, 14; among Indians, 226; and personal crises, 14; scores for rural adults, 205; self-perceptions of, 207; among Spanish Americans, 256; symptoms of, 204. *See also* Mental health; Morale

311